SIX SIGMA

SIX

**MIKEL HARRY, Ph.D., AND
RICHARD SCHROEDER**

SIGMA

The Breakthrough Management Strategy Revolutionizing the World's Top Corporations

■ ■ ■ ■ ■ ■ ■

CURRENCY

NEW YORK LONDON TORONTO SYDNEY AUCKLAND

A CURRENCY BOOK
PUBLISHED BY DOUBLEDAY
a division of Random House, Inc.

CURRENCY is a trademark of Random House, Inc., and DOUBLEDAY is a
registered trademark of Random House, Inc.

Six Sigma was originally published in hardcover by Currency in January 2000.

The Library of Congress has cataloged the hardcover edition of this book as follows:

Harry, Mikel J.
Six sigma : the breakthrough management strategy revolutionizing the world's top
corporations / Mikel Harry and Richard Schroeder.—1st ed.
xii, 300 p.; 25 cm.
Includes bibliographical references (p. [285]–289 and index)
ISBN 0-385-49437-8
1. Production management. 2. Quality control—Statistical methods.
I. Schroeder, Richard (Richard R.) II. Title.

TS155.H298 2000
658.5'62'015195—dc21
99-050021

ISBN 0-385-49438-6

PRINTED IN THE UNITED STATES OF AMERICA
First Edition: January 2000
First Currency Paperback Edition: April 2005

10 9 8 7 6 5 4 3 2 1

CONTENTS

The Six Sigma Phenomenon

We believe that Six Sigma is the most powerful breakthrough management tool ever devised.

What is Six Sigma? It is a business process that allows companies to drastically improve their bottom line by designing and monitoring everyday business activities in ways that minimize waste and resources while increasing customer satisfaction. Six Sigma guides companies into making fewer mistakes in everything they do—from filling out a purchase order to manufacturing airplane engines—eliminating lapses in quality at the earliest possible occurrence. Quality-control programs have focused on *detecting* and *correcting* commercial, industrial, and design defects. Six Sigma encompasses something broader: *It provides specific methods to re-create the process so that defects and errors never arise in the first place.*

Throughout this book, you will encounter new ideas and principles—some of which will run contrary to what managers have learned in school or professional practice. Six Sigma represents extraordinary sense, not ordinary or common sense; common sense rarely produces extraordinary results. It is our belief that once managers and their companies understand what Six Sigma is and how it works, they will begin to see that many well-accepted past management practices and quality-control methods are less than optimal, or are even wrong.

Industries are desperate to find new ways to buoy profitability. That is why companies as diverse as AlliedSignal, General Electric,

Sony, Honda, Maytag, Raytheon, Texas Instruments, Bombardier, Canon, Hitachi, Lockheed Martin, and Polaroid have adopted Six Sigma. Many of these companies are averse to management fads. But they have embraced Six Sigma because they believe the initiative will help them increase market share, decrease costs, and grow profit margins. As a result, they are beginning to tie quality directly to their bottom line.

Six Sigma produces superior financial results, using business strategies that not only revive companies but help them leapfrog ahead of their competition in terms of market share and profitability. By reaching for the seemingly impossible, companies *achieve* the impossible.

But the biggest reason for the incredible buzz about Six Sigma throughout the business community has been its astonishing success at dramatically improving a company's bottom-line profitability. As a result, Six Sigma has become the darling of Wall Street. Jennifer Murphy, an analyst with Morgan Stanley, Dean Witter, Discover & Co., spent three days at our ranch in Payson and at our Six Sigma Academy in Scottsdale, Arizona, a teaching facility we designed to educate and train executives in the principles of Six Sigma so that they can transform their companies into world-class organizations. Impatient with the negligible effect quality programs have had on the bottom line, Murphy was astonished by what she learned. "Six Sigma companies . . . achieve faster working capital turns; lower capital spending as capacity is freed up; more productive R&D spending; faster new product development; and greater customer satisfaction," she wrote upon her return. She estimates that by the year 2000, GE's gross annual benefit from Six Sigma could be as high as $6.6 billion, or 5.5 percent of sales.

Here are just a few reasons for the enthusiasm so many analysts on Wall Street voice:

■   General Electric's Jack Welch, a self-proclaimed cynic when it comes to quality programs, describes Six Sigma as "the most important initiative GE has ever undertaken." GE's operating income, a critical measure of business efficiency and profitability, hovered around the 10 percent level for decades. In 1995, Welch mandated that each GE operation, from credit card services to aircraft engine plants to NBC-TV, work toward achieving Six Sigma. GE averaged about 3.5 sigma when it introduced the program. With Six Sigma embedding itself deeper into the organization's processes, GE achieved the previously "impossible" operating margin of 16.7 percent in 1998, up from 13.6 percent in 1995 when GE implemented Six Sigma. In dollar amounts, Six Sigma delivered more than $300 million to GE's 1997 operating income, and in 1998, the financial benefits of Six Sigma more than doubled, to over $600 million.

■ Larry Bossidy, CEO of AlliedSignal Inc., brought the $14.5 billion industrial giant back from the verge of bankruptcy by implementing the Six Sigma Breakthrough Strategy. The company has now trained thousands of employees from every business unit and staff function in Six Sigma and the Breakthrough Strategy, with the goal of increasing productivity 6 percent each year in its industrial sectors. Broad-base Six Sigma initiatives allowed operating margin in the first quarter of 1999 to grow to a record 14.1 percent from 12 percent one year earlier. Since Bossidy implemented the program in 1994, the cumulative impact of Six Sigma has been a savings in excess of $2 billion in direct costs.

■ Former AlliedSignal executive Daniel P. Burnham, who became Raytheon's CEO in 1998, has made Six Sigma a cornerstone of the company's strategic plan. By pursuing Six Sigma quality levels throughout the company, Burnham expects Raytheon to improve its cost of doing business by more than $1 billion annually by 2001.

■ Since taking over GE's industrial diamonds business in Worthington, Ohio, in 1994, William Woodburn has increased the operation's return on investment fourfold and cut the operation's costs in half by employing the Six Sigma Breakthrough Strategy. He and his team have made their existing facilities so efficient that they have eliminated the need for new plants and equipment for at least another ten years. Woodburn and GE's industrial diamond business exemplify how Six Sigma can enable a company to cut costs, enhance productivity, and eliminate the need for new plant and equipment investments.

■   Polaroid Corporation's Joseph J. Kasabula, quality strategy manager for product development and worldwide manufacturing, believes that the most compelling reason companies embrace Six Sigma is its impact on the bottom line. While other programs may improve quality, Kasabula believes they do not focus on increasing a company's profits. With Six Sigma, companies focus on the processes that affect quality and profit margins on a project-by-project basis. Six Sigma is helping Polaroid to add 6 percent to its bottom line each year.

■   Asea Brown Boveri (ABB), which successfully applied the Six Sigma Breakthrough Strategy to its power transformer facility in Muncie, Indiana, has reduced measurement equipment error by 83 percent; piece count error from 8.3 percent to 1.3 percent; and no-load loss to within 2 percent. ABB also improved material handling, resulting in an annual estimated cost savings of $775,000 for a single process within a single plant.

We believe the Six Sigma Breakthrough Strategy should be of paramount interest to any forward-thinking executive, manager, and public administrator who wants to make his or her organization more competitive and profitable, and enhance its ability to drive change. Six Sigma principles apply to any business of any size. It applies to far more than just industrial processes—it applies to engineering, product design, and any commercial process, from processing mortgage applications, to credit card transactions, to customer service call centers. By attacking "variation" during the design of products and services, it's possible for any organization to achieve unprecedented profitability.

How does Six Sigma work? The first step in the Breakthrough Strategy is to ask a new set of questions, questions that take you out of your comfort zone, that force you to query what you have taken for granted, and that ultimately provide you with new direction. Six Sigma forces businesses to let go of bad habits. Bureaucracy becomes delayered. Those employees closest to the actual work and to the customer become motivated to meet or exceed consumer requirements. By questioning the speed with which products are produced and services are rendered, people begin to think about new systems that can be put into place to produce a higher-quality product or service in a shorter amount of time. As those closest to the work discover more effective and profitable ways of working, they are able to inform senior management about what changes need to be made, and as a result, push those higher in the organization to reexamine the ways in which they do business.

Six Sigma is about asking tougher and tougher questions until we receive quantifiable answers that change behavior. Through Six Sigma, companies relentlessly question every process, every number, every step along the way to creating a final product. Managers, employees, and customers ask different kinds of questions of each other than they've asked before. As Six Sigma takes hold across an organization, it creates an internal infrastructure that includes executives, managers, engineers, and operations and service personnel. When 50 percent or more of an organization's staff embrace Six Sigma, those individuals are able to mobilize massive changes in the way business is done, dramatically increasing profitability.

Questions, of course, are not meant to exist in a vacuum. The methodology behind Six Sigma is designed to pave the way to find the right answers for your company. In the classic children's story *The Wizard of Oz*, Dorothy's persistent questions about what she sees and where she is going lead her down the Yellow Brick Road and into the

Land of Oz. Similarly, when an organization starts to question what it does and why it does it, it too can begin to lay a Yellow Brick Road that will lead to its own long-term goals.

The fact is, organizations need ways of measuring what they claim to value. Measurements, or "metrics" as we prefer to call them, carry relevance to every member, for every activity, of an organization. You can't change what you can't measure. The foundation of Six Sigma uses metrics to calculate the success of everything an organization does. Enthusiastic speeches, colorful posters, and corporate mandates will not produce quantum change—only measuring the things a company values can do this. Without measuring a company's processes—and its changes to these processes—it's impossible to know where you are or where you are going. Six Sigma tells us:

- We don't know what we don't know.

- We can't do what we don't know.

- We won't know until we measure.

- We don't measure what we don't value.

- We don't value what we don't measure.

So, in a general way, Six Sigma is a process of asking questions that lead to tangible, quantifiable answers that ultimately produce profitable results. This book will share what Six Sigma is, how it is applied, and what it can do for your company, business, or organization. It will be your guide for transforming knowledge into a living vision.

To date, every company that has followed our Six Sigma methodology has achieved breakthrough profitability. Our intention in these pages is to pass on to you the knowledge that has taken us nearly two decades to learn.

We wish you well in your journey toward breakthrough profitability.

SIX SIGMA

CHAPTER ONE

Why Six Sigma?

Why Companies Are Embracing Six Sigma

What drives companies to implement Six Sigma? Contrary to what some believe, the goal of Six Sigma is not to achieve six sigma levels of quality. Six Sigma is about improving profitability, although improved quality and efficiency are immediate by-products of Six Sigma. Companies that implement Six Sigma do so with the goal of improving their margins. Prior to Six Sigma, improvements brought about by quality programs usually had no visible impact on a company's net income. Organizations that can't track the effect of quality improvements on profitability don't know what changes need to be made to improve their profit margins.

To date, every company that has implemented Six Sigma under our guidance has seen profit margins grow 20 percent year after year for each sigma shift (up to 4.8 to 5 sigma). Companies ranging from AlliedSignal to Dupont Chemical have come to us because despite improvements they made in quality, their profit margins were stagnating, if not shrinking. These companies could no longer afford to reduce prices to increase market share, and market competition would not allow them to raise prices to improve profit margins. They found themselves boxed into a corner. When they offered products and services with new features at no extra charge to the consumer, market share might increase but profit margins would shrink.

What Six Sigma Can Do for Your Company

While Six Sigma is a long-term, forward-thinking initiative designed
to fundamentally change the way corporations do business, it is first
and foremost designed to generate immediate improvements to profit
margins. Instead of projecting three or more years into the future, Six
Sigma focuses on achieving financial targets in twelve-month increments. Once those targets are met, companies will find that changes
in the market and Six Sigma's impact on their own financial landscape
have changed their internal dynamics so extensively that new financial targets must be set to keep the company moving forward. Companies operating at a three sigma level that marshal all their resources
around Six Sigma can expect to make one sigma shift improvement
each year. These companies will experience:

- a 20 percent margin improvement

- a 12 to 18 percent increase in capacity

- a 12 percent reduction in the number of employees

- a 10 to 30 percent capital reduction

Companies can expect to make one sigma shift improvement per
year up to 4.7 sigma, meaning that a three sigma company that
focuses all its resources on Six Sigma can expect to move to four
sigma during the first year of implementation. Companies already at
four sigma can expect to improve to 4.7 sigma during the first year of
implementation and deployment. The financial benefits of progress-
ing from 3 to 4 to 4.7 to Six Sigma are exponential, and experience has
shown that companies can achieve a sigma level as high as 4.7 sigma
without large capital outlays. In the second year, such companies can
expect to move from 4.7 sigma to 5 sigma, and in the third year they
will progress from 5 to 5.1. The closer companies come to achieving
Six Sigma, the more demanding the improvements become. At 4.8
sigma companies hit a "wall" that requires a redesigning of processes,

known as "Design for Six Sigma." However, the profit-margin increases between a 3 sigma level company and 4.8 sigma company are so dramatic, making these companies so much more profitable than their competitors, that they can selectively pick what plant, product, operation, or process they need to improve to attain five sigma or higher.

Companies often ask if Six Sigma savings are as significant in small companies as they are in larger companies. The answer is unequivocally yes. Larger companies are composed of smaller businesses or divisions, often with their own presidents, making them similar to stand-alone companies of comparable size. A large company with thirty business units may have fifteen business units with sales of $500 million or less. Whether a smaller business unit within a large corporation or a small-size stand-alone company, we have found that improved profitability depends far more on how rigorously Six Sigma is applied than on the size of the company's revenue.

Many companies ask if, as they improve their sigma level, subsequent projects will be as profitable as earlier projects. Since most companies start at roughly three sigma, virtually each employee trained in the Six Sigma Breakthrough Strategy will return on average $230,000 per project to the bottom line until the company reaches 4.7 sigma. After a company reaches 4.7 sigma, the cost savings are not as dramatic. However, improved profit margins allow companies to create products and services with added features and functions that result in greater market share. So while Six Sigma improves the quality of a company's products and services and, in some cases, catapults a company ahead of its competition, the overwhelming and most visible impact of Six Sigma is the immediate benefit to any company's profit margins.

Six Sigma Is About Making Money

As the business world has become intensely aware, Six Sigma has helped some of the nation's best-run Fortune 100 companies achieve dramatic financial results. How were the results achieved? What is the key to their success? The answer lies in human nature. As we pointed out in the preface, human beings measure what they value. Virtually everyone, for example, values money. Evidence of this value resides in everything from our nation's economic system to what we enter in our personal checkbook record—most of us write down and track our financial debits and credits religiously so that we can remain financially solvent. We track these "measurements" because we value financial solvency. Based on the numbers, we make decisions and take action. Measurements create a link between philosophy and action.

Companies, too, measure what they value. If we want to understand a corporation's values, we only have to find out what it measures, records, analyzes, reports, and takes action on. We would expect that an organization claiming to value growth would show the importance of this value in a measurement—such as by tracking and analyzing market share data, and sharing that information throughout the company.

Almost all organizations claim to be customer focused. But when there is no system of measurements in place to gauge customer satisfaction, can an organization genuinely say that its customers are a top priority? A company's business metrics can show if it values profitability over customer satisfaction. Organizations that do not measure what they profess to value don't know much about what they value. More important, they cannot control the outcomes of the things they value. Companies cannot improve what they don't measure.

Six Sigma starts with metrics—measuring the things that matter. Companies that value profitability will measure, report on, and react to escalating or falling profits. But do those same companies measure, report on, and react to the quality of their manufacturing and service processes, and how they affect customer satisfaction and profitability?

To Jack Welch, GE is not about numbers; it's about values. These values include employee satisfaction, customer satisfaction, and cash flow. GE knows that employee satisfaction translates into productivity; that high customer satisfaction means strong market share; and that cash flow means that employees have maintained the company's customer-focused vision, its passion for excellence, and its desire to push forward with energy and enthusiasm. GE backs up its values with performance-based metrics, complete with goals linked to executive incentive pay.

GE's values clearly show its determination to maintain a reality-based, customer-focused company. Commercial Finance, a division within GE Capital Services, uses Six Sigma to better understand customer requirements and thereby win more deals. The result has been a 160 percent increase in new transactions. Another division within GE Capital Services, Mortgage Insurance, developed a flexible new billing system that contributed to customer retention and was instrumental in winning $60 million in new insurance from just a single customer. In Japan, GE's Global Consumer Finance division helped customers overcome payment difficulties associated with limited banking hours, and saved money by establishing an alternate payment method through a network of 25,000 convenience stores, now used by 40 percent of its customers. Clearly, GE Capital Services knows what it means to value customer satisfaction, and it works steadily to measure how well it satisfies that value.

The New Definition of Quality

Past definitions of quality focused on *conformance to standards,* as companies strived to create products and services that fell within certain specification limits. Such definitions of quality assumed that if companies produced quality products and services, their performance standards were correct regardless of how those standards were met. In other words, performance standards may have been achieved after considerable rework of a specific part or service. In addition, previous definitions of quality often overlooked the fact that products or services rarely consist of a single element. Even a product or service made up of as few as five different elements that individually conform to standard may not work properly when put together. We call this concept "interacting standards."

The Six Sigma Breakthrough Strategy broadens the definition of quality to include economic value and practical utility to both the company and the consumer. *We say that quality is a state in which value entitlement is realized for the customer and provider in every aspect of the business relationship.* This new definition of quality focuses on achieving "value entitlement." In the world of Six Sigma, "entitlement" means that companies have a rightful level of expectation to produce quality products at the highest possible profits; for customers, "entitlement" means that they have a rightful level of expectation to buy high-quality products at the lowest possible cost. "Value" represents economic worth, practical utility, and availability for both the consumer and the company that creates the product or service. Economic worth refers to the fact that customers *want to purchase* products and services at the lowest possible cost, just as companies *want to produce* high-quality goods and services at the lowest possible cost. In addition, customers have every right to expect that the products and services that they purchase will be available when they need them and in the volume required. Providers have the same rightful expectation within their own businesses. Companies that produce products or services that do not conform to such standards are not achieving their economic and value entitlement.

Practical utility, as it applies to the customer, refers to the three areas of a finished product—form, fit, and function. All must meet the customer's needs. For example, new-car buyers look for "form"—they want an automobile that pleases the eye. They also look for "fit"—they expect the trunk lid to align with the body of the car, that there are no air or water leaks, rattles, or squeaks, and that engine noise be held to a minimum. Finally, car buyers look for "function," which means they are concerned with such things as gas mileage, automatic versus manual transmission, and the amount of horsepower the engine has.

While practical utility for consumers means that the product or service must possess a certain value, practical utility for companies refers to the fact that their processes must create value for the company. In other words, companies focus on process quality and consumers focus on the final product or service quality.

In the past, quality programs adopted by corporations focused on meeting the customer's needs at virtually any cost; many companies, despite poor internal processes, managed to produce high-quality goods and services. Even today, four sigma companies can produce six sigma products through enormous amounts of rework. However, they can't raise their prices to recapture these costs because they must price their products competitively. As a result, they suffer tremendous profit losses.

Business quality is highest when costs are at the absolute lowest for both the producer and the consumer. Six Sigma provides maximum value to companies—in the form of increased profits *and* maximum value to the consumer with high-quality products or services at the lowest possible cost. It is a business strategy and philosophy built around the concept that companies can gain a competitive edge by reducing defects in their industrial and commercial processes. Classically speaking, a defect is anything that fails to meet the customer's expectations or requirements. Again, Six Sigma takes a much broader view of defects. Within the framework of Six Sigma, a defect is anything that blocks or inhibits a process or service. For example, when a machine operator fails to change a gear during maintenance, it adversely influences the operation of a process, although it may not result in a defective product.

Within the Six Sigma Breakthrough Strategy that we developed over the last fifteen years are a series of established steps that (a) reveal how well products perform and how well services are delivered, and (b) show companies how to improve their processes and maintain the gains they achieve. The improvement process we have developed uses mathematical measurements to systematically reduce defects that occur in producing a product or service.

The sigma concept of measuring defects was created in the early 1980s as a way to develop a universal quality metric that applied regardless of product complexity or dissimilarities between different products. Higher sigma values indicate better products and lower sigma values represent less desirable products, regardless of what the product is. In short, the higher the sigma level, the fewer the number of defects per unit of product or service. The lower the sigma level, the greater the number of defects per unit. Products produced at a six sigma level of quality operate virtually defect-free—by definition, with only 3.4 *defects per million opportunities* (DPMO). As such, Six Sigma has become recognized as *the* standard for product and service excellence. This level of quality is in stark contrast to historical standards of what companies strived for, which was four sigma, or 6,210 defects per million opportunities. Six Sigma standards are about 1,800 times more demanding than the old standard. Common sense cannot create a 1,800 times improvement. Such extraordinary improvements occur only when people employ extraordinary reasoning—reasoning that results only from new questions being asked about how a product or service is created. As new questions emerge, new measurements are instituted. When the opportunities for nonconformance—defects—are brought to six sigma levels—whether in manufacturing, engineering, administration, sales, or service—companies can then take valuable resources once spent on anticipating, detecting, and fixing defects to perform activities that add value for customers and ultimately the company. Every time we produce a defect in a process, time, labor, capital equipment, overhead, and material have to be used to detect, analyze, and fix that defect. This cycle of detection, analysis, and correction ties directly back to the three elements of customer satisfaction—delivering the highest-quality product (defect-free products and services), on time (reduced cycle time), and at the right price (which impacts manufacturing costs). When the probability of a defect becomes so low that a company rarely encounters one, maintaining systems to detect, analyze, and fix defects are virtually unnecessary. Expenses drop dramatically. This is the ultimate goal of Six Sigma.

In today's competitive world, a great many companies conscientiously make improvements in product lines and delivery cycles, yet are unable to stay ahead of complex technological changes and escalating customer expectations. At best, these companies are just keeping pace. This explains why corporations, both in Europe and the United States, that operated at 3.5 to 4 sigma thirty years ago are still operating at that level today. Despite improvements, the evolution of technology, the complexity of product features, and more sophisticated customer demands have thwarted significant advances in how industrial and commercial processes are created, leaving the relative capability of organizations unchanged. History has shown that standards lag behind technology. Significant breakthroughs in technology, such as those we have seen in the past two decades, force companies to find new ways to meet customers' expectations.

As the phrase "six sigma quality" has increased in popularity, and more and more companies that have embraced Six Sigma have begun to achieve significant financial benefits, an increasing number of companies have become eager to jump on the bandwagon.

The Origins of Six Sigma

The quest to achieve Six Sigma had its birth at Motorola in 1979 when executive Art Sundry stood up at a management meeting and proclaimed, "The real problem at Motorola is that our quality stinks!" Sundry's proclamation sparked a new era within Motorola and led to the discovery of the crucial correlation between higher quality and lower development costs in manufacturing products of all kinds.

At a time when most American companies believed that quality cost money, Motorola realized that done right, improving quality would actually reduce costs. They believed that high-quality products should cost less to produce, not more. They reasoned that the highest-quality producer should be the lowest-cost producer. At the time, Motorola was spending 5 to 10 percent of annual revenues, and in some cases as much as 20 percent of revenues, correcting poor quality. That translated into a whopping $800 million to $900 million each year, money that, with higher-quality processes, could be returned directly to the bottom line. (Motorola's belief that high-quality products should cost less to produce has since been proven over and over again to be true.)

As Motorola executives began looking for ways to cut waste, Bill

Smith, an engineer at Motorola's Communications Sector, was quietly
working behind the scenes studying the correlation between a product's field life and how often that product had been repaired during
the manufacturing process. In 1985, Smith presented a paper that
concluded that if a product was found defective and corrected during
the production process, other defects were bound to be missed and
found later by the customer during early use of the product. However,
when the product was manufactured error-free, it rarely failed during
early use by the consumer.

Although Smith's findings were initially greeted with skepticism,
customer dissatisfaction with a product that failed shortly after it had
been purchased was very real. As a result, Smith's finding ignited a
fierce debate within Motorola. Was the effort to achieve quality really
dependent on detecting and fixing defects? Or could quality be
achieved by preventing defects in the first place through manufacturing controls and product design? Later data would show that a con-
certed effort at detecting and fixing defects would lead Motorola only
to four sigma—placing it only slightly ahead of the average American
company. At the same time, the company was finding that foreign
competitors *were* making products that required no repair or rework
during the manufacturing process.

Others at Motorola began to take a second look at Smith's work.
If hidden defects caused a product to fail shortly after the customer
began using it, something needed to be done to improve the manufacturing process. As a result, Motorola began its quest to improve
quality, and simultaneously reduce production time and costs, by
focusing on *how* the product was designed and made.

It was this link between higher quality and lower cost that led to
the development of Six Sigma—an initiative that at first focused on
improving quality through the use of exact measurements to anticipate problem areas, not just react to them. In other words, Six Sigma
would allow a business leader to be *proactive*, rather than *reactive*, to
quality issues.

The difference between previous total quality approaches and the

Six Sigma concept was a matter of focus. Total quality management (TQM) programs focus on improvements in individual operations with unrelated processes. The consequence is that with many quality programs, regardless of how comprehensive they are, it takes many years before all the operations within a given process (a process is a series of activities or steps that create a product or service) are improved. The Six Sigma architects at Motorola focused on making improvements in *all operations within a process,* producing results far more rapidly and effectively.

A quantum leap in manufacturing technology occurred at Motorola when it applied Six Sigma to the development of its Bandit pager—a name the company selected because those involved in the project "borrowed" every good idea they could find from products already on the market. Within eighteen months, and for a price tag of less than $10 million, Motorola's twenty-three Bandit engineers had designed a pager that could be produced in its automated factory in Boynton Beach, Florida, within seventy-two minutes from the time an order was placed by computer from any Motorola sales office. Pagers could be ordered with various options and could be custom-built for individual customers. Moreover, the Bandit's superior design and manufacturing process resulted in an average life expectancy for its pager of 150 years. The company's pagers were so reliable that product testing was ultimately eliminated; it was much more cost-effective to replace a pager, in the unlikely event that it failed, than to spend time and money testing a product that was virtually defect-free.

As Motorola saw a reduction in defects and in manufacturing time, the company also began to reap financial rewards from the Six Sigma concept. In other words, the company had higher-quality products and happier customers at a cheaper cost. Within four years, Six Sigma had saved the company $2.2 billion. Motorola's Six Sigma architects had done what most companies thought was impossible. By 1993, Motorola was operating at nearly six sigma in many of its manufacturing operations. Within a short time, Six Sigma began to spread like wildfire to other industries—and beyond manufacturing divisions alone.

What Is a Process?

Almost everything companies do involves a process. A process is any activity or group of activities that takes an input, adds value to it, and provides an output to an internal or external customer. Companies, regardless of their size, utilize thousands of processes every day to create their products and services. An *industrial process* is any process that depends on machinery for its creation and comes into physical contact with materials that will be delivered to an external customer. It does not include shipping, distribution, or billing processes. A *commercial process*, such as ordering materials, payroll, or processing customer orders, supports industrial processes, or may stand on its own as a separate and unique business. When at least 80 percent of a product's or service's value is derived from machinery, we consider this an industrial process. However, when 80 percent or more of a process depends on human activity, we consider this a commercial process. Airlines, employment agencies, accounting firms, fast-food restaurants, and the like are primarily commercial enterprises rather than industrial enterprises. The profitability of banks, insurance companies, brokerage firms, and the like depends primarily on the quality of their commercial process; manufacturing companies profit only when the quality of their industrial (and commercial) processes meets or exceeds their customers' expectations.

Six Sigma Applies to Products and Services, Not the Companies Who Create Them

Recent business history has shown that a company with six sigma products can still be in financial disarray. There is an important distinction between six sigma products and processes, and six sigma companies. The Six Sigma Breakthrough Strategy creates specific improvement goals for every process within an organization, allowing organizations to understand and incorporate technological advances lurking on the horizon. Six Sigma forces organizations to reexamine the way in which work gets done, rather than tweaking existing systems. It simplifies systems and processes, improves capability, and ultimately finds a way to control systems and processes permanently. Yet even a six sigma product will fail if brought to market late or into a market with no demand. This is why companies must achieve Six Sigma in *everything* they do.

Six Sigma Is a Performance Target

It's important to understand that Six Sigma is a performance target that applies to a single critical-to-quality characteristic (CTQ), not to the total product. When an automobile is described as "six sigma," this does not mean that only 3.4 automobiles out of a million will be defective. Six Sigma means that within a single automobile, the average opportunity for a defect of a critical-to-quality characteristic is only 3.4 defects per million opportunities. The more complex a product is— let's say we are comparing a paper clip with a sophisticated piece of medical equipment with complex subsystems—the greater the likelihood a defect will exist somewhere with the product. While a complex piece of medical equipment may have more defects per unit than the paper clip, at the "opportunity" level the paper clip and the piece of medical equipment can easily have the same sigma capability. So rather than stating that a product is six sigma, we say that the average opportunity for nonconformance within a product is six sigma.

Called on the Carpet

What exactly does Six Sigma—3.4 defects per million opportunities—mean? What is the difference, in practical terms, between, say, three sigma and six sigma? Let us give you an example. If wall-to-wall carpet in a 1,500-square-foot home were cleaned to the three sigma level (the average company operates at about a 3.5 to 4 sigma level), about four square feet of carpet (the carpet area under your average-size recliner chair) would still be soiled. In other words, a three sigma level would lead to a good number of disgruntled customers. If that same carpet were cleaned to the six sigma level, the soiled area would be the size of a pinhead—virtually invisible. The higher the sigma level, the less likely a process will produce defects. Each sigma creates an *exponential* reduction in defects. Consequently, as sigma increases, product reliability improves at a disproportionate rate. As a result, the need for testing and inspection diminishes, costs go down, cycle time decreases, and customer satisfaction goes up. Six Sigma is about as perfect as we can get in this world.

When describing Six Sigma and the number of defects that will occur at each sigma level to executives visiting the Six Sigma Academy, we often use this explanation: Each person sitting in the classroom is there because the airlines' record in getting passengers safely from one city to another exceeds six sigma, with less than one-half failure per million. However, for those whose bags did not arrive with them, it's because the airline's baggage operations are in the 6,000 to 23,000 defects per million range, or 3.5 to 4 sigma—which is typical of manufacturing and service operations (activities such as calculating restaurant bills, completing bank transactions, and filling medical prescriptions).

Customers are satisfied when they receive the value they expect. When products and services are produced at a six sigma level of quality, companies can be 99.99966 percent certain that each opportunity contained within the product will be created and delivered to the customer's expectation.

Taking Quality Personally

Former Motorola CEO Bob Galvin once told Mike that if a leader is to create true and lasting improvement, he or she must take quality to a personal level. Perhaps the path toward this goal should begin by looking at the chart on page 16. This form will guide you through the process of "sigma-tizing" one or more of your key processes, products, and/or services. The outcome may surprise you. At a minimum, it will give you a good benchmark of your key processes, products, and services as you progress through this book. It will place quality (and this book) on a more personal level.

To complete a form such as "How to Approximate the Sigma Capability for One of Your Processes," based on your criteria, there is little need for statistics or math of any kind—in fact, all that is required are some basic facts and simple arithmetic. So before reading on, let's find out what your sigma capabilities are.

Building a New Bottom Line

Again, the typical corporation today operates at a three to four sigma level. Companies below three sigma usually don't survive. At three sigma, the cost of quality is roughly 25 *to 40 percent* of sales revenue. To give you a sense of comparison, at six sigma, the cost of quality declines to less than one percent of sales revenue. Increasing profits by 20 to 30 percent of sales revenues creates massive savings and throws off significant increases to the bottom line. When General Electric reduced its cost of quality from 20 percent to less 10 percent—and raised its overall sigma level from four to five sigma—the company achieved a $1 billion increase in net income in just two years. This is money that goes directly to the bottom line. *This* is the reason corporations—and Wall Street—are so high on Six Sigma.

The Cost of Quality

For some companies, the cost to deliver a quality product can account for as much as 40 percent of the sales price. The laser jet printer you bought for $800 may have cost the manufacturer $320 in rework costs just to make sure that you took home an average-quality product. For a company whose annual revenues are $100 million, and whose operating income is $10 million, the cost of quality is roughly

| \multicolumn{4}{c}{**HOW TO APPROXIMATE THE SIGMA CAPABILITY FOR ONE OF YOUR PROCESSES**} |

STEP	ACTION	EQUATIONS	YOUR CALCULATIONS
1	What process do you want to consider?		Billing and charging
2	How many units were put through the process?		1,283
3	Of the units that went into the process, how many came out OK?		1,138
4	Compute the yield for the process defined in Step 1	= (Step 3) / (Step 2)	.8870
5	Compute the defect rate based on Step 4	= 1 – (Step 4)	.113
6	Determine the number of potential things that could create a defect	= N number of critical-to-quality characteristics (CTQs)	24
7	Compute the defect rate per CTQ characteristic	= (Step 5) / (Step 6)	.0047
8	Compute the defects per million opportunities (DPMO)	= (Step 7) x 1,000,000	4,709
9	Convert the DPMO (Step 8) into a sigma value, using the Sigma Conversion Chart at the back of the book		4.1
10	Draw conclusions		Slightly-above-average performance

25 percent of the operating revenue, or $25 million. If this same company could reduce its cost of achieving quality by 20 percent, it would increase its operating income by $5 million—or 50 percent of the current operating income. The following chart shows the benefits of reaching higher sigma levels.

THE COST OF QUALITY		
SIGMA LEVEL	DEFECTS PER MILLION OPPORTUNITIES	COST OF QUALITY
2	308,537 *(Noncompetitive companies)*	Not applicable
3	66,807	25 – 40% of sales
4	6,210 *(Industry average)*	15 – 25% of sales
5	233	5 – 15% of sales
6	3.4 *(World class)*	< 1% of sales
Each sigma shift provides a 10 percent net income improvement.		

Back to the Future

Why should companies focus on the process rather than the final outcome? Final outcomes or results are dictated by what happens during the process. When businesses create a better process, they eliminate opportunities for defects before they occur. By reducing variation during the creation of products and services, it's possible for *any* business to achieve six sigma quality. Every aspect of a business can improve its cost and profitability dramatically by using the Six Sigma Breakthrough Strategy.

Keep in mind, however, that Six Sigma and the Breakthrough Strategy are two distinct elements. Six Sigma is the philosophy and goal—3.4 defects per million opportunities. The Breakthrough Strategy provides the means to achieve that goal through a highly focused system of problem solving. Six Sigma is the Land of Oz; the Breakthrough Strategy is the Yellow Brick Road that takes us there.

Although companies pursuing Six Sigma through the Breakthrough Strategy will undoubtedly see a marked improvement in the quality of their goods and services, the most important impact of the undertaking will be on the bottom line. As one Polaroid executive put it, "Six Sigma gave our company universal tools that could be systematically applied to problems and then be used to gauge the results. In some ways, Six Sigma is one of the most misunderstood strategies ever to hit the business world. The focus is not so much on the number of defects per million opportunities, but a systematic road map to reduce variability in a process through assimilation and organization of information that increases bottom-line dollar savings. Although defects decrease as the process improves, Six Sigma focuses on the process that creates or eliminates the defects rather than the defects themselves."

Achieving Six Sigma is not easy. In fact, GE's Jack Welch calls Six Sigma the most difficult "stretch goal" GE has ever undertaken. But we are confident that Six Sigma will be the biggest, the most personally rewarding, and the most profitable initiative your company will ever undertake. The improved quality that results will translate not only into cost reductions but into increased sales and quantum leaps in profitability. By increasing quality levels, companies not only make more money for shareholders, they also acquire greater market share as a result of increased customer satisfaction. And that is a benefit no other reengineering or quality program can equal.

CHAPTER TWO

The Yellow Brick Road

Motorola had an unusual problem. In 1988, the inaugural year of the Malcolm Baldrige National Quality Award, Motorola was the first large company to win the coveted prize. The award came about, in part, as a result of former Motorola president Robert Galvin's 1981 challenge to the company that it achieve a tenfold improvement in performance over a five-year period. Motorola employees successfully achieved Galvin's goal and went on to win the Baldrige Award. But the company wasn't allowed to compete again for five years. As a result, the award couldn't serve as a driving force for continued improvement.

Four years earlier, Mikel Harry, a senior staff engineer at Motorola's Government Electronics Group (GEG), created a detailed road map for improving product design and reducing production time and costs within GEG. This represented the Yellow Brick Road to Six Sigma. Convinced that the initial concept of Six Sigma was valid, Harry pulled together a group of engineers within GEG to demonstrate its potential. Under his leadership, they began to experiment with problem solving through statistical analysis. Through this teachable methodology, the organization began to show dramatic results— GEG's products were being designed and produced faster and more cheaply. Subsequently, Harry began to formulate a method for applying Six Sigma throughout the company.

His work culminated in a paper titled "The Strategic Vision for Accelerating Six Sigma Within Motorola." The paper quickly made its way throughout the company, eventually landing on the desk of Robert Galvin. Galvin believed that achieving six sigma within Motorola was the incentive the company needed to raise the bar for quality. More-over, Galvin recognized the practical applications of applying statistical analysis to business problems.

In 1990, Galvin asked Harry to leave the company's Government Electronics Group in order to start up and lead Motorola's Six Sigma Research Institute in Schaumburg, Illinois. Other companies, such as IBM, Texas Instruments Defense Group, Digital Electronics, Asea Brown Boveri, and Kodak, would participate as well. The mission of the Institute was to develop Six Sigma implementation strategies, deployment guidelines, and advanced statistical tools that would work in a variety of companies and industries.

The Institute presented opportunities for further development of the Six Sigma Breakthrough Strategy that the actual factories could not. A real factory or work area is noisy and hectic. Moreover, many types of problems don't arise very often in the actual production of a product or service. The Institute did not have to worry about slowing down or stopping a manufacturing line or delivery of service to check or correct defects. The Institute allowed researchers to run simula-tions to show the effects of potentially costly mistakes. It created an environment where production problems from the factory floor could be translated into statistical problems to which the Six Sigma Break-through Strategy could be applied to find the cause of the problem and a solution.

Meanwhile, Richard Schroeder, vice president and general man-ager of customer service for Motorola's Codex subsidiary, heard about Harry and his accomplishments at the Government Electronics Group using Six Sigma. He decided to apply the methodology within Codex. Schroeder used Six Sigma to achieve a 58 percent reduction in cost of quality within the division, a 40 percent reduction in errors, and a 60 percent reduction in the time it took to design a product.

Excited by the potential to apply Six Sigma to other businesses, Schroeder convinced Harry to leave Motorola in 1993 and join him at Asea Brown Boveri's (ABB) transformer business, where they would help rebuild the Swiss manufacturing giant. While at ABB, they worked in tandem to shift the focus of Six Sigma from controlling defects to reducing costs, allowing for further refinement of the Breakthrough Strategy. By focusing the strategy on increasing ABB's net profits through improving product quality, performance, productivity, and costs, ABB achieved a 68 percent reduction in defect levels and a 30 percent reduction in product costs, resulting in an $898 million savings/cost reduction each year over a two-year period. Schroeder also helped many of ABB's suppliers apply the Breakthrough Strategy to their own products, ultimately reducing ABB's material cost purchases by $87 million. The two decided to join forces and henceforth be a team.

In 1994, Dr. Harry opened the doors to the Six Sigma Academy in Scottsdale, Arizona, taking on General Electric and AlliedSignal as the first clients. As the Breakthrough Strategy became known and applauded on Wall Street and in corporate boardrooms, the Academy has experienced phenomenal growth, attracting attention from Fortune 50 companies in a range of industries.

We are bombarded daily with requests from companies around the world that want more details on how the Six Sigma program works and how it can be applied to their organization. As a result, we developed a comprehensive Six Sigma training curriculum at the Academy to teach companies how to apply the Breakthrough Strategy to the processes that go into creating a product and/or service. At the Academy, and now, for the first time, in this book, we show how the Breakthrough Strategy affects six areas fundamental to improving a company's value:

1. process improvements

2. product and service improvement

3. investor relations

4. design methodology

5. supplier improvement

6. training and recruitment

A Breakthrough Strategy Overview

Six Sigma is a problem-solving venture. Every project has a process or design problem in search of a solution. The Breakthrough Strategy directs people's energies to finding solutions and improving bottom lines. It shows companies how much information (and therefore money) they are leaving on the table.

Using the Six Sigma Breakthrough Strategy to identify problems can be a daunting experience for corporate leaders. The Breakthrough Strategy takes executives through the maze of business, technology, manufacturing, quality, production, and delivery system issues. In doing so, it initially raises even more questions. Identifying a problem is simple compared with defining the underlying causes. Underlying causes are often masked by layers of skewed financial reports, irrelevant data, or a corporation's cultural bias.

There are eight fundamental steps or stages involved in applying the Breakthrough Strategy to achieve Six Sigma quality in a process, division, or company. These eight phases are Recognize, Define, Measure, Analyze, Improve, Control, Standardize, and Integrate. The four core phases (what we call M-A-I-C) of the Breakthrough Strategy—Measure, Analyze, Improve, and Control—are described here; Chapter 7 addresses each of the eight phases in greater detail.

The **Measure phase** includes a review of the types of measurement systems and their key features. Companies must understand the nature and properties of data collection and reporting. They must think about where errors in measurements can occur, as well as the potential impact faulty measurements can have on a project's success. In addition, companies must study the frequency with which defects occur and the process capability that governs the creation of defects.

In the **Analyze phase,** the Breakthrough Strategy offers specific statistical methods and tools to isolate key pieces of information that are critical to explaining the number of defective products. In the Analyze phase, practical business problems are turned into statistical problems. Is the problem sporadic or persistent? Is the problem technology or process related?

In the **Improve phase,** the Breakthrough Strategy focuses on discovering the key variables that cause the problem. The Improve phase encompasses the process known as Design for Six Sigma (DFSS), as well. Using DFSS, the processes that create the products or services are designed from the beginning or reconfigured in such a way that they produce six sigma—quality goods and services, much as Motorola designed a process to produce a virtually defect-free pager.

Finally, in the **Control phase,** the Breakthrough Strategy ensures that the same problems don't reoccur by continually monitoring the processes that create the product or service.

Realizing the full potential of the Breakthrough Strategy requires identifying and training key employees. Highly skilled employees known as Black Belts are trained in the Breakthrough Strategy and its tools. Working full time on Six Sigma projects, Black Belts lead teams through each of the four phases that affect key processes.

Six Sigma's Breakthrough Strategy

The Six Sigma Breakthrough Strategy is a disciplined method of using extremely rigorous data-gathering and statistical analysis to pinpoint sources of errors and ways of eliminating them. Six Sigma's heavy reliance on performance metrics coupled with statistical analysis eliminates the fluff found in other quality programs. Quality-improvement projects using Six Sigma are chosen as a result of customer feedback and potential cost savings, not fuzzy notions of continuous improvement. Improvements that have the largest customer impact—and the biggest impact on revenues—are given the highest priority. In other words, we focus first and foremost on the improvements that will have the biggest impact on your business. Again, unlike other quality programs, Six Sigma does not pursue quality solely for the sake of achieving quality. Six Sigma is about pursuing quality only if it adds value for the customer and the company.

The Breakthrough Strategy's methodology uses specific tools to reduce operating costs, improve capacity, improve margins, shorten

the length of time it takes to bring a new product to market, reduce
inventory, and process transactions in shorter time periods with fewer
errors. The Breakthrough Strategy applies a laserlike focus to improvement—first, through the short-term strategy of defect removal, and,
second, through the long-term strategy of refining the system. Remov-
ing critical defects will not only improve your bottom line in the short
term, but it will set the stage for eventually refining entire systems for
even greater profitability. Improving results requires that the processes
that generate the results also improve. When organizations recognize
that, they are already well on the way to achieving Six Sigma.

Six Sigma and Statistics

Understandably, most people believe that statistics are boring and
complicated. But some of the most interesting phenomena that occur
within organizations can be best captured and explained with the simplicity and beauty of statistics. Once people get beyond the symbols,
formulas, and charts, they usually find that statistics make problems
(and the questions) much clearer and simpler. Statistics can be creative, simple, important, and relevant, yet many people think statistics
only muddy the waters. It's just not true. It's really the simplicity of
statistics that allows us to measure, improve, and monitor the
processes within our organizations. Statistics are a tool that separates
commonsense reasoning from extraordinary reasoning.

H. G. Wells wrote in 1925, "Statistical thinking will one day be
as necessary for efficient citizenship as the ability to read and
write." We believe that statistical knowledge is to the information
and technological age what fossil fuel was to the industrial age. In
fact, the future of industry depends on an understanding of statistics.
Statistics are like a powerful microscope that make visible what has
previously been invisible. Without statistics, today's high-density
semiconductor chips could not be built. To an extent, statistics allow
us to see the future and introduce changes that permit us to redirect
or correct the way things develop. Statistics allow companies to solve

problems and form the backdrop for how they educate their employees. They allow companies to collect data, translate that data into information, and then interpret the information so that decisions can be made based on fact, rather than intuition, gut feel, or past experience. Statistics create the foundation for quality, which translates to profitability and market share.

Managers need to become more literate in statistics, but we also realize that statistical knowledge needs to be communicated in a format that makes it usable, so that people can extrapolate key data and apply it to their day-to-day work. But it's also important to recognize that the full benefit of statistics can be achieved only in a culture that looks at data with the right skills—hence, the Breakthrough Strategy. The more knowledgeable an organization becomes, and the more it allows its employees to use that knowledge, the more profitable it will become. Only knowledge put to use can create capital.

Because of the importance of statistics in achieving quality, industry is starting to devote huge amounts of money to training employees in statistical methods for quality improvement, as well as for other efforts. Unfortunately, our college and university curriculums still do not fully reflect the growing relevance of statistics in organizations of all kinds, and therefore give little emphasis to educating students in even some of the most fundamental aspects of how to apply mathematical statistics to everyday life in the workplace. Disciplines such as engineering and business should uniformly require statistical courses in the curriculum, but many do not, and may instead designate these courses as "electives."

Another problem is that many statistics courses are theoretical, and students are not given the opportunity to link theory to practical application. A lack of the right kind of statistical education at the university level is a major stumbling block to U.S. competitiveness in industry. While corporate-based education is certainly a way to overcome this problem, we also believe that our colleges and universities need to relearn the way they teach students so that when they enter the workforce they have the knowledge and skills to link theory to practice. On so many occasions, we have heard employees at organizations, particularly those employees just out of school, describe how their college statistics courses left them confused on how statistical tools apply to the real work world. If H. G. Wells is correct in his prediction about statistics—and we believe he is—the implications of his words for our educational systems and the future of our workforce are enormous.

Learning from Past Mistakes

Since World War II, the proliferation of programs and initiatives designed to improve productivity and increase profits has left much of American industry confused. The world has had enough of improvement programs and management fads based on intellectual models that don't have the tools or strategies to implement the new ideology. Organizations need standardized methods and tools designed to ferret out and exploit opportunities that will result in tangible financial gains. They need initiatives based on repeatable improvement. They need standardized road maps on how to implement and deploy the strategies, tactics, and tools, and the leadership necessary to create and sustain success.

Companies have tried downsizing, outsourcing, activity-based costing, new-product development, reengineering, material requirements planning, Kaizen,* and creating world-class factories. While none of these management methods are inherently bad—they have produced notable results—they are not designed to help companies improve their bottom line and simultaneously improve quality or performance.

Over the past fifteen years, American industry has been besieged by consultants and business books focusing on process improvement.

---

*Kaizen refers to gradual, unending improvement, doing "little things" better, and continually reaching for higher standards. It is Bombardier's belief that at a certain point the gain from basic Kaizen tools diminishes and the impact of Six Sigma takes off. Organizations that are between 3 and 3.5 sigma will see that some of their projects will look like Kaizen efforts, since Kaizen uses fairly basic tools. But once the Six Sigma methodology starts using tools such as Design of Experiments, companies make quantum leaps in performance not possible through Kaizen-type efforts. The gains from Six Sigma projects will be far greater than what can be achieved through Kaizen, particularly when companies begin to change the design of their products.

While such quality initiatives can have positive effects, none has the potential of Six Sigma and the Breakthrough Strategy.

One reason for this is that for most quality initiatives, people in the organization are not required to "own" the quality of their work. The quality of their products, product design, and industrial processes are so far removed from the financial aspects of the business that they have no reason to link their day-to-day activities to the overall financial state of the company. When design, manufacturing, sales, and quality control work independently, there is a great deal of resistance on the part of people to take responsibility for something that is not part of their job. While many quality programs work effectively within individual departments, they lack the ability to reach across the entire corporation in a unified and focused manner. To create synergy and shared goals and values, a quality initiative needs to infiltrate the mind-set and behavior of every employee in every corner of the organization. *The Six Sigma Breakthrough Strategy is a business initiative,* rather than a quality initiative; every employee throughout the corporation is accountable for understanding and implementing its methodology. When Six Sigma is implemented as a business strategy, the company uses financial measures to select projects for improvement and to determine the results. In other words, Six Sigma aligns the needs of the corporation and the customer with the needs of the individual.

For thousands of employees in hundreds of companies, Six Sigma is the place where science, technology, quality, and profitability meet. Common goals are forged between engineers and marketers, between companies and their customers, and between senior management and those who actually create the product or deliver the service. Six Sigma encourages employees to ask new questions and pursue answers with new and standardized investigative processes. As you learn how others have applied Six Sigma principles, we believe you may be forced to reexamine the ways in which your organization works, as well.

CHAPTER THREE

Being Better Is Cheaper

■   ■   ■   ■   ■   ■

Many companies—and managers—take refuge
in one or more of the following beliefs:

To err is human.
Excessive quality costs too much, takes too long.
Just beating last year's numbers is good enough.
Soft errors (like paperwork) are more excusable.
We are still better than our competitors.
Firefighting our way out of a quality emergency in the
nick of time is a badge of honor; it was even fun.

—ROBERT W. GALVIN

Every company (and customer) pays a penalty for less-than-perfect quality. Every defect is an economic detractor for the producer and customer. The results are costly when quality is not an intrinsic part of designing and producing a product or service. Most companies will find that the cost of quality, when properly evaluated, falls somewhere between 15 and 25 percent of total sales—not the 3 to 7 percent they estimate it to be. Their estimates are in error because their accounting system cannot trap most of the true costs associated with poor quality.

Activities such as inspection, testing, and review to prevent defective products from being shipped to the customer can increase these figures to between 20 and 25 percent of the total sales dollar. As we

noted earlier, the typical corporation produces products and services
between a 3.5 and 4 sigma level, which means that the cost of quality
is typically around 20 to 30 percent of each sales dollar. Enlightened
companies recognize the true cost of poor quality, and are setting out
to accurately measure it and reduce it.

The value in knowing the total cost of quality is that it provides a
starting point for management to compare courses of action and focus
decisions. For many, it's a wake-up call. Most companies do not know
the true cost of their own quality, so they remain asleep in the boiler
room or captain's quarters while the ship is slowly sinking. In fact, while
82 percent of U.S. companies are involved in quality programs, only 33
percent actually calculate the cost of quality. Executives who think they
have a good idea of the cost of quality at their company probably would
be surprised to learn that such a large percentage of their sales dollars are
consumed by quality-related costs. Many estimate their cost of quality to
be less than 5 percent. When executives get a realistic picture of the cost
of quality, they are shocked to learn how much revenue is lost.

"Lost" revenue is just that—lost. It's real money that shareholders
and corporations are entitled to but will never see. Worse yet, it becomes
the price customers pay for a company's inability to run its business in a
quality manner. Money that is "lost" in the factory will never earn interest and never add to the company's wealth. Poor quality creates a poor
"history." Customers cannot be confident that goods and services will be
delivered on time and will spend precious time and money recording,
processing, packing, and returning what never should have been shipped
this way in the first place. In the end, poor quality costs companies, customers, consumers, and society. It's very real—and pretty big—money.

The Cost of Quality

Since quality saves companies money—and lots of it—it makes sense
to produce a product or service with virtually no defects by doing it
right the first time. In 1995, when General Electric calculated its
overall sigma level to be 3.5, they discovered they were wasting $5 bil-

lion each year in the cost of quality. United Technologies Corporation chairman and CEO George David says that poor quality costs his company more than $2 billion a year.

Although some managers intuitively grasp the fact that poor quality is costly and that there is a great financial reward in preventing defects at the earliest possible stage or eliminating defects altogether, others see poor quality as a nebulous concept with little payback potential. Even if they do see it, they don't know how to get at it. They lack the "mind shovels" to dig it out, put it in buckets, and take it to the bank. For many executives who cannot create the Yellow Brick Road the way GE has, there is a tendency to discount what GE and others have done, or to minimize the importance of the lessons to be learned. Some deny with statements such as "You don't understand. Our company is different," or "Since we are already the market leader, we don't need Six Sigma."

The Cost of Quality Metric

Over the years, many companies have utilized the cost-of-poor-quality (COPQ) metric as a leading indicator of how well they are performing in the quality arena. In fact, some companies use this metric to the exclusion of all other indices of quality. When the COPQ index shows an operating level of 2 or 3 percent, corporate leadership mistakenly believes their product quality must be quite good; otherwise, the COPQ would be higher. We find three problems with conventional cost-of-quality theory.

- Costs do not increase in order for quality to improve, given a "Prevention" approach versus a "Detect and Fix" mentality.

- Many significant quality-related costs cannot be captured by most types of accounting systems.

- The conventional cost-of-quality theory ignores costly and avoidable inefficiencies that occur in the engineering, manufacturing, accounting, and service sectors of companies.

AN HISTORICAL PERSPECTIVE ON QUALITY IMPROVEMENT

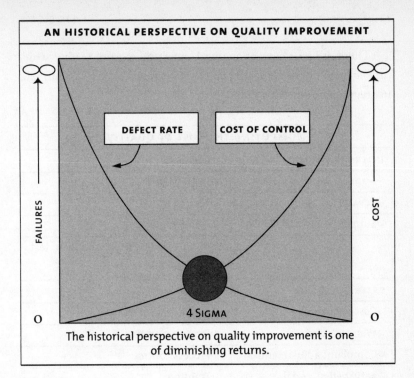

The historical perspective on quality improvement is one of diminishing returns.

THE NEW DEFINITION OF QUALITY

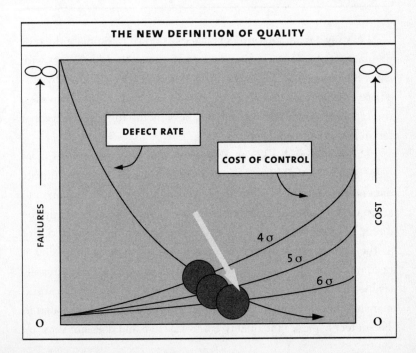

There are four categories that support the cost-of-quality structure. In general, the cost of quality is composed of costs due to failure, appraisal, and prevention.

COMPUTING THE COST OF QUALITY	
INTERNAL FAILURE	**APPRAISAL**
⇨Scrap	⇨Inspection
⇨Rework	⇨Testing
⇨Supplier scrap and rework	⇨Quality audit
	⇨Initial cost and maintenance of test equipment
EXTERNAL FAILURE	**PREVENTION**
⇨Cost to customer	⇨Quality planning
⇨Warranty cost	⇨Process planning
⇨Complaint adjustments	⇨Process control
⇨Returned material	⇨Training

Let's say a manufacturing manager sits down to estimate the cost of quality for his or her business, comparing traditional practices with a Six Sigma perspective. At first, the categories seem fairly obvious. There are warranty claim costs reported every month. In some cases, the manager tracks the cost his business incurs to fix products that fail in the hands of the consumer.

The manager also knows that scrap and rejects are a result of defects. To estimate these costs, he or she tracks down the quality data on the amount of scrap and rejects and uses this information to estimate the material and labor costs associated with it. Similarly, the direct labor required to rework defective parts can be estimated. But as the manager digs deeper into the nature of the cost of quality, it becomes clear that many of the other costs of quality are not readily visible. For example, when an "upstream" worker discovers a workmanship flaw, it is often "handed back" to the person who created it. The defect bypasses the quality-control system and does not show up in the quality information system, allowing the employee to avoid being penalized for poor workmanship.

Another example is when a manager knows that when the process produces a lot of defective parts, the length of time required to get completed components through the system increases. This increased cycle time has a real cost in terms of additional labor hours and inventory. However, this cost does not get assigned to the COPQ bucket and remains invisible from a quality perspective. There's also the cost of all hidden and nonroutine inspection and testing that has to be performed to try and catch the defects, not to mention unscheduled maintenance and downtime required to fix the problem. There is the important, but hard-to-quantify, cost impact of lost customers and reduced customer loyalty when faulty products are purchased. Although the manager isn't sure what economic havoc these defects are creating for the overall business, he knows that defective products lead to unhappy customers who, in turn, may take their business elsewhere.

To help generate relevant data and make estimates, the manager organizes the cost of quality into five cost groups:

1. The cost of failure in the field. This includes costs such as warranty claims, as well as the cost to service problems. The manager also has access to data on the costs incurred by the customer as a result of the failure, but decides to group these costs with opportunity costs.

2. The internal failure costs—the costs in labor and material associated with scrapped parts and rework. These costs include the additional inventory carried due to longer cycle time (the time it takes to move a product through the process).

3. The costs of appraisal and inspection. These are the materials for samples, test equipment, and labor costs to catch defects before they are shipped. These costs also include the costs related to quality audits, and those of monitoring outside vendors and dealing with their quality problems.

4. The costs related to improving poor quality, including the cost of equipment to better control processes and the cost of programs to improve quality.

5. The opportunity cost of producing more products with the same assets (by reducing the number of resources tied up in fixing defects and fighting fires, so to speak). This is in addition to the opportunity cost of lost customer loyalty and lost sales owing to poor quality in the past. The manager treats this category separately from the others, since these costs are lost opportunities that are more difficult to quantify.

The manager's first estimate of the cost of quality is very revealing. First, the overall total cost was higher than he ever dreamed possible, even without including the harder-to-quantify costs of customer ill will or extra inventory due to longer cycle times. Indeed, the total accounts for nearly 80 percent of the total cost of quality. The manager also noted that only 4 percent of the total costs was the result of efforts to prevent defects. At this point, it becomes clear that the whole system is upside down, and, as a consequence, is economically inefficient.

Overall, the estimate of the cost of quality was a good first estimate. There are some arguments about whether the cost of extra production days due to high scrap rates should be included. There are also some disagreements about whether or not to include overhead on top of the direct labor and material costs of the scrap and rework. In the end, the manager kept track of all these costs but put them in the "opportunity cost" category, since it wasn't clear how these costs could be tracked or captured. But the manager also began to realize that even if these costs aren't included, the total is starting to look enormous.

The one scenario that seemed to help identify the costs of quality was this: Suppose all the defects disappeared. Would the costs in question also disappear? What other costs would disappear or be reduced?

As the manager reviewed the cost-of-quality numbers for his business, he began to wonder how he could reduce the internal/external failure costs without growing the cost of appraisal and prevention. At a certain point, wouldn't it become uneconomical to improve quality? It would intuitively appear that there would be some point of diminishing return.

As the manager looks at the work done in his department, it becomes clear that a lot of effort is spent testing and inspecting for defects. If the business could reduce its defects, the need to continue to inspect would decrease; it could move toward sampling and audit-type inspections, and eventually completely eliminate inspection and testing. The manager noted that the cost-of-quality estimate they had prepared did not include many of the hidden costs and opportunity costs of quality, such as longer cycle times, increased inventory, and reduced customer loyalty.

The longer the manager compared the traditional views of poor quality with the Six Sigma view, the more obvious it became that by viewing variation as the driving force behind defects and the cost of quality, anything that strayed from the desired target became more expensive to produce or represented a loss.

One reason why some organizations are stuck at three or four sigma is that they believe that the costs of going beyond three or four sigma through defect reduction will exceed the benefits of reducing poor quality. Six Sigma holds that moving beyond four sigma is not only possible but profitable, because five and six sigma performance levels enable companies to dramatically reduce the cost of appraisal and prevention. We don't try to inspect our way to Six Sigma. Rather, we try to eliminate defects at the root source through better processes and better products and service design focused on meeting the needs of the customers. When we aim for this higher standard, we are forced to abandon minor adjustments in how we run our processes and consider entirely new ways of doing business.

COST OF QUALITY	
CURRENTLY MEASURED	**NOT CURRENTLY MEASURED**
Scrap	Increased maintenance
	Lost sales
Warranty expense	Customer dissatisfaction
	Downtime
Inspection costs	Engineering and product
	Development errors
Overtime	Bill of material inaccuracy
	Rejected raw materials

Designing for Six Sigma

George David, CEO of United Technologies, says that one of his company's plants has more inspectors than operators. "That's not my idea of how to achieve high quality. Our goal companywide is zero inspectors by placing more emphasis than ever before on quality at the design stage." Raytheon's Robert W. Drewes, too, acknowledges that most of his company's quality issues are traceable to design.

Numerous studies have shown that about 70 percent of a product's total cost is determined by its design. Some management consultants have put the estimate at as high as 80 percent. The higher the quality that is designed into a product, the lower its cost. In fact, 80 percent of quality problems are actually designed into the product without any conscious attempt to do so. Companies implementing Six Sigma find that the overwhelming majority of defects are created during the design process. To ensure that customer feedback is incorporated into improved designs of products, marketing and engineering need to compile more rigorous data about the performance of products in use. They also need to assess the capability of their processes and factor this into the design so that the finished configuration of a product or service is "producible" using existing technology. Whenever the capability of the process is less than that demanded by the design, equilibrium is achieved by part matching, sorting, and fixing. The cost of quality attributable to a poor design is extremely difficult to estimate; however, we do know it is very large.

Companies that win government contracts often spend 30 to 40 percent of their funds just on testing and correcting the product. These companies would be far more profitable if they designed their processes so that products did not have to be tested and reworked so extensively in the first place. If companies are going to manufacture to more demanding standards, clearly the answer is not to create more demanding inspection and testing requirements. However, if the process and design capability remains a constant, companies have no choice but to inspect and test more frequently and with greater precision—at increased costs to the customer and at lower profits to the company.

Among the reasons to adopt Six Sigma Breakthrough Strategy to improve a company's quality are the following:

- Businesses that achieve significant quality improvements earn 8 percent higher prices.

- Businesses that achieve a superior-quality position are three times more profitable as those with inferior levels of quality.

- Businesses that improve their quality gain 4 percent in market share each year.

- Each significant positive shift in process capability equates to ten times improvement in profitability.

SIX KEY AREAS TO ADDRESS WHEN IMPROVING THE COST OF QUALITY	
KEY DRIVERS	**BASIC ISSUE**
1. Basic organizational capabilities	• Skills and tools required to implement improvements in business processes are lacking
2. Industrial process variations	• Poor industrial process capabilities result in high COPQ (rework, scrap, field failure) • Customer demands are frequently not passed on to engineering • Inefficient front-end engineering
3. Business process variations	• Product cost estimation is often widely off the mark, resulting in poor financial performance and incorrect manufacturing decisions
4. Engineering/design process and documentation	• Engineering systems and design processes and documentation are often inadequate and flawed
5. Quality of specifications	• Specifications sent to suppliers/subcontractors vary considerably in their quality, resulting in poor-quality parts
6. Supplier capabilities	• Lack of quality suppliers, resulting in poor-quality parts/services, late deliveries, higher parts/service costs, etc.

ONE COMPANY'S EXPERIENCE:

General Electric 2000

. . . Six Sigma—GE Quality 2000—will be the biggest, the most personally rewarding, and, in the end, the most profitable undertaking in our history. We have set for ourselves the goal of becoming, by the year 2000, a Six Sigma quality company, which means a company that produces virtually defect-free products, services and transactions.

—JACK WELCH, GENERAL ELECTRIC'S 1996 ANNUAL MEETING

The best Six Sigma projects begin not inside the business but outside it, focused on answering the question—how can we make the customer more competitive? What is critical to the customer's success? Learning the answer to that question and then learning how to provide the solution is the only focus we need.

—JACK WELCH, GENERAL ELECTRIC'S 1997 ANNUAL MEETING

The media hoopla surrounding General Electric's embrace of Six Sigma has been a major catalyst in stimulating interest in Six Sigma at many organizations around the world. For years, Jack Welch's success in getting his ideas to work at General Electric has been closely watched by corporate America for information on the latest management thinking. Welch's 1996 announcement that he planned to lead the company to Six Sigma by the year 2000 created a lasting impression on other companies looking for new ways to prosper in a world in which value-oriented consumers demanded quality goods and services. Longtime GE observer and University of Michigan management professor Noel Tichy believes that Jack Welch has "set a new, contemporary paradigm for the corporation that is the model for the twenty-first century."

During his nearly twenty-year tenure at the helm of GE, Welch has guided the growth of GE's market value from $12 billion in 1981 to about $280 billion in 1998. He is regarded as one of the most successful and visionary executives of this century, having transformed GE from a predominantly manufacturing company to a much more diversified corporation with a broad spectrum of products and services. In 1990, 55 percent of GE's revenues came from sales of products such as jet engines, washing machines, CT scanners, and turbines, while the other 45 percent came from services. Today, GE Capital Services, with twenty-eight diversified businesses under its umbrella, contributes an extraordinary 40 percent to GE's total earnings and accounts for two-thirds of the company's revenues, making the division the most profitable financial group in the world.

Many factors have contributed to Welch's outstanding performance. Anticipating that by the year 2000 most of GE revenue would come from overseas sources, Welch positioned the company so that, unlike Motorola, Texas Instruments, and Xerox, it was not caught "in the eye of the Asian hurricane." Instead the company coped with the Asian boom by focusing on areas where it already held a competitive and technical edge, and abandoned businesses like consumer electronics where it did not. Welch built a management team of superstars, replaced cherished, but unprofitable, businesses with purchases of high-growth businesses, and pushed the company to focus more on its service technology than product technology.

But many observers believe that implementing Six Sigma is what has allowed Welch to transform the old-line industrial giant into a keenly competitive and agile growth company. Although General Electric had adopted quality programs prior to implementing Six Sigma, none had penetrated the company to the extent that Six Sigma has. In fact, prior to Six Sigma, Welch, a self-proclaimed cynic when it came to quality programs, felt that quality programs were heavy on slogans and light on results. But after hearing former GE vice chairman and current AlliedSignal CEO Lawrence A. Bossidy, a longtime friend and golfing partner, outline the benefits AlliedSignal was reaping from Six Sigma, which Bossidy launched at Allied in 1994, Welch wanted to know more. Welch learned that Six Sigma, unlike previous quality-control techniques, allowed AlliedSignal to focus simultaneously on *profitability*, through cost reduction, and on *defect reduction*, through decreased cycle time, inventory maintenance, and product improvement. Bossidy had the numbers to show that Six Sigma was doing exactly what it was designed to do. By allowing AlliedSignal's bottom-line growth to take precedence over quality, the company was creating higher-quality products at lower costs.

At home recovering from surgery, Welch asked Bossidy to take his place at GE's annual top management meeting in June 1995. Bossidy could talk about anything he wanted, as long as it lit a fire under GE executives. Choosing to share AlliedSignal's success with Six Sigma, Bossidy created such a positive and energetic reaction that when Welch returned to work in August, he decided to adopt Six Sigma at GE, with the ambitious goal of bringing each of GE's products and service operations to six sigma levels of quality by the year 2000, the year he is slated for retirement.

A cautious and thoughtful convert, Welch was candid about the magnitude of implementing Six Sigma. The Breakthrough Strategy would become one in a trinity of growth initiatives—globalization, services, and Six Sigma quality—that would take GE into the twenty-first century as the "best-in-class" corporation in the world. When GE decided to pursue Six Sigma, it discovered that overall its operations were running at somewhere between three and four sigma, or about 35,000 defects per million opportunities—a number consistent with the defect levels of most successful companies. The company would be required to go from generating products and services with an average of 35,000 defects per million opportunities (DPMO) to reaching and maintaining virtual perfection, or as close to it as one can get in this life—a formidable 3.4 defects per million opportunities.

Addressing shareholders at the 1996 annual meeting, Welch outlined what he called "GE Quality 2000: A Dream with a Plan." For GE to achieve Six Sigma quality by the year 2000, Welch told his audience, Six Sigma "will require us to reduce defect rates 10,000-fold—about 84 percent per year for five consecutive years—an enormous task, one that stretches even the concept of stretch behavior."

In 1996, the gap between being a three sigma organization and a six sigma organization was costing GE an astounding $7 billion to $10 billion each year in scrap, reworking of parts, correction of transactional errors, inefficiencies, and lost productivity. Achieving Six Sigma would reduce the error rate at GE to 3.4 defects per million opportunities—*or one ten-thousandth* of GE's error rate in 1996. But in order to raise GE's operations to six sigma levels of quality, Welch had to engineer one of the most sweeping changes in corporate history.

Launching a quality initiative that called for a massive investment for training tens of thousands of employees in a disciplined methodology based on applying statistics to problem solving was no small decision. But Welch knew that the program would go nowhere without training employees who could help to raise the level of quality throughout the organization. GE's Leadership Development Institute at Crotonville and other GE training centers located around the country had to be given the financial resources to train the company's employees in Six Sigma methodology.

Previous training and education investments made by the company paled in comparison with the $200 million Welch would commit in 1996 to training 200 Master Black Belts and 800 Black Belts in the Breakthrough Strategy. He also required that GE's 20,000 engineers be trained in Design for Six Sigma (DFSS), a methodology that would enable the company to literally design and build Six Sigma quality into every product and service, from fashioning an engine blade to answering a phone call about a credit card. GE realized that without the rigorous statistical processes required by DFSS, its products and services would never meet customers' standards of quality.

GE ended up dedicating far more than the initial $200 million the company spent. In 1997, GE invested $250 million in training nearly 4,000 Black Belts and Master Black Belts and more than 60,000 Green Belts out of a workforce of 222,000. But the massive investment would pay off. In 1997 alone, Six Sigma added $300 million to its 1997 operating income.

Since its wholehearted plunge into Six Sigma in 1996, when the cost to implement Six Sigma was slightly higher than the benefits, the company has begun reaping exponential returns. In 1998, the $500 million dedicated to the initiative were offset by over three quarters of a billion dollars in savings, and the company expects to save $1.5 billion in 1999.

Preparing GE for Six Sigma

Although he didn't know it at the time, Welch began laying the groundwork for Six Sigma in 1988 with a companywide initiative known as Work-Out. As Welch began to recognize that employees were an important source of brainpower for new and creative ideas, he wanted to create an environment that pushed the company's employees toward "a relentless, endless companywide search for a better way to do everything we do." The Work-Out program was a way to give *every* employee, from managers to factory workers, an opportunity to influence and improve GE's day-to-day operations. Much has been written about Work-Out's four major goals; the following list highlights those goals so we can see how they later helped lay the groundwork for Six Sigma.

> GOAL ONE Build trust. Employees were encouraged to speak out critically inside the company about GE and the way they performed their jobs without negative consequences to their careers.

WO Empower employees. The people who perform a
~~how~~ it intimately. To capitalize on employees' knowl-
~~nd~~ their unique perspective, Welch granted employees
~~power~~, in exchange for expecting them to take more
responsibility for their jobs.

GOAL THREE Eliminate unnecessary work. Welch wanted his
workers to work smarter, not harder.

GOAL FOUR Create a new paradigm for GE. Work-Out would
let GE employees define and create a boundaryless organization in which the entire workforce worked toward common
goals. Employees were encouraged to identify problems and
come up with solutions, and any manager who thwarted their
efforts risked being forced out of the company.

Work-Out allowed GE to reinvent itself. By the mid-1990s, GE
had become the strongest company in the United States and the most
valuable company in the world, as measured by market capitalization.
But even this accomplishment did not keep Welch from searching for
new ways to drive GE forward.

Work-Out turned out to be a natural conduit for GE's ready
embrace of Six Sigma. The program had unwittingly inculcated within
GE's culture the Six Sigma principles of openness to new ideas and
elimination of "not-invented-here" thinking, and encouraged people
to work more productively and efficiently. While Work-Out redefined
the way GE employees behaved, Six Sigma redefined how they work.

Although Six Sigma had initially been run on a "pilot" basis in
GE's Medical Systems division, the results it achieved were so convincing that the program was greenlighted for a companywide implementation. The vice president of business development at the time,
Gary Reiner, was assigned to head up the Six Sigma initiative. Reiner,
who joined GE in 1991, allocated resources, coordinated training programs, and ultimately drove an initiative that would indelibly and irre-
versibly change the work culture and the management style of GE as
it embraced Six Sigma. Each business unit within GE was expected to

identify and develop Champions, Master Bla[ck]
Belts.

GE did not allow its existing corporate cult[ure]
of implementing Six Sigma. The company re[invented the]
wheel in implementing the Breakthrough Strat[egy... com-]
panies that tailor Six Sigma to their existing cu[lture,]
made no effort to reconstruct the Six Sigma initiative to fit its corporate identity. This may be because GE's tendency is to continually dis-
mantle bureaucracy, create new cultures, and respond to new
challenges. Reshaping the Breakthrough Strategy to satisfy different
factions within the company would run counter to the company's fundamental values of learning, sharing, and spreading new ideas as fast
as it can. By taking a proven methodology and incorporating it into its
culture, GE was determined to provide its employees with the
resources they needed to succeed.

On March 12, 1997, Welch sent an e-mail message to every GE
manager throughout the world, stating that anyone interested in
being promoted to a senior management position within GE must
start Black Belt or Green Belt training by January 1, 1998, and complete the training by July 1, 1998. Until that message, many employees regarded Six Sigma as another "flavor of the month" initiative,
despite the fact that Welch had never let up chanting the mantra of
achieving Six Sigma by 2000. Even a company as lean and agile as GE
found that it took time for a new idea like this to take root among its
220,000 employees around the world. When told that some form of
training in the Six Sigma methodology was necessary for even the
most minimal advancement within the company, employees began
signing up for training in greater numbers. Welch's determination was
finally infiltrating the rank and file.

Today, Champions and Master Black Belts continue to undergo
training at the Crotonville facility, a pastoral, campuslike setting near
the Hudson River some thirty miles north of New York City. What
happens inside the training center, however, is far from peaceful. The
process of training and inculcating Six Sigma thinking, and learning
the skills necessary to implement it, involves candid, no-holds-barred

...sions as a key way of disseminating Six Sigma knowledge and ...ues to the more than 10,000 GE employees trained each year.

Although General Electric has launched a series of professional development programs over the years, training in GE's Six Sigma quality initiative has taken precedence over every other training program. GE trains its employees in-house in the Six Sigma methodology. But it is at the company-owned training facility at Crotonville that GE trains its Master Black Belts and Champions. GE purchased the estate of the Hopf Institute of Management in Croton-on-Hudson, New York, in late 1953 to provide more training facilities for its managers. Crotonville's environment not only encourages, but demands, that concerns and objections be aired. It can be a terrifying ordeal for even the most experienced and knowledgeable teacher. In what has been described as a "David and Goliath" environment, the instructor stands at the base of a semicircular amphitheater known as The Pit. The amphitheater holds up to 150 of the best and most aggressive business minds to be found anywhere in corporate America. These individuals are encouraged to speak candidly, and they do not suffer fools gladly. They see their mission as slinging stones at any new idea or concept that doesn't measure up. Instructors whose ideas or concepts survive a verbal duel from The Pit receive a mantle of credibility, and thereafter his or her ideas "count" within GE.

Welch is a regular participant at GE's senior-level management development courses, which outstanding managers attend by invitation. While instructors can be ruthless and unforgiving, candidness and outspokenness are expected on both sides.

Because Six Sigma was designed to focus on the customer, Reiner developed a tool that would become an integral part of GE's Six Sigma process. Known as the "Customer Dashboard," it solicited feedback from key customers to identify what they thought were the most critical-to-quality (CTQ) measurements of any of GE's products or services. Like the gauges on a car's dashboard, the Customer Dashboard gave GE employees a readout of how well they were meeting the customers' needs in quantifiable, objective terms, rather than relying on subjective and anecdotal information. One enthusiastic securities analyst reporting on Six Sigma at GE described the dashboard this way: "One arrow on several 'dials' on a dashboard indicates the level of quality that the customer is seeking. A second arrow measures how far the company is from meeting the requirement. Weekly, monthly, or quarterly dashboards are used to determine progress on solving problems for GE's most strategic customers. The data is shared across divisional boundaries and successful solutions applied to similar situations elsewhere in GE."

Reiner oversaw the development of an intranet site that helped employees stay focused on the Six Sigma process by providing information and status reports on projects, and by sharing with employees the best practices for completing these projects.

Six Sigma and the Service Industry

Since the days of Thomas Edison, GE had been in the business of manufacturing high-quality and innovative products. For more than a century, the service industry played no major role at GE. Today, Jack Welch sees the service industry as the key to GE's future, and service has become central to the GE business lexicon.

Six Sigma has been instrumental in raising the quality of GE services, whether the service comes from departments within manufacturing units or from divisions such as Capital Services and Medical Systems. As Gary Powell, general manager of global quality for GE Plastics, says, "Today people expect product quality. The area that becomes a differentiator is service. We've got about a third of [GE Plastics] resources working on projects in pricing, billing, and claims. When you think about what it costs us to process errant bills, it can add up to hundreds of thousands of dollars."

There is a tendency among those not familiar with Six Sigma to see it as a process that affects only the manufacturer of tangible products. But Six Sigma is equally effective in solving quality problems involving "soft" areas—service, invoicing, packaging, and so on. While many companies have set Six Sigma quality goals in their manufac-

turing and engineering divisions, General Electric was the first to
apply Six Sigma levels of quality to service as wholeheartedly as it did
to its manufacturing sectors. Moreover, GE took great strides in
focusing on the service aspects within its manufacturing divisions.
GE's manufacturing employees are keenly aware that the Breakthrough Strategy is meant to be applied not only to the quality of
products produced but to the quality of services provided, as well. GE
set out to accomplish what no company had tried before—applying
the Breakthrough Strategy to transactions and services.

As recently as ten years ago, the idea of measuring the quality of
service was virtually unheard of. Many companies weren't sure that
quality of service could even be measured. The key to measuring
quality is to clearly define the processes that occur in a service, and to
identify those processes important to customer satisfaction.

- Thanks to several Six Sigma projects, GE Capital's railcar-
leasing business achieved a 62 percent reduction in turnaround
time at its repair shops, resulting in an enormous productivity
gain for railroad and shipping customers. As a result, the business is now two to three times faster than its closest rival. In a
follow-up phase, Black Belts and Green Belts, working with
their teams, redesigned the overall leasing process, resulting in
a 50 percent further reduction in cycle time.

- GE Aircraft Engines in Canada uses Six Sigma Green
Belts to perfect paperwork when GE Canada imports a
marine and industrial engine, parts, or tooling for a Canadian
customer. In addition to cutting customers' costs, Green Belts
have reduced border delays by 50 percent.

- Some of the other service-based quality measurements
GE monitors include dead airtime on its NBC television network, whether salespeople have the right information at hand
when they return a client's call, and whether a contract at GE
Capital Services is executed on time and with the terms the
client expects.

To date, GE Capital has invested $6 million in the Six Sigma initiative, dedicated nearly 5 percent of its global workforce full time to quality, and has seen to it that 58,000 associates completed 28,000 quality projects to achieve Six Sigma levels of quality throughout its businesses. The benefits to GE's competitive position have been tremendous, and GE's responsiveness to its customers' needs has improved dramatically. Between 1990 and 2000, GE's total share of revenues from manufacturing has shrunk from 56 to 33.2 percent, while the share from financial services has grown from 25.6 to 45.8 percent.

GE Capital Services

As GE underscored the importance of applying Six Sigma to areas other than manufacturing, engineering, and design, its Capital Services division decided that Six Sigma was what it needed to make it the finest financial services organization in the world. Capital Services is a diversified financial division that offers comprehensive solutions to clients to help them increase productivity and efficiency through its twenty-eight independent business units in the areas of equipment management, consumer services, mid-market financing, specialized financing, and specialty insurance. Offering a remarkable variety of financial services and products globally, GE Capital Services' commitment to using Six Sigma Breakthrough Strategy to reduce "defects" as a way to control quality and increase customer satisfaction is unparalleled in the service industry. In fact, GE Capital Mortgage Insurance won the RIT/USA *Today* Quality Cup in 1998 for service businesses. The award spotlights companies that have achieved exceptionally valuable improvements in a system or process for achieving customer satisfaction.

In 1998, GE Capital Services generated over a third of a billion dollars in net income from Six Sigma improvements—double the figure for 1997. Each one of the business units in the Capital Services division lends strength to others as they work to enhance the value of their services to customers while increasing revenues and lowering costs. The person initially responsible for driving the Six Sigma initiative through-out GE Capital was GE Capital's then vice president and chief quality officer, Ruth Fattori. Fattori, who started out as a mechanical engineer, first encountered Six Sigma while working for Xerox sales agents in the United States and for the Zurich-based Asea Brown Boveri. Fattori's first task in adopting Six Sigma at GE Capital was to establish a rigor-ous and robust training program for Master Black Belts. Although GE's production divisions had plenty of quality-improvement experts, finan-cial services had none. After training a cadre of Master Black Belts, she expanded the training program to include a full complement of Black Belts, Green Belts, and Six Sigma team members.

Knowing that in the financial services industry the bulk of customer contact occurs over the telephone, Fattori devised a simple check sheet that allowed employees to keep a record of incoming calls. Still in use today, these check sheets are used to indicate what customers want — in other words, what their critical-to-quality characteristics (CTQs) are. Later the responses on the check sheets are statistically analyzed, and GE Capital is able to respond to the data collected.

Associates at GE Capital Mortgage Corporation, a business unit of GE Capital Services, field 300,000 calls annually from customers. For years they believed these calls were handled efficiently in person and through voice mail. Employees would conscientiously return calls promptly after having been away from their desks or handling other calls. But when a Master Black Belt–led team began to study GE Cap-ital Mortgage Corporation's service from the customer's perspective, they found that in many cases callers had talked to another lender by the time a Capital Mortgage associate got back to them. However, the Master Black Belt–led team also discovered that one of the forty-two mortgage branches had a near-perfect record of answering calls. The team analyzed this branch's system, process flows, equipment, physi-cal layout, and staffing—and then incorporated what they found into the other forty-one branches. Customers who once found themselves unable to talk with a GE Capital Mortgage associate nearly 24 percent of the time now have a 99 percent chance of speaking to a Capital Mortgage associate on the first try. Since 40 percent of such successfully placed calls result in business, the financial returns have accounted for millions of dollars in increased revenue.

Commercial Finance, another business within GE Capital Services, uses Six Sigma tools to help it win more deals through better understanding customer needs. The division developed a Customer Expectations Pact that has contributed to a 160 percent increase in new transactions.

Mortgage Insurance, another GE Capital Services division, developed a flexible billing system that not only contributed to customer retention but was instrumental in winning $60 million in new insurance from one customer alone. Black Belts in the Loan Work-Out Consistency team at GE Capital Mortgage Insurance applied Six Sigma to the process of working with delinquent borrowers to find alternatives to foreclosure. By cutting defects in the work-out process by 96 percent, GE Capital was able to offer borrowers quicker solutions while reducing claim payments by $8 million. In Japan, Global Consumer Finance, another GE Capital Services division, helped customers overcome payment difficulties associated with limited banking hours, and saved money by establishing an alternate payment method through a network of 25,000 convenience stores, now used by 40 percent of its customers.

Capturing the Voice of the Customer at GE Capital Fleet Services

Headquartered in Eden Prairie, Minnesota, GE Fleet Services is one of the largest corporate fleet management companies in the world, employing 3,400 people with more than a million vehicles under lease-and-service management throughout the Americas, Europe, Australia, and Asia. Fleet Services is a customer-focused business. While it provides fleets of vehicles to major customers such as Xerox, it's the many services surrounding the delivery of those vehicles that constitute Fleet Services' products. For example, Fleet Services provides around-the-clock service to customers whether they have leased a fleet of five vehicles or twenty thousand. These services include ordering of vehicles, financing, fleet repairs, and an electronic fuel card program that allows fleet managers to control and monitor fuel consumption. Fleet Services provides competitive and uniform pricing; it even goes so far as to train drivers, develops a personal mileage program that provides quarterly and year-end reporting for tax purposes, and sells the vehicles at auction or through other resale channels at the end of the lease.

Anita Lefebvre, Master Black Belt and head of GE Capital Fleet Services' Canadian operations, launched and coached ten Sigma Black Belt projects between March 1996 and May 1997. Collectively, these projects returned $1.2 million to the division's bottom line. Not one to rest on her laurels, Lefebvre then initiated and managed eleven Black Belt and twelve Sales Green Belt projects that increased the Sales processes from 1.2 to 3 sigma in less than a twelve-month period. Fleet Services' goal today is to attain 4.5 sigma in each of its seven core processes, which include Product Management and Marketing, Sales, Customer Service, Fleet Management Solutions, Vehicle Ordering, Invoice and Remittance Services, and Remarketing Services.

Lefebvre describes GE's use of the Breakthrough Strategy in this way:

> We [GE as a whole] were the first service company in the world to roll out Six Sigma. That included applying statistical analysis and rigorous application of data to the services industry—a process that would present a unique set of challenges. We quickly found that measuring something as fluid and intangible as information is quite different than measuring how well a product works. In GE Capital Fleet Services, our challenge is tracking customer response time through call centers as opposed to tolerance variations on a manufactured part. For us, a critical-to-quality was not how well customers thought our products worked, but how quickly and accurately we responded to their service expectations.

Sigma levels are calculated on a weekly basis and the core service process adjusted so that mistakes and defects do not recur. Lefebvre and other Master Black Belts have trained their Black Belts and Green Belts to pinpoint how and where processes falter. Black Belts, Green Belts, and Core Process "Owners" are expected to internalize the Breakthrough Strategy to the extent that it becomes a way of life, rather than a last-ditch endeavor resorted to when all else has failed.

Lefebvre believes in systematically listening to and addressing key issues from customers. The Quality Team has been instrumental in helping GE Capital Fleet Services determine its customer expectations and priorities, or critical-to-quality measurements. For example, GE Capital created "ScoreCards" to track and measure customer expectations versus GE Capital's performance. First, customers indicate on a ScoreCard what processes they would like GE Capital to measure. Then they rate GE Capital on those measurements, indicating what their performance expectations are. GE Capital incorporates that data into a rigorous system called Quality Process, which tracks and measures each business unit's level of performance versus customer expectations.

Now, instead of just leasing a van to a customer, GE Capital Fleet Services will bring that van to whatever location the customer requests and with the added features the customer wants. Service is not just being friendly; it's anticipating and satisfying customers' needs.

Through the use of quality tools, GE Capital Fleet Services was able to identify causes of variation—defects—in the purchasing process that could potentially result in delays. By using the data from ScoreCards to generate solutions, the team implemented a series of improvements to slash the cycle time on stock purchases and factory ordering by more than 80 percent.

In an effort to further simplify the ordering process, a Black Belt team assembled an Order Optimization Guide for GE Capital account managers that would assist customers in preparing and submitting an order. The personalized guide was created to bring all the ordering tools together so that the sales teams could easily communicate to customers the most appropriate order methods. The result has been more complete and accurate orders, increased customer knowledge and satisfaction, improved productivity at GE Capital, and higher levels of customer service. GE Capital Fleet Services applies the following Six Sigma processes to improve its interaction with customers step by step:

- determining its customer needs

- identifying opportunities for improvement within the company

- meeting with the customer to set expectations and develop an action plan

- designing and executing Six Sigma projects to improve its services

- communicating progress to the customer on a regular basis

- meeting or exceeding customer expectations

Lefebvre says that Six Sigma training at GE Capital Fleet Services has been extremely aggressive and extensive. Senior management, acting as "Champions," are committed to providing resources and time to train employees in Six Sigma methodology. Currently, the North American team of Fleet Services consists of six full-time Master Black Belts, eighteen full-time Black Belts, and thousands of part-time Green Belts. Master Black Belts and Black Belts frequently meet with their Quality Teams in what is called the "war room," which functions as a think tank for reviewing customer input, evaluating existing processes by applying the Breakthrough Strategy, and making changes to improve service. Customers who visit Fleet Services' global headquarters often begin their day in the "war room," where they can see their specific needs and feedback implemented in process-improvement initiatives.

Six Sigma from the Outside In

As GE heads into its fifth year of the Six Sigma revolution, there is no question that the program is here to stay. In his address to shareholders at the company's 1999 annual meeting, Jack Welch again underscored the role of Six Sigma within GE: "Six Sigma means fixing processes so they are nearly perfect . . . and then controlling them so they stay fixed. The common objective in virtually all Six Sigma projects is the elimination of variance."

But Welch also understands that GE isn't the only company to benefit from Six Sigma. GE's customers are clamoring to see the impact of Six Sigma on their businesses, as well. In response, GE is focusing the full power of Six Sigma toward it customers by applying the Breakthrough Strategy to what it calls Design for Customer Impact (DFCI). Both Six Sigma and Design for Customer Impact demand that the company start with the customer as the initial point of every process. GE has to look from the "outside in" by rigorously measuring customer needs and the customers' processes before it can begin to eliminate variation.

Anita Lefebvre describes GE's goal in the Design for Customer Impact initiative this way:

> In 1997 and 1998, the customer's critical-to-quality characteristic was that we be able to factory order and deliver a Ford Taurus within four days. Today they are asking not about the four-day mean [delivery time], but what are we doing about the range of variance between delivery of a car in a day—and delivery of a car in eight days. Or ten days. When it comes to our customers and our ability to help them improve their businesses, we view any variation as the worst of all evils.

The powerful effect of applying Six Sigma to improve service within GE's manufacturing divisions can be seen in the following story concerning GE Lighting, the division that handles the company's traditional business of manufacturing and selling light fixtures and bulbs.

Wal-Mart, a key GE customer, had been complaining for years about the number of mistakes in the invoices GE sent the company. Alan Watson of GE Lighting, in a meeting with a Wal-Mart representative in February 1996, tried to verify the fact that from GE's perspective 95 percent of the invoices GE sent the retail store were correct.

"Nope" was the Wal-Mart's representative's reply. "From where we stand, it's more like 70 percent." Given that Wal-Mart received about 12,000 invoices from GE each year, that meant about 3,600 invoices contained at least one error. Watson immediately put together a Black Belt team and flew them to Wal-Mart's headquarters to tackle the problem.

As it turned out, Wal-Mart's preference—which most suppliers honored—was to receive one invoice for each shipment of goods. However, GE Lighting issued separate invoices for each type of product. It was this that led to the enormous discrepancy in Wal-Mart's perception of the number of incorrect invoices. Watson's team resolved the situation by altering GE's invoicing procedures to meet Wal-Mart's needs. The Black Belt team also developed a software program so that invoices could be issued online to speed up the billing process for both parties.

Six months later the error rate on invoices had dropped to below 2 percent. While Watson admits that the process has yet to reach a six sigma level, he emphasizes the single most important lesson he and his Black Belt team learned: Never assume anything about your customer. "Listening to what customers have to say is more important than anything else. Finding out how true that is has been the biggest result," says Watson.

Jack Welch described the event this way:

> We had a billing system at GE Lighting that worked just fine from our perspective. The problem was it didn't mesh very well electronically with the purchasing system of Wal-Mart—one of our best customers. Our system didn't work for them and was causing disputes, delaying payments, and wasting Wal-Mart's time. A Black Belt team using Six Sigma methodology, information technology, and $30,000 in investment tackled the problem from Wal-Mart's perspective—and in four months reduced defects in the system by 98 percent. The result for Wal-Mart was

higher productivity and competitiveness with fewer disputes and delays—real dollar savings. The result for GE was a return many times that of our investment.

Many quality programs focus on improvement in areas of manufacturing, but they are not designed to help resolve customer complaints about late shipments, inaccurate invoices, or having the wrong product shipped. Customers want speed and accuracy. But as GE Lighting found out, the supplier (in this case, GE) doesn't necessarily understand what the customer (Wal-Mart) needs. Identifying critical-to-quality characteristics tackles this problem by identifying and then prioritizing areas of customer dissatisfaction.

Another example comes from GE's Medical Systems Division. The division's application of Six Sigma to improving the life of CT scanner X-ray tubes used in hospitals is detailed in Chapter 12. But providing *service* in the form of repairs and upgrades to Medical Systems equipment is just as vital, and contributes a substantial portion of the division's profits.

Twenty years ago, most businesses didn't question where their profits came from. If they made a good product, chances were it would be profitable. But many things have changed over the last two decades. Profits are moving away from products to services. GE's Aircraft Engines Division, for example, provides customers with an obvious product—jet engines. But the larger percentage of profits for the division are derived from financing, service, spare parts, and overhauling old engines. In light of that, the manufacturing of jet engines is only part of Aircraft Engines' business. Many companies that run unprofitable product-centered businesses have not yet caught on to this.

GE Capital Services' vice president and chief quality officer, Dan Henson, has ordered everyone inside Capital Services to stop focusing on the mean. "What we must achieve is zero variance," he says. To this end, Jack Welch instituted a new mandatory training program at Crotonville for all Business Leaders and their direct reports. The program is called "The Roadmap To Customer Impact"; it is a two-day applied statistics workshop aimed at getting functional leaders to

reduction. GE senior managers are required to work a
ect during the course, using statistical tools to solve a
ed by unacceptable variance. The course reinforces
stomer Impact by forcing managers to focus on eliminating variations in order to "delight the customer."

GE's LightSpeed CT scanner and TrueTemp electric range are
drawing unprecedented customer accolades because of the emphasis
placed on Design for Customer Impact (DFCI). Both products, in
essence, were designed by the customer; they have all of the critical-
to-quality performance features (CTQs) that customers wanted in the
products, and these CTQs were subjected to the rigorous statistical
Design for Six Sigma process.

Six Sigma Delivers

The financial headlines in GE's 1998 Annual Report suggest how
great an impact Welch's daring commitment to Six Sigma has had
since its inception in 1996:

- Revenues have risen to $100 billion, up 11 percent.

- Earnings have increased 13 percent, to $9.3 billion.

- Earnings per share have grown 14 percent, to $2.80.

- Operating margin has risen to a record 16.7 percent.

- Working capital turns have risen sharply to 9.2 percent, up from
  1997's record of 7.4.

This performance generated $10 billion in cash flow, which, in
combination with an AAA bond rating, enabled GE to invest $21 bil-
lion for 108 acquisitions.

Welch was able to give Six Sigma a glowing report card. "The financial returns from Six Sigma have exceeded expectations. In 1998 we
achieved three quarters of a billion dollars in Six Sigma–related savings

over and above our investment . . . and this year [1999] that number will go to a billion and a half . . . with billions more to be captured . . . from increased volume and market share as customers increasingly 'feel' the benefits of GE Six Sigma in their own businesses."

Summary

GE has blazed a new trail by applying the Breakthrough Strategy to each division's products and services. Today Six Sigma has transformed every product and process that touches GE customers. New terms—such as CTQs, "critical-to-quality" measurements important to customers; D-M-A-I-C, Define, Measure, Analyze, Improve, and Control; DFSS, Design for Six Sigma; and DFCI, Design for Customer Impact—have become common language within the company.

Despite its success, however, GE knows that good financial numbers are not achieved through success stories and graphics. Rather, they are the product of people executing manufacturing and service in such a way that dollars are driven back to the company's bottom line. Welch's willingness to acknowledge, invest in, and leverage GE's most important asset—its intellectual capital—remains unparalleled. Knowing that quality products and services are produced by educated and empowered employees, GE continues to dedicate more resources to training throughout the corporation than does any of the other top fifteen largest corporations in the United States. Although reaching Six Sigma by the year 2000 may be, as Welch says, the toughest challenge GE has had to face since its creation in 1892, few doubt that the company will reach its goal.

FOUR

Benchmarking: Discovering Who Is Really Best

■   ■   ■   ■   ■   ■

We benchmark every day.

—LAWRENCE A. BOSSIDY

How important is it to gain an edge over your competitors? As the following story makes clear, it can be the difference between life and death. A group of cowboys were moving a herd of cattle from Texas to Arizona. Although aided by a helicopter and several well-trained dogs, they still faced daily hardships as the results of inclement weather and the difficulty of finding enough pasture and water for the cattle. Late one night, the cowhands were awakened by an angry black bear about to charge their campsite. All but one of the cowhands frantically pulled on their boots and took off running. One of the cowhands saw the remaining cowhand sitting on a log lacing up a pair of running shoes. "Hey, forget those running shoes," he called. "They aren't going to help you outrun that bear." The cowhand with the running shoes replied, "I don't need to. I just need to outrun you."

In a business environment, the commitment to being the best is like those running shoes keeping us one step ahead of the pack. Companies today have increasing amounts of information available to them to aid in decision making. Since competitors have access to the same data, the companies that transform data into knowledge and then organize and use that knowledge to their benefit have an advantage. The Six Sigma Breakthrough Strategy shows companies how to scientifically measure their key processes and products, as well as those of their competitors, so they can determine where breakthrough is required and the extent to which they must improve in order to leapfrog to the front of the pack.

Companies that strive to achieve Six Sigma quality have the potential to place themselves so far ahead of the competition that they are continually the best. While a 4.2 sigma company can lead a pack of 3.8 sigma companies, we suggest that companies not settle on being just "good enough." Although the one-eyed man in the land of the blind has a distinct advantage, he'd be foolish to pass up the opportunity to see with both eyes (much less utilize night-vision technology). Similarly, corporations need to develop full vision in all spectrums of their business.

There are those who say, "Why should we benchmark? We are already the best in the business." Or they claim, "We are unique. We can't compare our business with others." What these companies fail to realize is that the majority of their processes are virtually identical or quite similar to those found in other companies that produce dissimilar products or services. For example, a billing and charging process in a company that produces lightbulbs is fundamentally the same as the billing and charging process in a company that produces pencils or a company that delivers a standardized service. If the company that produces lightbulbs discovers that the pencil company has 100 times fewer billing and charging errors, clearly the right thing to do would be to investigate why the pencil company is so much better at a similar process. Senior management must know exactly where their company stands relative to competitors and other companies with similar processes. The very nature of *any* organization requires that it successfully deliver its products and services. Whether large or small, government agency or nonprofit association, organizations have business processes in common with other industries. For instance, the human resources operation in one industry is usually very similar to that of another. Benchmarking with another industry allows your business to elevate its own human resources practices to even higher standards. The net effect is that after implementing changes from your benchmarking study, you will be able to become the new industry leader in that process.

Ultimately, benchmarking allows companies to leapfrog their key industrial and commercial processes. It also lets companies define what world class really is, with unbiased, repeatable measurements, and assess their current performance relative to the "best." They can identify performance targets that they seek to surpass. Successful benchmarking incorporates sharing information and best practices in order to implement meaningful, measurable change.

What does an average company—a company operating between 3.5 and 4 sigma—look like?

PROFILE OF THE AVERAGE COMPANY
It is profitable and growing.
Its market prices are declining.
Its competitors are increasing.
It has a quality-assurance program.
It spends 20 to 30 percent of sales dollars repairing or reworking products before shipping.
It is unaware that best-in-class companies have similar processes that are over 100 times more defect-free.
It believes that achieving the goal of zero defects is neither realistic nor desirable.
It contracts with ten times the number of suppliers necessary.
Five to 10 percent of the organization's customers are dissatisfied with the product, sales, or service and will not recommend the product or service to someone else. Today we know that only one out of twenty-five dissatisfied customers will express dissatisfaction to the company, but that same dissatisfied customer will tell seven to ten others of his or her dissatisfaction.

What Is Benchmarking?

Companies should always know who their strongest competitors are on a process-by-process basis, as well as at the product and business levels. They should consciously seek to understand how their strengths and limitations affect customer satisfaction and profitability. Benchmarking is a powerful tool to help organizations compare their processes with those of their competitors, and understand what makes another organization's product or service superior. This can provide improvement solutions. Benchmarking is an essential part of Six Sigma projects when used during the Measure and Analyze stages, or after a process has been identified for improvement. Benchmarking can answer what it means to be the best, and what it takes to get there. It can bring to light questions and insights that lead to breakthrough.

Benchmarking is not a one-time event, a quick and easy process. It must be done continually. The results of benchmarking must be incorporated into day-to-day operations so that organizations can begin to think differently about how they work and solve problems. Benchmarking that does not result in process improvements is a waste of time, money, and energy. Prior to Six Sigma, many companies think they are one of the best. Their long-standing reputation in the industry reinforces this belief. However, when companies discover their true sigma capacity, they discover that their quality is quite average.

Six Sigma companies view benchmarking as an essential tool and use it as a stepping-stone toward Six Sigma. AlliedSignal CEO Lawrence A. Bossidy tells his employees that they must work under the assumption that every one of their competitors does at least one thing better than Allied. To Bossidy, benchmarking means looking at specific practices, getting the benefit of other companies' expertise, and bringing the best practices back to one's own company without having inhibitions about adopting a better practice from the outside. And he believes in letting people know where a borrowed practice came from. Bossidy requires his senior managers to visit as many companies as they can, something he does himself as well.

But Bossidy does not believe that you have to go into competitors' factories to benchmark effectively:

> *In industries where performance is relatively mediocre, you don't want to benchmark, anyway. I've heard, for example, that receivables at one of the largest credit card companies are managed extraordinarily well—so that's the place to benchmark receivables. Go to the world-class computer and peripherals companies to look at new-product development. Go to people in any and every industry who, you have reason to believe, are better at some processes than you are. And bring back what you can. There's no company in the world you can benchmark to learn everything. The trick is to look at a lot of good processes in multiple companies, then select from those, bring them back, and implement them.*

However, when mediocrity does not prevail, companies should not blindly incorporate another organization's business practices based on hearsay or speculation. This is *not* benchmarking. Benchmarking is the process of examining best practices, sifting through the results, and adopting only the practices that will add value to *your* organization. Benchmarking can be accomplished through literature searches that uncover best-in-class performance. In many cases, companies can benchmark through computer searches or articles and technical papers to establish the sigma capability of their competitors. Site visits and interviews can provide the most specific and focused insights.

While discovering who is world class in a particular process requires research in a variety of sources, companies first need to determine which type of benchmarking they wish to perform.

INTERNAL BENCHMARKING compares common processes among diverse functions within a single company, such as how efficiently and accurately orders are processed between divisions.

COMPETITIVE BENCHMARKING looks at direct competitors and their processes, and measures levels of customer loyalty, customer satisfaction, and market share. Competitive benchmarking can also assess companies as potential candidates for mergers and acquisitions, and determine how well other companies are identifying trends and meeting changing customer needs and preferences. Competitive benchmarking can reveal what customers value most about your goods and services and how well your customers think you are doing in the areas that matter most to them.

FUNCTIONAL BENCHMARKING focuses on the process itself, and organizations with similar processes, regardless of their industry. Functional benchmarking will reveal a plant's overall manufacturing strategy, the average number of annual training hours required of employees, a plant's scrap and rework costs as a percent of sales, the extent that scrap and rework costs have changed over the past five years, a plant's warranty costs as a percent of sales, and a plant's on-time delivery rate.

Motorola's development of the Bandit pager illustrates the benefits of functional benchmarking. Working together as a group dubbed "Team Bandit," employees from the Boynton Beach plant spent eighteen months benchmarking a wide variety of products and services around the world before settling on a comprehensive manufacturing design for a Motorola pager. They traveled as far as Italy's Benetton, the sweater company that keeps pace with its customers through a computer system that notifies factories of what styles and colors are selling quickly in Benetton's stores around the world. The plant then implemented a very similar system to track and respond quickly to its style-conscious pager users.

Functional benchmarking also led Team Bandit to implement a system where orders for pagers coming in from field offices were assigned a bar code that indicated the customer's specific requirements. The factory had a series of computers and robotic equipment that read the bar code; with this information, customized pagers could be built and shipped out the door in under two hours.

Benchmarking and Six Sigma

The practice of benchmarking is not new, but the notion of quantitative benchmarking *is* relatively new. Quantitative benchmarking

UNDERSTANDING BENCHMARKING
It represents a tool for the identification of best practices.
It is an effective approach for guiding improvement.
It is a formalized way to manage change.
It helps determine the most important things to improve.
It helps determine the best approach to use.
It establishes best practices.
It is not a single-person activity that can be done alone.
It is not a one-time program that is used and then forgotten.
It is not competitive intelligence or market research.

allows companies to evaluate performance in every division on a level playing field, using standardized indices of performance and capability, and then compare performance not only between divisions but also with other companies considered "best-in-class." Quantitative benchmarking seeks to establish two things. First, it determines the yield or defect rate for a particular product, service, or transaction. Second, it reveals how many opportunities for defects exist in that product, service, or transaction. These two pieces of information allow companies to assess the sigma capability per opportunity and provide opportunities to compare disparate things with varying degrees of complexity. Not surprisingly, as the complexity of a product increases, the likelihood of detecting a defect decreases.

For example, suppose we did a literature search on a particular process and discovered that Product A has a final yield of 85 percent and there are 600 opportunities for defects contained with the product; then the average yield per opportunity for a defect is $.85^{1/600} = .99973$, or 99.97 percent. This means that the average capability for each of the 600 opportunities for defects is equivalent to 3.5 sigma. Given this level of capability, 15 percent of the units produced would contain one or more defects. Another way of describing this phenomenon is to say that a product containing 600 opportunities for defects at a 3.5 sigma level would produce approximately one defect for every 1.2 units produced.

Now let's take Product B, a dissimilar product made using a similar process, which has 48 opportunities for defects and shows a final yield of 96.8 percent. In this case, the average yield per opportunity would be $.968^{1/48} = .99973$, or 99.97 percent. As with Product A, the yield level per opportunity converts to 3.5 sigma. Therefore, we can conclude that Product A has the same capability per opportunity as Product B, despite the differences in function and complexity. Thus, we are able to benchmark the quality of similar processes producing dissimilar products despite different yields and the number of opportunities for defects.

Many factory managers with highly complex products have been penalized for low yield because the number of opportunities for defects is significantly higher than that of other products within the company. Six Sigma creates a level field for benchmarking regardless of the complexity of a product. Again, Six Sigma allows companies to work smarter and still outrun the competitive bears.

Companies should begin benchmarking processes that have the most potential for improvement both financially and in terms of quality. Benchmarking for Six Sigma involves studying the best-in-class processes and then implementing measurable change. Once benchmarking has been completed, the process can move deeper into the Breakthrough Strategy.

What Should Companies Benchmark?

Knowing what products and services are provided to customers, and understanding which are most important to customer satisfaction, helps organizations determine what areas to benchmark. Other concerns to address when deciding what to benchmark include identifying internal and external areas of competition, identifying the organization's major cost drivers, determining which processes can be quickly and easily improved, and understanding which products and processes make you different from your competitors. Benchmarking quickly identifies the critical-to-quality characteristics (CTQs) most important to the customer and then focuses on comparing those characteristics with those known to be best-in-class or world class.

Benchmarking as a way to achieve Six Sigma is not a one-time or periodic event. It should be a continuous activity across all departments, locations, and divisions. Results should be shared across the organization and the results continually recalibrated quickly as process improvements are made.

CHAPTER FIVE

Changing What Companies Measure: A Six Sigma Credo

We don't know what we don't know.

We can't act on what we don't know.

We won't know until we search.

We won't search for what we don't question.

We don't question what we don't measure.

The Power of Measurements

In 1891, British physicist Lord Kelvin wrote, "When you can measure what you are speaking about, and express it in numbers, you know something about it; but when you cannot measure it, when you cannot express it in numbers, your knowledge is of a meager and unsatisfactory kind: it may be the beginning of knowledge, but you have scarcely, in your thoughts, advanced to the stage of science." Lord Kelvin clearly believed that progress is difficult without a way to measure it. The progress of measurement is, in fact, the progress of science. Trying to improve something when you don't have a means of measurement and performance standards is like setting out on a cross-country trip in a car without a fuel gauge. You can make calculated guesses and assumptions based on experience and observation, but without hard data, conclusions are based on insufficient evidence. Imagine going to a basketball game without a scoreboard—not knowing the score as the game progresses, only to have a winner declared when the final buzzer sounds. Imagine being the coach at season's end—trying to assess what has happened over the year without any numbers to guide and support your analysis. Similarly, companies cannot improve quality and customer satisfaction without the right metrics to tell them where they are and whether they are making progress.

Companies that measure customer opinions, and then link those measurements to their processes, are more likely to come out with successful products or services that satisfy the customer. Companies that measure quality and efficiency of their processes will be able to produce higher-quality products at lower costs. Companies that measure employee satisfaction (and take action as a result) are more likely to have higher employee retention rates. So why is it that companies claiming to be customer focused fail to measure customer satisfaction? Why is it that companies measure and report on profits and growth, but fail to measure and report on the key processes that create the profits and growth? How well do companies consciously attempt to create a connection between how their processes work, customer satisfaction, and profitability? Many companies that claim to value quality either don't measure their quality or don't follow up on their quality measurements. This behavior sends a message to employees and shareholders that the company doesn't really value quality after all.

Most companies have not attempted to establish how their performance metrics statistically cross-correlate to each other. They only assume that a correlation exists. For example, when training corporate executives, we ask how much weight they place on first-time yield. (The concepts of first-time yield and rolled throughput yield are explained in Chapter 6.) They universally respond that they believe first-time yield to be valid and important. When we ask if that metric correlates to cost, the answer is inevitability "yes." We then show mathematically and empirically that the correlation between first-time yield and costs is very low, but that the correlation between rolled throughput yield and costs is quite accurate. Most executives are stunned into silence when they realize how little first-time yield correlates to costs, and again realize that "companies don't know what they don't know."

Organizations that can't describe their processes in the form of numbers can't understand their processes. And if they don't understand their processes, they can't control them. Measuring processes with metrics that correlate to the company's fundamental economics is the only way to improve quality and increase customer satisfaction. Improvements cannot be made without product data. Products and services "talk" in the form of data. Without data, products and services are mute and companies are deaf. But data, properly assembled and summarized with the aid of statistics, create a "tool" for understanding defects. This is the language of breakthrough.

Statistics provide insights into what the data says about a product or service. Data are the alphabetical letters of the product's language. The words are formed by using statistics to metaphorically arrange alphabetical letters into words and finally sentences that, in turn, communicate information about the product. Through statistical analysis of product and process data, we are able to hear what the product is telling us. We are able to form concepts on the basis of the statistics and take action. However, the best statistical analysis in the world is useless if those handling the information are paralyzed by corporate fear. When the data clearly suggest one direction, but corporate culture or convention dictates another, fear can rule and the potential for change is lost. Only strong leadership can eradicate the fear factor and allow an organization to realize its potential. Statistics alone cannot achieve breakthrough. However, it is a very powerful tool that can alter a company's playing field.

Why Do We Need Metrics?

Metrics create a common language for communication and allow process measurements to be communicated openly and candidly. We need metrics in order to:

- establish the difference between perception, intuition, and reality

- gather the facts for good decision making and provide the basis for sound implementation of those decisions

- overcome the limits to our current thought processes and move us toward boundaryless thinking

- identify and verify problem areas or bottlenecks that have remained undetected

- better understand our processes and determine which factors are important and which are not

- characterize our processes so that we know how inputs and outputs are related

- validate our processes and determine whether they are performing within the required specifications

- evaluate customer satisfaction and establish the links to our key processes

- document our processes and then communicate them to others

- provide a baseline for process performance and cost correlation

- see if our processes are improving, and retain the gains for those that are

- determine if a process is stable or predictable and determine how much variation is inherent in the process

The Role of Questions

Since companies don't know what they don't know, asking new questions is an integral part of the Breakthrough Strategy. To change results, a company's leadership needs to ask new questions about the quality of its products, services, and processes. New measures lead to new questions. New questions create new vision. New vision guides activity.

The pursuit of Six Sigma requires that processes be measured differently. In the same way, measurements are drivers of what an organization values. The question becomes, What are we currently measuring and what should we be measuring? The organization's leadership needs to question process capability, product design, and overall quality, rather than outputs and budgets. The success of Six Sigma depends on creating new knowledge by asking new questions. This focus drives new measurements.

The right statistical measurements are a surefire way to trigger new reactions and responses within a company. This philosophy leads to cost improvements and, more important, customer satisfaction.

Let the Product Do the Talking

The Breakthrough Strategy requires companies to pose questions and look for the answers within data. Companies wanting to improve their processes cannot depend on past experience, observation, or general consensus. For example, if we assume that there is a relationship between an outcome (Y) and a potential cause (X), we must collect and analyze data to prove our hypothesis. Simply believing it's true does not make it true. *If we want to change an outcome, we need to focus on the X, not the Y.*

Traditional metrics focus on profit margins, scrap, and rework. When management asks, "Have we met our financial targets?" and the answer is "Yes," no one questions how the goal was met. The actual reasons for success are speculative at best. We spend a lot of time and resources designing products and processes, but little on the creation of valid business and performance-measurement systems. In a four sigma business, the focus is on the final product or service— the Y factor, or the symptom. But a six sigma company focuses on the X variables, or the processes that generate the problem. The Six Sigma Breakthrough Strategy drills down into the key process that governs products and business performance and examines it through a new set of questions. As an organization begins to examine and correct the many processes—the X factors—that create a product or service, the need to inspect and test Y begins to diminish.

Black Belts tackle the mathematical relationship of $Y = f(X)$, with Y (the problem) being a function (f) of X (the cause of the problem). Project by project, companies reduce costs, cycle time, late deliveries, and customer complaints to limit defects and improve their overall productivity and efficiency.

Inspect and Test the Process, Not the Product

All products and services are the results of processes, which is why Six Sigma monitors the processes, not outcomes. When the process isn't right, the final product or service won't be right. It's by testing and inspecting the process that creates the product or service that companies circumvent problems before they appear. Process inspection includes not only equipment but such things as procedures and employee skill levels. Educators that focus on SAT scores rather than the processes that lead to learning are focused on outcomes and not the processes that create the right results.

Using the Measure, Analyze, Improve, and Control (M-A-I-C) approach consistently across diverse businesses and processes has allowed companies to leverage the power of the Breakthrough Strategy's tools to achieve significant financial results. The Breakthrough Strategy's rigorous, systematic, disciplined approach to problem solving and process changes provides a common language to allow different business units to talk to one another, share lessons learned, and, in general, move forward as an organization. It also enables companies to compare the effectiveness of their processes and levels of quality with those of companies with dissimilar products—let's say airplane engines and dishwashers—through common metrics. When employees in a corporation begin to see, in the form of sigma values, how they compare with other companies, products, and services on a level playing field, emotions generate internal discussions and questions that inevitability lead down the path toward Six Sigma improvement.

Finding Critical Leverage Points

Companies can no longer afford to focus solely on products and services. Rather, they need to focus on creating processes with strong metrics. For example, if an organization claims that customer satisfaction is a value, it needs a way to continually measure that value. To do this, these companies must first define who their customers are and then what it is they value most about these customers. Companies expansively say, "We value our customers." But what does this phrase really mean? What exactly is it—other than money—that a company values about its customers? Many organizations are stymied when they begin to explore this question. While admitting that they never examined or really understood the claim, they insist that it's a core belief. Although many organizations sincerely believe they value their customers, Six Sigma forces them to identify and define exactly *what* they value about their customers and then link metrics to each value. Only then can they begin to understand *how* they value their customers.

Next, organizations must determine what is critical to customers' satisfaction. These factors are called "critical-to-quality" characteristics, or CTQs. Then companies must clearly define how these critical-to-quality characteristics will be measured and reported. Finally, companies must correlate the critical-to-quality measurements to the key process variables and controls so that they can determine how to improve the process. To do this, companies must have process metrics—ongoing measurements that reflect how well processes are creating products and services. When companies can quantify how well their processes are performing and their customers' satisfaction levels, they can link the two, isolating which processes have a significant impact on customer satisfaction and which do not. They know which knobs to turn to make things better. When this happens, companies can take meaningful and focused action to improve their processes. They can "manage by fact" rather than "manage by feelings."

Surveys can help companies calculate customer satisfaction. But too often the results are sketchy and not shared throughout the organization. Even worse, the information gleaned from customer-satisfaction surveys is rarely linked to the processes that occur on factory floors or in administrative offices. Factory managers can report on process yield, but they cannot show how these yield measurements correlate to costs, reliability, and customer satisfaction. As we will see in the following chapters, process yield (the ratio of output to input) has only a slight correlation to cost or customer satisfaction—something we have learned through years of data collection, statistical analysis, and rigorous application of mathematical models in business economics.

The Customer Is King

Organizations are hard-pressed to make quantum, noticeable improvements in customer satisfaction without measurements. Customer satisfaction is ultimately connected to factory performance, and factory performance is linked to process performance. Process performance is a function of capability, which translates to an understanding of the interaction between machinery specifications, procedures, and employee knowledge. You can't sell a customer a good cup of coffee without considering the quality of the beans; how the beans are processed, roasted, and ground; the amount and quality of water used to brew the coffee; whether the coffee is left on the burner too long; and so on until that steaming cup of coffee is handed to the customer. An organization's profitability is determined by *what* it chooses to measure and *how* it measures it.

Several years ago we were preparing to give a seminar to the CEO and the executive leadership of a well-known corporation. As we flipped through several annual reports and other impressive promotional material, we couldn't help but notice the descriptive language;

words such as *quality, competitive pricing, innovation,* and *integrity* were scattered throughout the reports and brochures—all words that connote some kind of value. These words were carefully selected to reflect the values this organization wanted to communicate to its customers, suppliers, employees, and shareholders. But they were the values the company *wanted* to possess, not necessarily those that it *did* possess. How did we know this? Because of what the reports and brochures told us the company measured, tracked, reported, and reacted to.

The three areas of customer satisfaction—delivering high-quality products, on time, at the lowest possible cost—need to be focused on at all levels of an organization. Factory workers have told us that they are measuring production time and counting how many products meet performance standards when they should also be measuring and recording the number and types of defects, and where and how these defects occur in the manufacturing process. Accountability is lost. When a customer returns a defective product, there is no system to "source trace" the cause of the problem. The trail has disappeared and employees resort to "hunt-and-peck" methods of problem solving, wasting time and precious resources.

Competing in tomorrow's marketplace will require organizations to focus on process measurements and the technology that supports those processes. Processes can't be ignored in the pursuit of new products and services. While *product technology* led Americans to invent the video camera and the fax machine, and the Dutch to invent the CD player, a lack of *process technology* cost both countries sales and profits. Other companies in other countries quickly came to "own" these products with the development of effective and efficient processes. Good process technology paves the way for escalating sales, employment levels, and profits. Unlike a number of decades ago, when companies bringing new products to market could create a monopoly that allowed them to set higher prices and earn higher profits, today's competitors possess the technology to re-create another's products, usually at a lower price. Historically, corporations have made innovation a top priority and paid only passing attention to the need for producibility. But in today's world, producibility is the cornerstone of success. Both values are crucial, and they work hand in hand. Innovation can be viewed (and compared) in terms of uniqueness and features. How is the producibility of design alternatives established and weighed? Many companies profess to consider producibility, but few know how to measure and track it throughout the design process. The message is clear. The winners are those who can provide their customers with high-quality, innovative products and services on time at the lowest cost. To do this, companies must focus on the producibility of those products and the deliverability of those services.

CHAPTER SIX

Unmasking the Hidden Factory

As a young engineer, Mike managed the starter motor field coil operation for a large division of a major automobile manufacturer. Several weeks into the job, Mike discovered that the company's mantra was "Meet production schedule at any cost"—meaning that the penalties for not delivering a certain number of field coils by a specified date to the assembly plant were far greater than incurring additional costs to produce the field coils on time. Mike's success as a front-line manager depended on production speed and quantity, and he was rewarded with promotions and salary increases for pushing his employees to build more field coils rather than examining and correcting the root causes for defective field coils, which led to yield loss. As long as he met the production schedule, little was said about the process yield. Recognizing Mike's ability to consistently meet production and scheduling requirements (with no regard to cost), the company rewarded him for being such an efficient and dependable manager, and seldom questioned the operation's escalating overtime, materials, inspection, and rework costs. Focus was placed on the outcome (Y), rather than the process (X). This philosophy did not allow any time to improve the process, but focused on keeping the line running.

Companies that produce products and services at four sigma and lower levels of quality spend an extraordinary amount of time and money practicing what we call detection and correction of mistakes and errors. So pervasive is this practice that companies unwittingly create hidden factories—ad hoc systems and processes set up to correct errors made during the manufacturing process. They take up unnecessary space, time, and resources. A hidden process can be as simple as Mary, in Department B, returning a defective part back to Jane, in Department A, before it is noticed by management. Although employees may think they are acting responsibly when they hand back a defective product or service, often they are masking a bad process from management. Consequently, processes are never fixed, while hidden processes become more efficient and less visible.

Data recorded by employees in their weekly or monthly nonconformance reports for extra material and labor costs are not hidden factories, since these costs are measured and recorded in a visible way. Costs that are not made known to management are part of the hidden factory. Costs that cannot be broken down and traced to specific operations are also hidden. Hidden factories are not exclusive to manufacturing. They exist in all parts of an organization, and, although they often function with the best of intentions, they are responsible for longer cycle times, increased costs, and inefficient use of resources. Like defending against stealth fighter planes, companies cannot fight what they cannot see or trace.

Every defect takes additional space, time, materials, money, and manpower for detection, inspection, analysis, and defect repair. As defect rates increase, hidden factories in a company or process tend to proliferate, and costs escalate. Most executives don't realize how expensive hidden factories are. As discussed before, costs in this instance refer not only to financial dollars but to quality, customer perception, and return business—all of which are interdependent. Businesses that are able to prevent defects through better control of process capability, rather than waiting to detect defects at the end of production or completion of a service, see enormous improvements in their profit margins, as Motorola did with its highly profitable Bandit pager.

Bringing Visibility into the Hidden Factory

Customer surveys, rejection reports, returned goods, and warranty claims all provide companies with data on how well their processes are performing. They are able to count the number of product or service units that went into a process and the number that successfully came out. Traditionally, companies use this type of data to calculate a metric called yield—the number of units that pass a particular inspection, compared with the total number of units that pass through that point in the process. Essentially, this metric boils down to a simple concept—output divided by input—the amount of good stuff companies are able to make contrasted to the total amount put through the system.

This measure of operational efficiency has very strong intuitive appeal and is quite easy to calculate, but it is a major managerial trap. It has the ability to gravely mislead and deceive. It is the cloaking mechanism that allows hidden operations, processes, and factories to exist. Its virus is embedded in many commonly used indices of performance—first-time yield, first-pass yield, and final yield, just to mention a few. The basic idea of contrasting output to input lies at the heart of all such metrics. To better understand how this idea can mislead and deceive, let's consider two scenarios.

In the first scenario, imagine two units of product that were recently produced at some point in a manufacturing process—say, unit numbers 101 and 102, respectively. These two units have just arrived at our inspection station for evaluation. Unit 101 is free of defects; however, unit 102 contains two defects. In the second scenario, we shall consider unit numbers 103 and 104. Here, unit 103 is error-free, but unit 104 contains eight defects.

When considering the two units described in the first scenario, the first-time yield would be computed as output (1) over input (2), or .5, which in percentage terms equals 50 percent. In the second scenario, the first-time yield would be the same—50 percent. From this perspective, both processing scenarios are rated at the same level of performance; however, from a quality perspective, they are different. In the first scenario, the total defects per unit, the TDPU, would be computed as two defects divided by two units, or 2/2, which equals 1.0. For the second scenario, we would compute the TDPU as eight defects divided by the two units, or 8/2 = 4.0. Since each repairable defect within a product must be detected, analyzed, and fixed, it is obvious that the cost of production in the first scenario is less than that of the second. Thus, total cost correlates to TDPU but not to first-time yield. In other words, yield can remain constant while cost varies, whereas there is a strong correlation between defects and costs. Hence, we can be seriously deceived when we gauge our success on the basis of classic yield calculations. Stated more scientifically, yield is a function of defects, not output and input. In short, the given method of yield calculation is wrong and masks the hidden factory.

Rarely are products or services created in a single step. Final yield is the same calculation as first-time yield, but after the last step in a series of steps in a process.* Hence, many companies use the term "final yield." Much like first-time yield, final yield does not accurately measure process performance.

Unfortunately, the vast majority of industrial operations measure first-time yield to calculate the efficiency of each process. On the surface, first-time yield has strong intuitive appeal and is easy to calculate. However, it ignores cycle time, overall product quality, and the cost to produce it. The following is another illustration of why first-time yield is an unreliable metric:

Imagine that a company produces plastic cups through an injection process, and that ten cups can be produced in the same mold. A typical plastic injection process consists of plastic pellets (input) going into a mold with cavities; through pressure and temperature changes, the cups are formed (output), and a blade is used to trim the

---

*In many industrial settings, final yield is the only process performance metric that is measured and reported. This single measurement is used to report on how well the process is working. This type of yield can be thought of as "post-process" yield because it can be assessed only at the end of the process. Its corollary in the Six Sigma world is rolled throughput yield. In general, final yield is the probability that a "unit" will successfully pass all of the system-level requirements assessed at the end of the process, whereas rolled throughput yield is the probability of passing all in-process requirements as well as end-of-line requirements.

excess plastic from around the edges. However, the operator oversee-ing the process notices that five out of the ten cups are defective, and he places the five bad cups into a shredder, knowing that the plastic can be reused, and sends the five good cups on to inspection.

In this scenario, first-time yield will be 100 percent, because of the five cups tested each will pass inspection. Further, no materials were wasted. The defective units were recycled back into the process to pro-duce good units and the rejected cups were never recorded in a non-conformance report. The time spent remaking the defective cups is not captured in any cost structure. As such, it constitutes a hidden factory.

How to Measure Process Performance

The way companies measure and calculate performance can reinforce the use of costly "hidden" factories. To expose the unnecessary and cost-intensive rework and repair processes, one must have the right performance measures. The wrong or inappropriate metrics can deceive and mislead, while the right metrics can act like an X-ray machine—exposing operational diseases and management malignan-cies. Essentially, there are three fundamental metrics that, when used collectively, can expose even the smallest inefficiencies in a process or facility. These metrics are *throughput yield*, *rolled throughput yield*, and *normalized yield*. Each of these yield measurements is based on the defects produced, whereas the more classical measures of yield are based on the number of units produced. At first glance, one might be inclined to conclude that there isn't really that much difference. Upon deeper investigation, however, the opposite is seen to be true. Understanding this difference is what separates a four sigma process from a six sigma process.

UNDERSTANDING THE SIX SIGMA PROCESS METRICS

Throughput yield is the probability that all defect opportunities produced at a particular step in the process will conform to their respective performance standards. It is the likelihood of "doing all things right" at a given point in the process. *Rolled throughput yield* is the probability of being able to pass a unit of product or service through the entire process defect-free. Expressed differently, rolled throughput yield is the likelihood of doing all things right at each step across an entire series of process steps. Six Sigma also makes use of what is called *normalized yield*. Normalized yield can be thought of as the "average" throughput yield result one would expect at any given step of the process—it represents the "typical" yield one could expect. In this sense, normalized yield is a baseline measure. It is the base metric from which a sigma measurement is computed.

CONTRASTING FIRST-TIME YIELD TO THROUGHPUT YIELD

Most companies currently utilize two measures of yield—first-time yield and final yield. Companies that use these measures often find that they have high yield rates, and assume, sometimes mistakenly, that their processes are operating effectively.

There are important distinctions between the classic measures of yield and those advanced by the Six Sigma school of thought. As discussed above, while it is true that first-time yield can reflect process efficiency, it most often does so only *after* the influence of the hidden factory. Throughput yield, on the other hand, measures process efficiency *before* the hidden factory. First-time yield is based on the total number of units produced, regardless of the number of opportunities for defects contained within a unit. Throughput yield, however, is based on the total number of critical-to-quality characteristics per unit and not the number of units produced.

In other words, first-time yield is "unit sensitive" and throughput yield is "defect sensitive." First-time yield is not sensitive to product complexity; it simply looks at the quantity of units produced. Throughput yield is extremely sensitive to product complexity as well as to the total number of defect opportunities contained in a unit of product or service.

In other words, while first-time yield measures how well companies "process units," throughput yield measures how well companies "process quality." This is why the Six Sigma yield measurements have a high statistical correlation to labor, costs, cycle time, and work in process (inventory), while classic measures show little correlation.

CONTRASTING FINAL YIELD TO ROLLED THROUGHPUT YIELD

Although final yield, too, is a widely used metric, it has several drawbacks. Like first-time yield, final yield is based on the total number of units produced, while rolled throughput yield is based on the total number of defect opportunities produced. Here again, final yield is based on results calculated after the "defective units" have been processed through the hidden factory (repair and rework loops). Rolled throughput yield does not suffer from this limitation, because it measures yield independent of any influences from the hidden factory.

Interestingly, there is no connection between first-time yield and final yield—they are independent measures. In other words, first-time yields cannot be used to calculate the final yield. There is, however, a direction correlation between Six Sigma measures of yield, because all of these measures are based on defect data. Throughput yield is based on defects-per-opportunity data, and rolled throughput yield is based on defects-per-unit data. In this case, both measures are dependent on quality information rather than production volume.

In essence, final yield reports on the proportion of product or service units that pass inspection, while rolled throughput yield reports on the likelihood that any given product or service unit will pass through the entire process error-free. Final yield tells us what we did and rolled throughput yield tells us what we will do. Inevitably, rolled throughput yield is substantially less than final yield.

APPLYING THE METRICS: THROUGHPUT YIELD

Again, throughput yield tells us the statistical likelihood that a unit of product or service will pass through a certain process step error-free. It is the probability of achieving "conformance to standards" for all of the critical-to-quality characteristics (CTQs) in a particular step in a process.

Suppose we have a process consisting of five steps. Let's assume 100 units have just passed through Step 3 of the five-step process. Let's also assume that each of the units has 20 CTQs, or "opportunities" for defect, which we will designate by the letter M. Let's assume that we have just observed 5 defects across the 100 units. At this point, we compute the defects per unit (DPU) to be DPU = 5/100 = .05, or 5 percent. Given that there are 20 CTQs per unit, the defects per opportunity (DPO) would be DPU/M = .05/20 = .0025. Using this calculation, we can say that the probability of creating a defective opportunity is .0025, or .25 percent. Thus, the opportunity level yield would be $1 - .0025 = .9975$, or 99.75 percent. We could compute the defects per million opportunities, a standard Six Sigma measurement, as DPMO = DPO × 1,000,000 = .0025 × 10^6 = 2,500. This converts to 4.3 sigma capability per opportunity using a standard sigma conversion chart. Now we can say that if every opportunity is 4.3 sigma capable and there are 20 opportunities per unit, then we should anticipate an average of .05 defects per unit for those units passing through Step 3.

In other words, 5 out of every 100 units created at Step 3 of the process will contain one or more defects and, consequently, fail to "yield." This gives us a throughput yield of 95 percent—95 out of every 100 units created will pass through Step 3 of the process with zero defects.

Now compare this with first-time yield. If only 1 of the 100 units produced contained all 5 of the observed defects, the first-time yield would be computed as 99 good units out of 100 total units started, or 99 / 100 = .99, or 99 percent. On the other hand, if the 5 defects occurred in 5 different units, the first-time yield would be 95 / 100 = .95, or 95 percent. In other words, first-time yield is highly dependent on how the defects are distributed across the sample units. Throughput yield, on the other hand, remains constant, and therefore offers a more accurate assessment of a particular step in a process.

This is the primary difference between first-time yield and throughput yield. In many cases, these two methods of yield calculation can reveal a very different sense of the process. First-time yield is almost always equal to or higher than throughput yield. In this sense, throughput yield is the "ground floor" of first-time yield. Thus, first-time yield can provide a more optimistic and rosy picture of process efficiency, while throughput yield provides a "defect-sensitive" picture that is highly correlated to things such as cost, inventory, and cycle time.

APPLYING THE METRICS: ROLLED THROUGHPUT YIELD

Because rolled throughput yield gives us the probability of zero defects across an entire process, it is important to better understand this concept and see how it is different from final yield. Consider the following example:

A Black Belt is working on a transactional process that involves five independent steps and she wants to compute the rolled throughput yield of the process. The Black Belt must first gather defect data on each CTQ produced at each of the five steps. With these data in hand, the Black Belt would have all the necessary information to compute the throughput yield for each step (as in the previous illustration).

The Black Belt computed the throughput yields for each step of the process and recorded the yields as 98 percent, 93 percent, 95 percent, 98 percent, and 94 percent, respectively. To compute the rolled throughput yield, the Black Belt simply multiplied all of the individual throughput yields—$.98 \times .93. \times .95 \times .98 \times .94 = .7976$, or approximately 80 percent. This tells us the likelihood of passing a unit of product through all five steps error-free.*

Rolled throughput yield can rapidly decrease as the number of steps increase. This is why a company, plant, or service operation must have high throughput yields at each step in the process in order to achieve a high rolled throughput yield. It must also try to minimize the overall number of steps and CTQs. While throughput yield is only sensitive to the number of CTQs in a product (product complexity), rolled

---

*At this point in our discussion, the reader may wonder why we don't simply aggregate the first-time yields. Generally speaking, the simple cross-multiplication of first-time yield values reflects the probability that any given unit of product will pass all functional test points in a process. It does not reveal the probability of passing a unit of product through the entire process defect-free. Only rolled throughput yield can provide this information. If one is truly "customer focused" and concerned with "value entitlement," then the measure of process efficiency selected should reflect not only the likelihood of product functionality but form and fit as well. In other words, rolled throughput yield is the probability of meeting all requirements throughout the process, not just those requirements related to product functionality. After all, a product could be 100 percent functional at the end of production cycle but still contain defects that may cause the customer problems during or after the warranty period.

throughput yield is sensitive to both the number of CTQs and the number of process steps (process complexity). True value entitlement can only be realized when rolled throughput yield is at its entitlement value. Getting there is what the Breakthrough Strategy is all about.

APPLYING THE METRICS: NORMALIZED YIELD

Normalized yield is a single and equivalent value that is assigned to a series of process steps involved in making a product. This is used to collectively characterize all the steps involved in manufacturing a product when the total defects per unit at the final step is known. In this sense, we say that normalized yield represents a "kind of average" yield value per step for a series of process steps, and is used to "sigmatize" processes and products. Adopting metrics such as throughput yield, rolled throughput yield, and normalized yield helps companies measure, uncover, and eliminate hidden factories.

Here is how normalized yield is calculated:

A Six Sigma Black Belt from Human Resources is analyzing a particular process involving a form. He knows that there are ten steps involved in the process and calculates that the rolled throughput yield is equal to 36.8 percent.

When the team wants to assign yield values to each of the ten steps, one member suggests dividing 36.8 percent over ten steps. They quickly realize that this is not the correct method to calculate the normalized yield. Another member suggests, incorrectly, that since the rolled throughput yield equals 36.8 percent, then all steps should have the same throughput yield (36.8 percent).

After several discussions, the Six Sigma Black Belt points out that the normalized yield is equal to the kth root of the rolled throughput yield, where k equals the number of process steps. He explains to the team that this is a form of "average" that represents an equalized value applicable to all steps of the process. The team then calculates the 10th root of 0.368 and concludes that each step has a normalized yield equal to 90.5 percent. The Black Belt now recognizes that 90.5 percent normalized yield is the perfor-

*mance baseline for each of the ten steps that comprise the
"process." This is true because* $.90510^{10} = .368$, *or 36.8 percent.*

Throughput yield, rolled throughput yield, and normalized yield
have important business implications. Using these yield measurements allows companies to much more accurately assess the performance of their industrial or commercial processes. For many
companies, these yields paint a surprising and disturbing picture.
Companies who calculated their final yield at 90 percent might find
that their rolled throughput yield is only 2 percent. Once companies
understand their true yield, they can begin to set breakthrough targets
and track improvements with measurements that tell the whole story.
Calculating rolled throughput yield will far more accurately reflect
quality, cycle time, and cost because calculations are done at each
step in the process and not just at the unit level, as is the case with
first-time yield.

As a final point on rolled throughput yield, we need to take a closer
look at this metric's relationship to cost. To illustrate, let's look at the
following example. Suppose that a certain process displays a rolled
throughput yield (Y.rt) of 70 percent. To compute the number of equivalent units that must be started to produce one defect-free unit
(assuming that all defects are repairable), we use this formula: $1 + (1
- Y.rt)$, or, in this case, $1 + (1 - .70)$, which equals 1.30. In other words,
we must start an equivalent of 1.3 units in terms of material and effort
in order to send one good unit on to the customer. If the defects are not
repairable and the "unit" must be scrapped (owing to one or more
of the defect types), then we would use the slightly different formula
of $1 / .70$, or 1.43. In other words, we would need 1.43 units. As you
may have guessed, the higher the defect rate, the lower the rolled
throughput yield, which, in turn, decreases capacity. As a result, more
"equivalent" units must be created in order to produce a good unit.

If everything in a process goes right, production time is kept to a
minimum. This minimal or optimal production time is referred to as
cycle-time entitlement, or the rightful level of expectation, which we
abbreviate as "T.min." We abbreviate the *actual* length of time it takes

to produce the units as "T.actual." We can compute the actual process-ing time per units as T.actual = T.min times the rolled throughput yield. If the optimal time—T.min—is 10 minutes, then the actual time is 10 × 1.3, or 13 minutes. This means that, on average, a "unit" requires 13 minutes to process, versus the entitlement time of 10 minutes. Since inventory is equal to cycle time times process volume, if the schedule requires that 1,000 units be produced each day, we need enough resources to produce the equivalent of 1,300 units a day to get the 1,000 units we need to meet the production schedule. This allows us to track work-in-process costs and labor costs, which, of course, relate directly to the bottom line. By now it should be clear that there is no way to calcu-late this kind of relationship for first-time yield or final yield.

So why do companies continue to use first-time yield as a basis for measuring how well their processes work to create products and ser-vices? Because it is easy to calculate, can be calculated using readily available data, and most companies don't recognize the difference between first-time yield and rolled throughput yield. Again, *we don't know what we don't know, and we can't do anything about what we don't know*. Six Sigma is about working smarter, not necessarily harder. Six Sigma is about doing what is right, not necessarily what is easy.

Are You Efficient or Effective?

Effectiveness focuses on results. Efficiency focuses on activity. Com-panies, like people, can do the wrong things with great efficiency. There's a small town in Arizona where life revolves around horses and cattle, and not much happens that the town's sheriff doesn't know about. One night several years ago, the local sheriff, new to the town and not yet familiar with all the streets, was awakened by a caller informing him that there was a dead horse in the middle of the road and that the horse needed to be moved right away. The sheriff said he'd be right over, and asked the caller to give him the name of the street. The caller said that the horse was lying in the middle of Man-zanita Street. "How do you spell that?" the sheriff asked. "I dunno," the caller replied. "But I'll find out." Ten minutes passed before the caller finally came back on the phone and said, "Sheriff, I couldn't get the correct spelling of Manzanita Street for you, so I done moved that dead horse over to Easy Street. That's spelled E-A-S-Y."

Efficiency means turning the crank right. Effectiveness is turning the right crank. In other words, you may be turning your cranks faster than anyone else in the industry, but you need to *turn the right cranks* to be effective. The Breakthrough Strategy shows companies how to be effective. Moreover, it has the potential to help companies redesign products and services so that no cranks need to be turned at all because there are no defects to fix.

Virtually all executives and managers can be educated in the Six Sigma Breakthrough Strategy. But those who have this year's financial bonus or incentive package tied to the first-time-yield metric may have built-in incentives to continue using old methods. Management needs to consider the kinds of actions they are rewarding or penalizing. Rationalizing business practices that are flawed can impede the implementation of Six Sigma, and has nothing to do with what will best improve a company's long-term performance.

Polaroid Flashes Back

Like many companies, the venerable Polaroid Corporation had implemented a series of quality programs. While each initiative improved product quality—and in 1996 alone the company saved $10 million through variability-reduction processes—Polaroid had never encountered a program with the depth and far-reaching effects of Six Sigma. Although instant photography remained the backbone of the organization, research and development had provided Polaroid with a wealth of other imaging applications—and the success of these applications would depend heavily on Six Sigma.

In 1995, Gary DiCamillo was named CEO of Polaroid Corporation. DiCamillo announced that his goal was to turn a company from one that had not sustained any "real" growth for ten years (from 1985 to 1995) into one that was growing every year. The effort was dubbed "Polaroid's Renewal"; achieving the "new" Polaroid would rely heavily on Six Sigma. DiCamillo believed that Six Sigma was the fastest and most effective path to improving product quality, widening the company's customer base, and improving profitability.

Retaining Polaroid's Heritage

During a Santa Fe, New Mexico, family vacation in 1944, Edwin H. Land's young daughter asked why she had to wait to see the pictures

her father had just taken of her. As Land, Polaroid Corporation's
founder and CEO, walked alone through town later that day, he
mulled over the problem his daughter had unwittingly posed, and
finally pieced together a way to create a camera with instant self-
developing film. Three years later, on February 21, 1947, Land stood
before the Optical Society of America and took a picture of himself.
In less than a minute, Land peeled back the negative and presented
an instant picture to an enthusiastic audience. Land's invention was
splashed across the front page of *The New York Times,* was given a full
page in *Life,* and received attention in the international press.

Within two years, on November 26, 1948, the Cambridge-based
Polaroid Corporation sold its first instant camera in Jordan Marsh,
Boston's oldest department store, profoundly changing the history of
photography. The camera weighed five pounds when loaded, and sold
for $89.75. For an additional $1.75, shoppers could purchase film
with eight sepia-toned exposures. By the end of the day, demonstra-
tors had sold all of the 156 cameras, and shoppers were clamoring for
more. During the next year, Polaroid's instant cameras sold as quickly
as the factory could produce them, with sales exceeding $5 million.
By 1950, more than four thousand dealers sold Polaroid cameras,
film, and accessories, when only a year earlier Kodak had virtually
monopolized the U.S. photography market.

More than fifty years and more than 165 million cameras later,
Polaroid is in the midst of similarly profound changes both within the
company and in the field they now call imaging.

Today Polaroid is a company with more than $1.8 billion in sales,
primarily in instant cameras and film. The company is spread out over
seventeen locations around the world and employs more than 8,500
people. But like every company in the photographic imaging business,
Polaroid is in the process of transforming itself into an electronic and
digital imaging business. To date, companies in the photographic imaging business have made their margins around film, but consumer
demand for new photographic technology has essentially created a
kind of culture shock in the imaging industry. To Polaroid's credit, it
has managed to ride the crest of the wave by continuing to introduce

new instant and digital products designed to appeal to a wide range of consumers around the world. It continues to be the leader in photographic identification and is now the leader in electronic identification. In West Virginia, Polaroid has created a driver's license ID system using facial-recognition technology to reduce driver's license fraud—a first for the United States. The process begins with a high-quality Polaroid digital photo, which is taken when a new applicant applies for a driver's license. The system "reads" the photo and retains digital information about the applicant's facial features in a secure central database. When a license is renewed or replaced—both prime opportunities for license fraud —a new photo is compared against the file for verification of the applicant's identity. The Polaroid system also stores digitized fingerprints of West Virginia drivers who elect this option as a secondary, antifraud screening device. Polaroid is transitioning from a company whose skill base lies in chemistry and engineering to one whose skill base lies in electronics and digital imaging.

In addition, Polaroid is shrewdly leveraging existing products by adding features that don't require substantial investments in research and development. For instance, SpiceCam, an instant camera that capitalizes on the famous Spice Girls brand name and is based on the Polaroid 600, targets the young adult market. SpiceCam is manufactured in special girl-power colors—violet, pink, orange, and silver—and comes with a customization kit so that kids can add their personal design to the cameras. Teenagers can purchase the 600 AlterImage film, which allows them to write notes on the photographs or draw in backgrounds. Another film produces photos that can be turned into stickers, a product popular with Japanese girls. Polaroid is also marketing black-and-white film to the youth market—a novelty to a generation whose parents documented their children's lives solely on color film.

Polaroid and Six Sigma?

The financial shrewdness and pragmatism of the then executive vice president of Polaroid's Commercial Imaging Group, Carole J. Uhrich, made her one of the company's most effective change agents. A chemist by training, Uhrich's first engineering tour de force at Polaroid was overseeing the design and manufacturing of Polaroid's 600 Series camera and film system, the first integrated camera and film system not personally directed by Ed Land. The 600 Series camera remains the largest single revenue generator in Polaroid's history.

When Uhrich, who sits on the boards of directors for Ceridian and Maytag Corporations and is a trustee for Northeastern University, heard about how successful Six Sigma has been at General Electric and AlliedSignal, she wanted to know more. Concerned for Polaroid's profitability and market position, and a staunch proponent of customer satisfaction, Uhrich sent quality strategy manager Joseph Kasabula on a fact-finding mission. He was charged with defining quality from the customer's point of view and then finding a way to translate those expectations into Polaroid's products. After studying best practices in the industry for quality, Kasabula convinced other Polaroid senior executives that the Six Sigma Breakthrough Strategy would best help Polaroid reach its goal. In 1996, executives internally assessed the sigma capability of each of the company's divisions and came up with a company average. Based on their assessment, not only did they feel that taking the company to six sigma by the year 2001 was a realistic goal, but they believed that the Breakthrough Strategy would dramatically improve Polaroid's profitability and increase customer satisfaction.

For nearly twelve years, from 1983 to 1995, when Polaroid phased out its last quality program, the company had engaged in a series of variability-reduction efforts. One was an internally designed program called Statistical Engineering Training Program (SETP), which was combined with a Design of Experiments course called Product Process Optimization (PPO). Although these programs had some effect on the bottom line, none attacked companywide quality issues to the extent that Six Sigma does. These programs focused on product and process, but they didn't provide road maps to implement the programs or the tools to gauge their total financial impact on the company. Polaroid needed a program that would focus on dollar savings, not just defects.

Uhrich was adamant that the Six Sigma Breakthrough Strategy not be treated as another course where employees sat through several days of classes and then put the course materials on a shelf, never to be used again. One senior executive displays a *Dilbert* cartoon showing Dilbert hoisting a hefty notebook into a bookcase, with a caption in which he describes his new training manual as a "living monument to temporary knowledge." It's not unusual for people who attend training seminars without having the opportunity to put knowledge into action to soon forget what they have learned.

First, Uhrich sent out word throughout the company that Polaroid would train in the Six Sigma Breakthrough Strategy only people with an approved project. Projects would enforce action-based learning and force people to demonstrate proficiency. In other words, this would not be another ticket-punching program. Second, Uhrich demanded that all participants begin Six Sigma training with a project that would return a significant amount of money to the bottom line. Employees were made to understand that bottom-line dollar results were the program's focus and that dollar savings were going to be studied meticulously.

Uhrich also emphasized that, unlike earlier quality programs that focused on middle-level managers and engineers, often leaving senior management in the dark, the Six Sigma Breakthrough Strategy would require active involvement from senior management. Management needed an in-depth understanding of the program. Without this understanding, the program would lose momentum and could not be pushed down throughout the company as it needed to be. "Our executives needed to understand the importance of sigma capability before they could understand what it could do to their bottom line," said Uhrich. She believes that the Six Sigma Breakthrough Strategy is the only program that enforces the rigorous demands required for a company to achieve six sigma.

After convincing Polaroid chairman and CEO Gary DiCamillo that the Six Sigma Breakthrough Strategy could help Polaroid, Uhrich positioned herself as the key driver behind Polaroid's Six Sigma program, taking responsibility for ensuring management goodwill and financial backing for each Black Belt project. Since 1993, Polaroid had been achieving an impressive year-on-year 6 percent productivity increase. Uhrich believed that not only would Six Sigma make it easier to sustain this level of productivity, but it could be the catalyst to drive the number even higher while keeping assets level. Polaroid began training its first wave of Black Belts* in June 1997. Polaroid management advertises Six Sigma to its employees as an operational initiative that leads to variability reduction, reduced costs, and increased profitability. They readily admit that achieving that 6 percent year-on-year has not been easy, but are working feverishly to take the company to six sigma by 2001.

Project Selection

Polaroid's project selection was based on dollar savings, not defect reduction. Thus, projects were chosen with high dollar impact, or with the highest payback potential. Ultimately, projects were recommended by plant and development managers who felt that the project carried significant potential to increase customer satisfaction and profitability. Initial projects were essentially action learning projects with review. In a nutshell, this meant that Black Belts would spend one week in class studying the measurement phase of their project, then spend three weeks applying what they had learned in the measurement class; they would then present their measurement-phase application and results in the first session of the Analyze phase. This process would continue for four months, until each Black Belt had taken his or her project through each of the four phases of Measure, Analyze, Improve, and Control. Each Black Belt project was reviewed weekly by a Champion, reviewed monthly by a plant manager, and reviewed quarterly by Commercial and Consumer Manufacturing vice presidents.

---

*Polaroid refers to its Black Belts as "Variability Reduction Leaders," or VRLs; it feels the term flows logically from past quality-control efforts. "The phrase 'Black Belts' seems to require a definition within our organization, whereas the phrase 'Variability Reduction Leader' is immediately understood," says Joseph Kasabula, quality strategy manager for product development and worldwide manufacturing.

A Polaroid Case Study

A conversation with almost anyone within Polaroid quickly reveals that the company does not believe its mission is photographic imaging as much as it is to re-create an event or an emotion in a way the customer wants to remember it. Photographs anchor memories to a particular time, place, or event, and Polaroid's goal is to create a snapshot of reality in a way that triggers a positive response.

Polaroid's instant cameras are remarkable pieces of technology. From the time the shutter-release button is pushed and the film sheet emerges from the camera to create that "perfect" instant photograph, an astounding 25,000 functions take place within a single self-contained one-minute processing lab where the internal temperature can reach between 120 and 150 degrees Fahrenheit. Needless to say, those within Polaroid responsible for designing and creating the "perfect" photograph have a daunting task in ensuring that the customer is satisfied with the final product.

Let's say you have just purchased a box of Polaroid instant film with ten exposures. Each exposure consists of two important sheets. One sheet is called the *negative* and the other sheet is called the *positive*. The *negative* sheet captures the original image and will transfer that image to the *positive* sheet, where the photograph will appear. Between the negative and the positive are three layers of emulsions. The first layer is sensitive to blue light, the second layer is sensitive to green light, and the third layer is sensitive to red light. Sandwiched between these three layers are developing agents. During exposure, light enters from the top layer and passes through the next two layers to create the photograph. Through use of the three color-sensitive layers, the entire color spectrum can be reproduced in a single photograph.

After the photographer has pushed the shutter-release button and the picture has been taken, a "pod"* ruptures as the film passes through two metal rollers and exits the camera. Developer (or "reagent") from

---

*The pod is a very complex package of chemicals found in the bottom portion of the white frame surrounding the picture. Barely perceptible to human touch, the pod consists of sixteen layers of materials, including polyester, aluminum, vinyl, adhesives, and paper.

the ruptured pod spreads evenly between the positive and negative sheets to create the image. As color dyes from the negative migrate upward to the positive, the picture gradually forms and is complete within about a minute.

One of Polaroid's primary concerns centers on "sensitometry"— a process that measures how sensitive film is to light and whether colors and brightness are accurately reproduced. Because of the importance Polaroid places on the quality of its instant film, it first chose to apply the Six Sigma Breakthrough Strategy to measuring the sensitometry of its film. Polaroid's manufacturing division uses a series of measurements to determine whether the light and color levels will reproduce accurately in a photograph. Making sure that the measurement system performs accurately and precisely is pivotal to guaranteeing the film's consistent performance throughout a range of conditions.

The role of the Champion in any Black Belt project is to make funds available and free Black Belts from their regular duties so that they can focus solely on applying the Breakthrough methodology to their project. Realizing the extent of the challenge to create and enforce a uniform measurement system throughout each of Polaroid's plants, the company assigned two Champions and five Black Belts to the task.

The five Black Belts selected to work the project brought diverse, but complementary, skills to the project. Ken Pickering, a technical supervisor, Tom Lumenello, a technical manager, and Howard Worzel, a photographic scientist and engineer, each longtime Polaroid employees, were responsible for running the tests on film and determining what variations in the process affect the results. MIT graduate Mark Wilen, a relative newcomer to Polaroid, was charged with documenting the process so that once the correct process had been determined, it could be replicated. And finally, engineer Mike Hart, a twenty-eight-year veteran in Polaroid's Consumer Imaging Manufacturing Division, was responsible for ensuring that the results were implemented consistently throughout every lab in each Polaroid plant.

Despite Polaroid's concern with providing customers with a film that produces consistent results, the profusion of earlier variability-reduction work within Polaroid had decentralized its measurement systems and equipment and made it increasingly difficult for measurements at one site to agree with another. The Six Sigma Breakthrough Strategy was crucial to reinforcing uniformity and central standards. Howard Worzel described the problem like this:

> If you go back into history, you will find that the Egyptian definition of a cubit* equaled the distance between one's fingertips and elbow. Now if every Egyptian adult's arms and hands were the same size, this would be a fairly accurate measurement. But, in reality, the distance between a six-foot man's fingertips and elbow is going to be significantly longer than that of a five-foot woman. Now what if that man and woman are each asked to build a ten-cubit house? Obviously the woman's house is going to be significantly smaller than the man's house. So even though both individuals have followed the directions meticulously, using what they believed to be a standard measurement, the final products are going to vary substantially.
>
> Similarly, if I am responsible for a certain part of the film-making process that always gets great results, and then I am transferred to a new position within the company and someone else takes over my job, the process may start to drift. Chances are, the person who has taken over my job may not know what the problem is, much less how to fix it, because the process has never been documented. Six Sigma first corrects the process, and then documents the process so that anyone with the "cookbook" can keep the process under control. What we are trying to do is reminiscent of my grandmother, who made some great meals with a pinch of this and a scoop of that, but no one else in the family could replicate her recipes. The Six Sigma methodology is quite literally a cookbook for getting perfect results every time.

---

*A cubit is an ancient measurement unit used to measure length, and is based on the length between the elbow and the tip of the middle finger, usually equal to about eighteen inches in length.

A story that highlights the importance of "road mapping" centers around how technicians in the manufacturing lab were mixing ingredients to create the reagent. When the pod ruptures, the reagent (acting as a developer) spreads evenly between the positive and negative sheets to re-create the photographic image. Technicians were stymied as to why batches of reagent varied so drastically despite the fact that each batch was made with identical ingredients in identical amounts. Finally, the technicians were asked to create a detailed road map describing each step of the process they went through to create a batch of the reagent.

Amazingly, without even applying statistical analyses to the process, the technicians discovered that the different road maps revealed crucial information. It was discovered that some technicians added a powdered chemical called DA56 to a vat of liquid. During the course of the chemical being added, small amounts were sucked up into the ventilation system and a fine film of the chemical clung to the rim of the vat, reducing the amount of chemical actually added to the process. Other technicians were taking the same amount of powdered chemical and making a paste before adding the rest of the liquid. Although all the technicians were following the same formula, even a variation as seemingly innocuous as the order and the way in which identical ingredients were combined created an impact on the final product. If not enough of the powdered chemical made it into the batch of reagent, the resulting film wouldn't develop properly. If too much of the powdered chemical went into the batch, the plant would waste money on the extra chemical.

Howard Worzel summed up the value of mapping out the Breakthrough Strategy this way:

> If we can catch a problem with a chemical from our supplier before we use it, we lose only two cents. If we don't find the problem with the chemical until it has been added to the rest of the solution, it may cost us $10 in time and materials to go back and fix the problem. But if we don't catch the problem until the reagent has gone into the film and is ready to be packaged and shipped out to our customers, the expense of correcting that problem may exceed the entire cost of manufacturing that product.

Experience has taught Polaroid that its Black Belt project teams have to be made up of people on the floor who actually do the work, the design people who create the process around theory, and the manufacturing people—so that knowledge and actual practices are shared. Getting people to talk to one another and share what they know (and don't know) is crucial to the success of the Six Sigma methodology.

Mike Hart, the Black Belt engineer responsible for seeing that the Six Sigma measurement processes are implemented consistently from laboratory to laboratory and from plant to plant, describes the Six Sigma Breakthrough Strategy this way:

> The Breakthrough Strategy gives new structure to the tools we already had. Structure has been the key element missing in Polaroid's drive for quality. I keep telling my people that the Breakthrough Strategy cookbook tells us how to use time-tested ingredients in new ways. It takes the same ingredients that we've been using for years, but combines them in new ways to get different results. Now, instead of pouring eggs, sugar, chocolate, and milk into a bowl to make chocolate pudding, we take those same ingredients, separate the yolks from the egg whites, beat the egg whites, combine the ingredients in a very specific order, cook at precise temperature, and come out with a chocolate soufflé. For us, the results from the Breakthrough Strategy have been quick and powerful.

Strobe Exposure Variation

Another Six Sigma project that produced impressive results within a short period of time focused on improving the accuracy of strobe exposure in Polaroid's 600 Series camera line. Richard James, David Sproul, and Alaster McDonach led a team of twenty highly qualified employees from within the Consumer Hardware Division to resolve an inconsistency in strobe exposure. Since the majority of Polaroid photographs are taken indoors at lower light levels, the use of a strobe is extremely important in creating a properly exposed picture—one that is not too light or too dark. The 600 Series camera line is one of Polaroid's lower-priced models, and its popularity accounts for nearly 90 percent of Polaroid's camera sales. Previous quality efforts had raised the camera's internal exposure system to a 3.5 sigma level; within eighteen months of applying the Breakthrough Strategy, the product had jumped to a 5 sigma level.

With an admirable lack of ego and a willingness not to assume that it knew what the customer wanted, Polaroid hired an outside research firm, the Home Testing Institute, to survey its customers prior to applying the Breakthrough Strategy to its product. The Home Testing Institute's role was to act as an unbiased party in contacting current customers of the 600 Series camera line, providing them with film, and then asking these consumers to rate their satisfaction with the camera and film. Polaroid wanted to know what features were pleasing to the customer and what features left the customer dissatisfied. The firm believed that if it asked, "What is the customer looking for? How can we give the customer what they want?" it could prevent the customer from purchasing cameras and film from a competitor, thereby increasing customer use of Polaroid products.

The Home Testing Institute's survey revealed four critical-to-quality characteristics (CTQs) of particular concern to consumers of the 600 Series camera and film.

- Is the film exposure too light or too dark?

- Is the color balanced and does it show the proper hues?

- Is the picture sharp and clear?

- Does the camera work properly?

Exposure, in particular, turned out to be an important critical-to-quality characteristic for the consumer. The nature of instant imaging necessitates that Polaroid's exposure requirements be much more exact than those of conventional cameras and film, particularly since there is no opportunity to adjust exposure later on during the developing and printing process, as there is when developing the more traditional 35mm film.

David Sproul and his coworkers gave particular attention to the camera's photometric system. The photometric system determines how the film is exposed within Polaroid's instant imaging cameras. Sproul and his team worked to refine the camera's internal exposure system so that exposure could be adjusted in smaller increments to ensure that the customer received a perfectly exposed snapshot.

Once again, those working on the 600 Series camera quickly realized that they could not improve exposure performance without accurate and consistent test equipment. They first upgraded their test equipment, then standardized the equipment itself, and ultimately implemented a new level of standardization in each plant around the world.

Before each 600 Series camera is packaged and shipped out to the consumer, its exposure capabilities are measured and, if necessary, adjustments are made so that each camera leaves the factory with the same internal exposure capabilities. Standard test equipment is extremely important in making sure that all cameras are subjected to the same testing conditions. Variation in the measurement system would mean there would be variation in quality from camera to camera. Alaster McDonach and his team at Polaroid's Vale of Leven, Scotland, plant improved the accuracy of the measurement-calibration system and then implemented a uniform measurement system across all assembly modules. This ended the daily, time-consuming practice of requiring employees to manually calibrate each piece of exposure test equipment and closed the door on significant variation in the measurement system. Worldwide use of Breakthrough Strategy tools to statistically identify and eliminate the sources of variation reduced testing variation within plants and from plant to plant significantly.

Polaroid realized that it could increase customer satisfaction and ensure that its customers purchased more Polaroid film by improving the quality of each picture's exposure. A 3.5 sigma level indicates approximately 22,750 defects per million opportunities. When one considers that Polaroid makes five million of the 600 Series cameras each year, this translated into more than 100,000 cameras that gave the customer a picture less than perfectly exposed. By taking the process from 3.5 sigma to a 5 sigma, and reducing defects to 233 parts per million, this variability-reduction team guaranteed their division an annual $1 million in sales through increased "repurchase intent." In other words, by satisfying the customer, they increased the probability that consumers would purchase more Polaroid cameras and film. As Richard James explains it:

> Many consumers have several different brands of cameras sitting in a drawer at home. If they are confident that our camera and film will give them a consistent quality photograph, and that they will have a properly exposed photograph in their hands in less than a minute, they are more apt to use our camera and film over our competitor's. But if consumers believe there is even the slightest risk that our product will not deliver the kind of photograph they expect, they are likely to reach for our competitor's product. From a product standpoint, the Breakthrough Strategy improved our quality, and customer complaints decreased over whether the pictures were too light or too dark. On the manufacturing side, employees were no longer recalibrating the test equipment before each day's production began.

In addition to guaranteeing customer satisfaction, the variability-reduction team is annually saving over $200,000 in operating expenses—in this case, rework costs (again, the hidden factory) and the cost of having employees continually check the measurement system for consistency and accuracy—with, as James emphasizes, a minimum financial investment to (1) upgrade test equipment, (2) make minor changes to the product, and (3) make improvements to the manufacturing process.

So not only did James, Sproul, McDonach, and their team improve the product by using a better photometric system to create a better adjustment capability, they also improved the manufacturing process through improving the test equipment calibration process. Applying the Breakthrough Strategy turned out to be a win-win situation both for customers (they were getting photos with better exposure) and for Polaroid's manufacturing division (the manufacturing plant no longer had to devote time and manpower to recalibrate equipment each workday), thus lowering costs and ensuring consumer retention.

An interesting side note to this story is that early on in Richard James's Polaroid career, he had been assigned the task of improving exposure for Polaroid's SX-70 camera. James is the first to admit that, working alone, although he made several improvements to the camera's exposure system, he never succeeded in improving the exposure process to the extent achieved by applying the Breakthrough Strategy. Today he sees the difference between his limited success at improving the exposure process and his success in using the Six Sigma Breakthrough Strategy as a great example of what happens when you bring together a team from across the company with different technical expertise, who can then collectively apply the comprehensive tools to solve a problem. James's experience reinforces our belief that Six Sigma projects must be a team effort, where everyone's talents are used synchronously to give the customer a better product, reduce operating costs, and boost profitability.

Prognosis

Polaroid's receptiveness to change, particularly change brought about by Six Sigma, is remarkable. Each initiative has generated positive changes within the Polaroid culture, allowing the company to see its business as a series of intertwined processes, instead of thousands of separate functions. Six Sigma has been the final stepping-stone. Unlike companies whose divisions essentially turn themselves into "warring tribes," with different sectors attacking each other's product and procedures, Polaroid has used Six Sigma to operate as a well-oiled machine and communicate in a common language. Today, Polaroid sees Six Sigma as a way to reach its goal of a 50 percent reduction in the time required to bring product ideas from inception to market. The company is already beginning to see results.

Although those within Polaroid know that market competition will not allow them the luxury of basking in past glory, they see Six Sigma as a natural conclusion to the work Edwin Land started more than half a century ago. Land refused to accept that something could not be done. He believed that 90 percent of solving a problem was asking the right questions. Once the right questions have been asked, he said, the problem can be solved. Land would have been a whole-hearted proponent of taking a process, breaking it down into its fundamentals, figuring out which parts of the process are most important, and experimenting to improve them. As Polaroid begins to control crucial processes, it is realizing its most challenging goals. Ultimately, Polaroid's goal is to so thoroughly understand and define quality from its customer's point of view that quality is immediately translated into its products.

Polaroid has eagerly embraced the Six Sigma philosophy. The company believes that Six Sigma is the best strategy for bridging product development, manufacturing, and customer service, while also creating a common language around Six Sigma at all levels within the organization.

The Breakthrough Strategy

There are eight fundamental steps or stages involved in applying the Breakthrough Strategy to achieve Six Sigma performance in a process, division, or company. These eight stages are Recognize, Define, Measure, Analyze, Improve, Control, Standardize, and Integrate. Each phase is designed to ensure (1) that companies apply the Breakthrough Strategy in a methodical and disciplined way; (2) that Six Sigma projects are correctly defined and executed; and (3) that the results of these projects are incorporated into running the day-to-day business.

Almost every organization can be broken down into three basic levels. The highest level, the umbrella of a corporation, is the *business level*. The second level is the *operations level*. The third level is the *process level*. While the Breakthrough Strategy applies to each level of a company, at each level it achieves different, although complementary, results. The success of Six Sigma is defined as the extent to which it transforms each level of an organization to improve the organization's overall quality and profitability. In essence, the Breakthrough Strategy is a fluid methodology that works its way up and down the hierarchies of an organization. This is one of the reasons why Six Sigma, unlike other quality initiatives, needs to be understood and integrated at every level of the organization if long-term, companywide improvements are to be made.

One way of understanding how the Breakthrough Strategy works at various levels in an organization is to picture the way gears work.

Gears exist in just about everything that has spinning parts, from clocks to car engines and VCRs. Each of these products has a number of gears of different sizes that move simultaneously but at different speeds. A nondigital clock, for example, has several hands on its face representing hours, minutes, seconds, and sometimes a moon phase. The hour, minute, and second hands move at different speeds, as a result of the different sizes and shapes of the gears. The shafts that drive the gears are aligned to create a fluid motion. If one gear, shaft, or spring fails, the entire mechanism fails or becomes ineffective.

The way the Breakthrough Strategy affects different levels of an organization is similar to this, with each level or "gear" moving in synchronicity but at different speeds. For example, it may take companies at the business or corporate level—under the direction of a Deployment Champion—three to five years to fully implement and deploy all eight stages of the Breakthrough Strategy. At the operations level—a smaller-sized corporate "gear"—it will take a Project Champion roughly twelve to eighteen months to cycle through the eight phases. At the process or individual project level, Black Belts can run through the Breakthrough Strategy in six to eight weeks as they apply it to specific projects, generating immediate cash to the bottom line. Like individual gears in a clock connected to one another through a gear train, each level of a company applies the Breakthrough Strategy independently, and at different speeds, as it works toward a larger, common purpose, driven by the mainspring of reward and recognition.

Executives at the business level use Six Sigma to improve market share, increase profitability, and ensure the corporation's long-term viability; managers at operations level use Six Sigma to improve yield, eliminate hidden factories, and reduce labor and material costs. At the process level, Black Belts utilize Six Sigma to reduce defects and variation and improve process capability in ways that tie in with the business and operational goals, leading to improved profitability and customer satisfaction. Although each level of the organization applies the Breakthrough Strategy differently, it is done in tandem and coordinated so that the overall strategic business goals are met. So while everyone from executives at the business level down to Black Belts at the process level work through the Recognize, Define, Measure, Analyze, Improve, Control, Standardize, and Integrate phases, they do so with a different focus and in a different time frame.

For example, during the Measure phase at the executive level, leadership is concerned with measuring operating margins and overall profitability; operations managers are responsible for measuring labor costs and controlling material costs and overhead; Black Belts, at the process level, measure cycle time, yield, and defects per unit, and so on. Each level of measurement flows into the other in a very specific and connected manner.

Similarly, during the Improve phase, the goal of those at the business level might be a companywide deployment of Six Sigma, while managers at the operations level might focus on Black Belt training and project selection, and Black Belts at the process level might conduct Design of Experiments (DOE)—the direct manipulation of variables to see how they affect a critical-to-quality characteristic.

During the Control phase, the executive leadership at the business level might take steps to ensure that Six Sigma gains are maintained; at the operations level, managers might focus on devising a reward and recognition system to ensure Black Belt retention; and, at the process level, Black Belts might document procedures so that improvements to process performance are maintained. Again, each level connects to the next in a smooth and hierarchical fashion.

So while increasing profitability requires companies to improve their processes at their most basic levels, the long-term goal of Six Sigma is to integrate and standardize companywide system improvements at every level in order to raise the overall "sigma" performance. Companies such as AlliedSignal, Dupont, and General Electric have all found that the benefits of Six Sigma have been expedited by focusing their human and financial resources solely on Six Sigma. These companies have realized that Six Sigma is the organizing agent for other initiatives. Through Six Sigma, they discover which initiatives drive beneficial change and which initiatives generate uncorrelated results. Six Sigma aligns and focuses the power of their overall improvement efforts to reap maximum business leverage.

An Integrated View of the Breakthrough Strategy

The eight primary components of the Breakthrough Strategy fall into one of four categories. The Recognize and Define phases fall under the category of *identification*, where companies begin to understand the fundamental concepts of Six Sigma and get a sense of the Breakthrough Strategy as a problem-solving methodology with a unique set of tools. Managers and employees begin to question inputs—the processes that go into creating a product or service—rather than simply inspecting the final product or service that is delivered to the customer. Management can then create opportunities and an environment for change. In the Define phase, Black Belts identify specific Six Sigma projects, based on product and process benchmarking. Through top-down product and process benchmarking, senior management considers what industrial or commercial lines might be the best initial focus of Six Sigma projects. These decisions are made within the context of the industry and business-specific issues facing the organization.

The Measure and Analyze phases fall under the category of *characterization*, where critical-to-quality characteristics in the process are measured and described. The Improve and Control phases fall under *optimization*, because these two phases maximize and maintain the enhanced process capability. And, finally, the Standardize and Integrate phases are part of *institutionalization*, where the results of applying the entire Breakthrough Strategy are woven into the corporation's culture.

IDENTIFICATION STAGE

Business growth depends on how well companies meet customer expectations in terms of quality, price, and delivery. Their ability to satisfy these needs with a known degree of certainty is controlled by process capability, and the amount of variation in their processes (these processes can be any kind of process, ranging from administrative to service to sales to manufacturing). Variation has a direct impact on business results in terms of cost, cycle time, and the number of

THE SIX SIGMA ROAD MAP			
STAGE	**BREAKTHROUGH STRATEGY PHASE**	**OBJECTIVE**	
Identification	Recognize Define	Identify key business issues	
Characterization	Measure Analyze	Understand current performance levels	BLACK BELTS / PROJECTS
Optimization	Improve Control	Achieve breakthrough improvement	
Institutionalization	Standardize Integrate	Transform how day-to-day business is conducted	

(left margin vertical: BREAKTHROUGH STRATEGY)

defects that affect customer satisfaction. Identification allows companies to recognize how their processes affect profitability and then define what the critical-to-business processes are.

CHARACTERIZATION STAGE

Characterization assesses where a process is at the time it is measured and helps to point to the goals a company should aspire to achieve. It establishes a baseline, or benchmark, and provides a starting point for measuring improvements. Following the Measure and Analyze phases that make up characterization, an action plan is created to close the "gap" between how things currently work and how the company would like them to work in order to meet the company's goals for a particular product or service. In characterization, Six Sigma Black Belts select one or more of the product's key characteristics and create a detailed description of every step in a process. The Black Belts then make the necessary measurements, record the results on process-control cards, and estimate what the short-term and long-term process capability is.

OPTIMIZATION STAGE

Optimization identifies what steps need to be taken to improve a process and reduce the major sources of variation. The key process variables are identified through statistically designed experiments; Black Belts then use these data to establish what "knobs" must be adjusted to improve the process. Optimization looks at a large number of variables in order to determine the "vital few" variables that have the greatest impact. Using various analyses, Black Belts determine which variables have the most leverage or exert the most influence. The final goal of optimization in the Breakthrough Strategy is to use the knowledge gained to improve and control a process. Results may be used to develop better process limits, modify how certain steps of the process are performed, or to choose better materials and equipment. In a nutshell, optimization improves and controls the key variables that exert the greatest influence on a product's key characteristics. This provides the organization with an array of improvements that ultimately improve profitability and customer satisfaction, as well as increase shareholder value.

INSTITUTIONALIZATION STAGE

The Standardize and Integrate phases that make up *institutionalization* address the integration of Six Sigma into the way the business is managed on a daily basis. Six Sigma involves more than just focusing on each phase of a project to completion. It also offers a way to step back and look at how the collective results of smaller projects affect the large, high-level processes that run the day-to-day business. As companies learn what kinds of measures and metrics are needed to drive improvement, these insights have to be integrated into management's thinking and intellectual capital.

The Standardize phase ties together the many Six Sigma projects within a business and works to identify best practices and to standardize those practices within and across businesses. As companies improve the performance of various processes, they should standardize the way those processes are run and managed. Standardization allows companies to design their processes to work more effectively by using existing processes, components, methods, and materials that have already been optimized and that have proven their success.

The Integrate phase modifies the organization's management processes by taking advantage of the best practices identified through Six Sigma projects to support overall Six Sigma philosophy. For example, companies typically find that their current cost-accounting methods need to be changed to better track the "hidden factory" and cost of poor quality (COPQ), as well as to trace the direct and indirect benefits of Six Sigma.

Each business needs to identify best practices, judge when it makes sense to standardize a particular policy, practice, and/or process, and then disseminate the new standard throughout relevant parts of the organization. In essence, organizations can share their experiences and learn from one another. These new practices and policies need to be incorporated into the appropriate management processes and business philosophy. Six Sigma is about more than successfully completing individual projects. It requires the coordination and integration of these projects into the practices, policies, and procedures of corporate management. Over time, as hundreds of Six Sigma projects are completed, management coordinates standardization. For example, as Six Sigma projects characterize and optimize processes, the organization develops a set of best practice processes and standardizes them (such as when a company identifies the best process for handling capital requests or the best way to perform a certain type of riveting). As companies identify and establish new standards, they integrate them into how the day-to-day business is run. By systematically identifying key processes and improving the capability of those processes, the Breakthrough Strategy is able to attack and eliminate the overwhelming majority of persistent problems.

The strength of the Breakthrough Strategy comes from interaction at each level of an organization. Each phase of the Breakthrough Strategy is designed to ensure that companies apply the Breakthrough Strategy across organizations in a methodical and disciplined way. Doing so through all vertical levels ensures "leveraged success." While the Breakthrough Strategy always retains its basic form and objectives, the structure allows for flexibility within any given phase (particularly since projects rarely mirror one another).

The Breakthrough Strategy: Business Level

The business-level application of the Breakthrough Strategy focuses primarily on making significant improvements to the informational and economic systems used to "steer" the business. Systems that measure customer feedback and supplier quality are examples of business-level systems that influence business focus. Without customer feedback or supplier performance systems, it would be impossible to effectively achieve breakthrough performance. To achieve breakthrough at the business level requires a consistent and focused application of the Breakthrough Strategy at the business systems level for three to five years. The executive leadership's role in applying the Breakthrough Strategy is as follows:

BUSINESS PERSPECTIVE OF THE BREAKTHROUGH STRATEGY

R Recognize the true states of your business.

D Define what plans must be in place to realize improvement of each state.

M Measure the business systems that support the plans.

A Analyze the gaps in system performance benchmarks.

I Improve system elements to achieve performance goals.

C Control system-level characteristics that are critical to value.

S Standardize the systems that prove to be best-in-class.

I Integrate best-in-class systems into the strategic planning framework.

RECOGNIZE THE TRUE STATES OF YOUR BUSINESS. A business "state" describes global business conditions created by the systems used to guide and manage a business. These underlying systems have the ability to independently or interactively impact the top- and bottom-line economics of a business. Once management begins to measure their business states, they can begin to improve. Again, companies cannot improve what they do not measure. When the measurement is "fuzzy," so are the improvement efforts. Companies first need to identify the various states of their business before they can be measured.

As mentioned earlier, customer satisfaction is a reflection on the state of the business and depends on three things: (1) delivering a defect-free product or service; (2) delivering a product or service on schedule; and (3) delivering a product or service at the lowest possible cost. Each of these three elements can be translated into "systems." For example, the delivery of a defect-free product or service depends on how companies measure quality. On-time delivery of a product or service requires a sound material acquisition system, as well as a reliable scheduling system. Delivering a product or service at the lowest cost requires good accounting systems, management systems, and so on. In other words, most business states are virtually inseparable from a company's business systems.

Many organizations conduct customer-satisfaction surveys and use this information to create simple bar charts and frequency tables that display at a glance which options were most frequently selected for each question. While this kind of analysis allows companies to see the "state" of the customer—or how pleased he is with their products and services—it provides minimal understanding on how to improve low scores and "transplant" the success factors behind high scores. Companies that lack the capability to explore and analyze data are forced to read between the lines and draw superficial, and sometimes inaccurate, conclusions. Because they cannot properly "mine" the data, they cannot see how the various (and often dynamic) dimensions of customer satisfaction correlate to the business systems used to create, deliver, and support their products and services. In other words, the surveys they use can prohibit or restrict the cross-correlation of customer data to their business systems. Because they cannot fully determine the true state of their system capability, they are unable to forecast their ability to improve customer satisfaction.

Let's say a company has carefully authored a customer survey for a particular product or service that will allow it to statistically trace the level of satisfaction to one or more of its business systems. Through analysis of the data, a company might find that low customer satisfaction can be attributed to some aspect of the engineering system, rather than the manufacturing system. Knowing this, a company can leverage its management efforts and business resources to find the seemingly elusive state of "total customer satisfaction."

WHAT PLANS MUST BE IN PLACE TO IMPROVE? Once companies have defined and characterized the various states of the business, they can begin to creatively think about how to achieve a higher level of performance. If they discover that they do not know (statistically and practically) how customer satisfaction relates to key business systems, they can initiate plans to find out.

Companies might ask, "Does the customer's experience best correlate to our manufacturing capability, design capability, and/or service capability?" A company needs to formulate the right questions, and develop a strategic plan, to guide it while it pursues these answers. For example, let's suppose that Company X wants total customer satisfaction and it knows its engineering systems are a key element in customer satisfaction. If it discovers that its customer-satisfaction scores are low, the company needs to develop a strategic plan to increase its engineering systems' capability. Asking the right questions and implementing a strategic plan requires that each system be well defined and accountable.

MEASURE THE BUSINESS SYSTEMS THAT SUPPORT THE PLANS. This step often appears to be much easier than it actually is. While the idea of measuring is eloquently simple, we have consistently seen companies encounter three obstacles when attempting to measure. The first obstacle is knowing what to measure. The second obstacle is knowing how to measure. The third (and perhaps most formidable) obstacle is gaining executive commitment to go after the right measurements.

An industrial example of this is "engineering systems capability" where "product design capability" is one facet. Product design capability is the ability of a product or process design to meet the customer's requirements, conform to internal cost and timing constraints, and be "manufacturable" and "robust" using existing process technologies.* Let's say we've discovered that we must measure five key elements in order to establish product design capability. We must measure our ability to (1) meet or exceed customer requirements and expectations, (2) be at, or below, the "hard" costs targets, (3) meet or exceed established engineering schedules, (4) achieve consistently high process yields, and (5) tolerate normal process variations during production.

Once companies overcome the obstacle of defining *what* to measure, they can determine *how* to measure these elements. Let's look at the first element, "meet or exceed customer requirements and expectations." To measure this aspect of product design ability, we must establish some performance metrics. In this case, we will determine (1) the percent of engineering drawings in which the critical-to-quality characteristics (CTQs) have been identified, (2) the percent of CTQs that have been analyzed using Six Sigma methods, (3) the percent of CTQs that have been analyzed and statistically optimized, (4) the percent of optimized CTQs that perform at five sigma or higher, and (5) the percent of five sigma CTQs that are robust to normal variations in process centering.

These five performance metrics are hierarchically linked together and can be transformed to the "sigma" scale of measure. As stated earlier, the final obstacle is achieving the executive leadership's commitment to obtaining these measurements. Perhaps the best way to generate this support is by example—taking a few measurements, creating the benchmarks, and sharing the results. Benchmarking, for example, can set the stage for new questions, which, in turn, can motivate the executive leadership toward common action.

---

*Robust design refers to a design's ability to tolerate process "hiccups" without a significant change in any of the key characteristics of the product or service.

ANALYZE THE GAPS IN SYSTEM PERFORMANCE BENCHMARKS.
Once a company has measured its business systems, knows its capabilities, and has linked the capability measurements to the various
states of the business, it is ready to diagnose capability measures and
assess the performance gaps. For example, if a company discovers
that the typical customer requirements for one of its key products or
services is operating at a 3.4 sigma level, and that a similar product or
service generated by another business operates at a 4.6 sigma level, it
would then analyze the gap to uncover what the 3.4 sigma process
business does differently than the 4.6 sigma process business. Why
does one perform better than the other? Once this secret is uncovered, the company can transfer the knowledge and/or technology to
its own business.

Suppose a manufacturer of large-scale transformers discovers
through customer surveys that customers are dissatisfied with the
company's speed and competency in responding to complaints. The
company's response is to create a strategic plan that would improve
customer satisfaction by focusing on the complaint process within the
customer service system. It measures the customer service system
and finds that it operates, on average, at a 3.9 sigma level, and the
complaint process of the system operates at a 3.7 sigma level.
Nonetheless, it also discovers that the CTQ called "complaint
response time" is at a 3.2 sigma level (well below average).

If the company is to improve the overall system, it must close the
gap with respect to the complaint process, which, in turn, will require
the company to substantially improve the sigma level of the response
time. But suppose that in small-scale transformers, the company discovers that the CTQ called "complaint response time" is higher—say,
4.3 sigma capable. In this case, the company would have one segment
of the business performing far better than others with respect to the
same CTQ. Let's say that this company benchmarks several external
businesses with similar systems, subsystems, or processes and finds
that one of these external businesses has a complaint process that
operates at 5.3 sigma.

Given this, this company would realize that its internal level of entitlement—the level it should achieve—is at least 4.3 sigma, and that it could achieve a sigma level as high as 5.3 sigma. It becomes obvious that the company's next step should be to improve the system elements that limit overall system performance, thus improving CTQ sigma level and "customer satisfaction."

IMPROVING SYSTEM ELEMENTS TO ACHIEVE ENTITLEMENT PERFORMANCE. Improving any aspect of a business system is a fairly straightforward task. Let's look at a quality information system, or "QIS," for short. This type of system is used as a repository for the data on defects collected from all of the processes within an organization. Obviously, a company should refer to this database to understand the root causes of problems. Unfortunately, most QIS systems fall short of this capability, producing too little data, too late, and at too high a cost.

Before a company can improve a system, it must define its measuring system. To start, the company could make a list of analytical and reporting requirements the system must be able to produce. Then it could create a measurement instrument much like a customer-satisfaction survey that uses a comprehensive screening system. Once the measurement has been put to use and the necessary data collected, it could analyze the data and prioritize various efforts at improvement. Let's assume that the biggest problem is related to the system's inability to collect information from the database in a way that shows how different financial data affect the materials planning system.

If the company could solve this problem, it would know which types of quality problems are most related to labor costs, scheduling bottlenecks, missed shipments, and so on. This type of problem can be solved by a Black Belt and support team reporting to a Champion or Master Black Belt, and the resources necessary to fix this type of problem are minimal when compared with the dividends.

CONTROL SYSTEM-LEVEL CHARACTERISTICS THAT ARE CRITICAL TO VALUE. The QIS system provides an example of a "system level" critical-to-value characteristic (CTV)—the system's ability to collect data in a way that can be easily used. The elements used to create the solution need to be monitored over a period of time.

If a Black Belt discovered that a demographic field within the QIS system called the "date of data collection" was present, but saw that the system did not possess any type of "select if" capability, the system will not be able to create and summarize "time-bounded" intervals that would match the time intervals used by the accounting system and material acquisition system. There would be no apples-to-apples file structure to match that of other database systems.

If the Black Belt is able to structure the database so that comparative analyses can be done, then the black Belt can identify the system-level characteristics that must be monitored and controlled over time to ensure that the database can work in conjunction with other databases. To do this, Black Belts may need to reconduct the survey at periodic intervals to ensure that the QIS customers are continually able to cross-correlate data and information. In other words, the Black Belt's principle control mechanisms would be regular "system level audits."

STANDARDIZE THE SYSTEMS THAT PROVE TO BE BEST-IN-CLASS. Building on our QIS example, once the critical-to-value characteristics (CTVs) have been identified, characterized, optimized, and properly controlled, the *optimal* performance of the QIS system can be compared with similar systems. In this case, the company may find that the Black Belt's solution to a problem is so effective that other strategic business units should follow suit. When this is the case, the company can "standardize" the improved QIS system across the company to capitalize on the potential savings from the Black Belt's efforts.

While standardization can occur in many ways, the common denominator seems to be how technology is transferred. It is one thing to discover which QIS system is best-in-class, and quite another to adopt it. When the change involves time and money, many executives are slow to act, particularly when their bonuses are affected by the proposed change.

INTEGRATE BEST-IN-CLASS SYSTEMS INTO THE STRATEGIC PLAN-NING FRAMEWORK. Many times companies have difficulty getting the organization to adopt and use a new or improved best-in-class system. The psychology of this behavior is discussed in greater detail in Chap-

ter 14; here we will look at several steps management can take to
diminish or sidestep resistance to change.

First, the executive leadership must fold new or improved systems
into the strategic plan of the business in such a way that it becomes
critical to achieve new immediate or long-range business aims, goals,
objectives, and targets. When this is done, the organization's thinking
begins to move forward and an internal debate will take place. A rea-
sonable period of debate is crucial if the change is to be adequately
institutionalized.

Second, the success of the Six Sigma initiative must be strongly
tied to the company's compensation. When bonuses or stock options
are based on Six Sigma improvements, change can be better managed
during and after deployment.

Regardless of the methods used, Six Sigma must be incorporated
into the strategic planning framework to ensure that accountability is
well established and the resources required to promote change are
allocated in a timely fashion.

Critical thinking and systems diagnostics are key to implementing
Six Sigma at the business level. Executives must begin to reason and
think statistically in order to create breakthrough at the business
level; they can no longer afford to guide their companies based on
economic indicators, intuition, and experience. Six Sigma is not just
for Black Belts. It is a business process that helps companies reexamine the way in which the work gets done. Rather than tweaking the
system, they learn to reexamine how the business support systems
function and how they interact with other systems. Six Sigma offers a
way to work smarter in a world where we are often forced to work
harder and longer.

The Breakthrough Strategy: The Operation Level

Many of us have heard an operations manager say that he or she "has
an issue with that." While we may understand what the manager
means in general, the use of the word "issue" masks something deeper

and more convoluted. We believe that an "operational issue" (such as a quality issue) is simply a collection of higher-level problems (and potential solutions) that become confounded. Once companies recognize that an issue is really a set of interrelated problems, they can begin to decompose the "issue" into its components. Only when this is done can a company begin to adequately define problems, formulate plans, and take positive actions. The manager's, or Project Champion's, role in applying the Breakthrough Strategy is as follows:

OPERATIONS PERSPECTIVE OF THE BREAKTHROUGH STRATEGY

R Recognize operational issues that link to key business systems.

D Define Six Sigma projects to resolve operational issues.

M Measure performance of the Six Sigma projects.

A Analyze project performance in relation to operational goals.

I Improve Six Sigma project management system.

C Control inputs to project management system.

S Standardize best-in-class management system practices.

I Integrate standardized Six Sigma practices into policies and procedures.

RECOGNIZE OPERATIONAL ISSUES THAT LINK TO KEY BUSINESS SYSTEMS. Often the tactical solution to an operational issue is masked by the underlying support system. The system itself can blind companies to operational issues that are persistent and predictable. Persistent and predictable problems are easily masked by the architecture or operating constraints and requirements of the support system. Companies are often quite good at firefighting sporadic problems or picking the low-hanging fruit. However, the sweetest fruit is always at the top of the tree. The ability to reach that fruit requires companies to classify their operational issues into two categories—those issues that are systems dependent and those that are not. Only then can companies reduce the number of sporadic operational issues that plague the business.

To better understand this, consider a factory or service unit that experiences a low "end-of-line" yield. In order to "work the issue," we have four basic options. The first is to ignore the issue and help it eventually resolve itself—an unlikely occurrence. The second is the "hunt-and-peck" method, where businesses "twist the knobs," hoping they will stumble on the one that will make the quality issues disappear.

The third approach is statistical, rather than tactical and tool driven. This approach relies on using well-established quality problem-solving methods and tools such as Pareto charts, failure mode effects analysis (FMEA), Design of Experiments (DOE), statistical process control (SPC) charts, and so on. However, this approach is *a posteriori,* or after the fact, by nature. Those charged with reducing defects must wait for them to occur before there is sufficient data and information to take definitive action. Companies are trying to resolve issues that no longer exist in "real time and space." Returning to our QIS illustration, the effectiveness of the company's problem-solving methods and tools is largely governed by the limits of QIS to provide the relevant data. In this case, the QIS does not offer access to the types of data needed for *a priori,* or before-the-fact, analysis. While applying the tools might solve an array of problems, because the problems are sporadic in time and nature, they will reappear. So while improvements will occur and specific problems will be solved, quality remains an issue and the overall sigma level of an operation remains constant.

The fourth approach to resolving quality issues is more tactical. In the QIS illustration, the persistent nature of the reoccurring quality issues could be better resolved by installing an in-process quality measurement system that connects to the end-of-line QIS. This connection provides the business with an overall quality system far more capable of forecasting (and subsequently preventing) sporadic end-of-

THE BREAKTHROUGH STRATEGY

125

line defects before they occur. This also allows the business to statistically correlate in-process events and phenomena to end-of-line results.

Although a business may not always be able to predict the specific number or kinds of defects, the goal is to forecast the onset of quality-related problems. This allows the business to "get in front" of the issues. It also provides a way to more effectively focus and utilize the inherent power of statistical tools and better leverage the knowledge base of the workforce. With this approach, underlying problems can be uncovered and dealt with in "real time and space." Businesses are positioned to take action on the process rather than taking action on the product or service. Again, we call this *a priori* action, or action before the fact. While marginal improvement can be made by taking action after the fact, breakthrough improvement requires action before the process begins.

SIX SIGMA PROJECTS AT THE OPERATIONAL LEVEL. It's at this point that a business can begin to fully leverage its Black Belts. As we discuss in Chapter 13, Six Sigma projects are identified and selected based on certain criteria, such as (1) the extent of cost savings to be realized, (2) the degree to which an operational issue is connected to larger critical-to-quality issues, (3) the degree to which an operational issue is connected to the efficient and effective operation of a business support system, and (4) the expected length of time necessary to resolve a specific problem or issue. Business leadership must select projects carefully in order to retain focus and momentum toward achieving Six Sigma goals and objectives.

While there is no "model" criterion, one common factor is money—setting specific and "hard" financial targets. In most cases, focusing on financial targets necessarily involves operational issues and business systems. When businesses focus on reducing defects for the sake of improving quality alone they seldom see significant improvements to operational issues and virtually never improve the underlying business support systems. Six Sigma projects should focus on resolving operational issues, since these issues inevitability directly or indirectly impact bottom-line profitability.

Many times an organization's leadership will want to focus on its biggest and toughest problems. Labeling these problems as "projects" can be seductive. But the greater the scope and depth of an issue or problem, the greater the number of Black Belts, resources, and time needed to properly apply the Breakthrough Strategy. If Black Belts are not properly trained, or are too few in number to adequately tackle the job, and if resources are scarce, Black Belts can become discouraged, management will suffer disappointment, and problems will persist. It is much more realistic to see these kind of projects as long-term projects, and to break the larger problems down into smaller, more manageable, projects.

MEASURING THE PERFORMANCE OF SIX SIGMA PROJECTS. Businesses must quantitatively gauge how well projects are doing in both an absolute and relative sense. In other words, they must see the specific benefits provided by the projects (individually and collectively) as well as how those benefits stack up against a company's performance goals. They must regularly review or monitor a project's progress and assess how well a project is doing. To do this, businesses need to establish project metrics and specific performance goals. This can be done using a standard survey to regularly assess things such as morale levels among Black Belts, as well as to determine what restraints they are experiencing that keep them from even higher levels of performance. The business might also measure and track the total number of projects undertaken and what phase each project is in. Businesses might track the "yield" of Black Belt and Green Belt projects, or the percentage of the forecast achieved. In this sense, the rolled throughput yield would represent the probability that all projects will achieve their respective targets. The list of things to measure is endless, and it is governed only by our business needs and creative thinking.

Measuring project performance requires the collection and analysis of data. To do this, businesses need a project tracking system that is capable of "slicing and dicing" data in many different ways. Companies must be able to hierarchically pool data to the appropriate business levels.

ANALYZING PROJECT PERFORMANCE AT THE OPERATIONAL LEVEL. Evaluating project performance may seem simpler than it is. It entails far more than looking at the Black Belt project and comparing actual savings with projected savings. It also involves comparing the performance of a number of Black Belt projects with the operational goals of the business. For example, if one of the operational goals is to reduce cycle time across the board 10 percent, management would want to know what percentage of Black Belt projects exceeded the larger operational goal.

Management might also want to investigate the relationship between cycle time and quality. They might ask, "What proportion of our cycle-time improvements can be explained by defect-reduction projects?" If the operational goal is to reduce the cycle time and a large portion of the cycle-time improvements can be explained by defect reductions, then management may want to shift the focus from cycle-time projects to defect-reduction projects.

IMPROVING THE SIX SIGMA PROJECT MANAGEMENT SYSTEM. Once management has successfully translated the key operational issues into Black Belt projects and instituted a project management tracking system, they are ready to improve and refine the system. Let's say a business has been tracking the project savings within and across business units. At this point, it might want to correlate project cost forecasts to the actual project costs. Or management might want to track other variables, such as net savings, project scope, project completion time, and so on. By tracking the right data, it is possible to build a statistically based prediction model that allows a business to adjust its project-selection criteria to maximize outcomes.

There are many other elements of the project management system that a business might want to improve. For instance, experience has shown that there is a small, but significant, fallout of Black Belts in an organization pursuing Six Sigma. With proper planning and analysis, the reasons for this fallout could be uncovered and system-level changes instituted to reduce the fallout. As an organization moves forward with the implementation and deployment of Six Sigma, the identification and realization of such system improvements will occur naturally.

CONTROLLING THE PROJECT MANAGEMENT SYSTEM. Once a business has discovered the key inputs to an effective and efficient project management system, it must institute regular system audits. Standards must be established and consistently met. Bringing about improvement is one thing; sustaining it is often more difficult and requires greater diligence.

STANDARDIZE BEST-IN-CLASS MANAGEMENT SYSTEM PRACTICES. Standardization at the operations level is no different from standardization at the business level. Once the business has uncovered a best-in-class management practice, it should seek to standardize it and transfer the knowledge to all relevant sectors within the business.

If the Black Belt retention within one business is at 4.6 sigma, but falls below 4.0 sigma in other businesses, practices and policies pertaining to Black Belts in the 4.6 sigma business would be studied and standardized into the other businesses. A business might discover that the Black Belt retention rate of a dissimilar profession outside its business is at 5.2 sigma. The best-in-class practices of the other business can be investigated and applied, allowing the company to leapfrog its way to a higher retention rate. Once a company has standardized a particular Six Sigma practice, it must integrate the practice into the fabric of its operations, reinforcing it through reward and recognition systems.

INTEGRATE STANDARDIZED SIX SIGMA PRACTICES INTO POLICIES AND PROCEDURES. Integration at the operations level is no different from what takes place at the business level. Once a Six Sigma practice is standardized, it must be integrated into the fabric of the operations. Practices become institutionalized when their cross-applicability is interwoven into operating policies and procedures and then reinforced through reward and recognition systems.

The Breakthrough Strategy: The Process Level

Black Belts focus on *processes*, working to recognize poor processes that result in warranty problems, functional problems, high labor costs, poor supplier quality, and form, fit, and function errors and defects. Like those at the business and operations level, Black Belts discover what

methods correct problems, then standardize those methods to ensure
that those problems don't reoccur. Once these methods become established procedures, they are shared throughout the operation and can
even be transferred cross-functionally across the organization.

The Black Belt's role in applying the Breakthrough Strategy is as
follows:

THE BLACK BELT PERSPECTIVE OF THE BREAKTHROUGH STRATEGY	BLACK BELT APPLICATION PROJECT						
BREAKTHROUGH COOKBOOK	1	2	3	4	5	6	7
Measure							
1 Select CTQ characteristic							
2 Define performance standards							
3 Validate measurement system							
Analyze							
4 Establish product capability							
5 Define performance objectives							
6 Identify variation sources							
Improve							
7 Screen potential causes							
8 Discover variable relationship							
9 Establish operating tolerances							
Control							
10 Validate measurement system							
11 Determine process capability							
12 Implement process controls							

Note: For most Black Belt projects, all twelve steps of the Breakthrough Strategy will be completed; however, the types of tools used and sequence of application within any given cell of the matrix will vary from project to project.

R   Recognize functional problems that link to operational issues.

D   Define the processes that contribute to the functional problems.

M   Measure the capability of each process that offers operational leverage.

A   Analyze the data to assess prevalent patterns and trends.

I   Improve the key product/service characteristics created by the key processes.

C   Control the process variables that exert undue influence.

S   Standardize the methods and processes that produce best-in-class performance.

I   Integrate standard methods and processes into the design cycle.

RECOGNIZE PROBLEMS THAT LINK TO OPERATIONAL ISSUES. Let's say that employees executing a billing and charging process are confronted with an operational issue involving the billing cycle for a particular customer. Moreover, the department has not been getting its bills into the mail on schedule. This issue involves several independent, but interrelated, problems. One of the problems might be related to billing accuracy. Given this, bills that contain errors must be corrected (repaired). This means that the department needs additional processing time to detect, analyze, and correct the errors, which can create bottlenecks that increase cycle time and contribute to the fact that bills are consistently sent out late.

It's important to understand the hierarchical nature of process problems. Process problems are interconnected to operational issues, which, in turn, are tied to the support systems that are ultimately linked to business issues such as customer satisfaction, profitability, and shareholder value.

DEFINE THE PROCESSES THAT CONTRIBUTE TO THE PROBLEM.
Functional problems can be classified as one of three basic types: (1) product problems, (2) service-related problems, or (3) transactional problems. All three problems are created by one or more of the processes required to create the product, service, or transaction.

All processes consist of a series of steps, events, or activities. Individually, these steps are incapable of creating an outcome. In most cases, they are repetitive by nature and designed to maximize the efficiency and effectiveness of how labor and/or materials are used to deliver a product or service.

Too many organizations are complacent in comparing processes. There is a tendency to focus on outcomes rather than the process itself. How often does your organization "map" its processes? How often are such processes linked to common operational issues and problems? Too many critical processes are never mapped and linked. When the process breaks down sporadically, teams are brought in to correct the problem, but without creating process maps, persistent problems continue unrecognized.

By mapping a product or service process, a company can create a "data flow" map. The company could then see how this information affects accounting, material acquisition, and engineering processes, for example. The very act of "mapping a process" can lead to improvement. Again, we don't know what we don't know, and we won't know until we search. In order to effectively search, businesses need a map.

MEASURE THE CAPABILITY OF EACH PROCESS THAT OFFERS OPERATIONAL LEVERAGE. Most organizations fail to recognize the importance of measuring the capability of each process. They do not know the capability of their major process, much less their less visible, backroom, support processes. A company that cannot express how well a process is performing in the form of a measurement does not understand its processes. If it does do not know the capability of a process, it doesn't know the capability of the business.

Process capability impacts every aspect of a business. Poor process leads to quality problems. Quality problems, in turn, affect cycle time and inventory. These problems lead to low morale, which, in itself, can affect process capability. To understand their process capability, businesses must break apart the elements of the process, identifying the critical characteristics, defining and mapping the related processes, understanding the capability of the processes, discovering the weak links, and then upgrading the capability of the processes. It is only by taking these steps that a business can raise the high-water mark of its performance.

Once a product or service has been broken down into its various elements, the critical-to-quality characteristics (CTQs) become apparent. A CTQ could be the dimensions of a part in an automobile transmission (a manufacturing application), dirty windows after your car goes through the car wash (a service application), the accuracy of information related to a specific "box" on an administrative form (a transactional application), or the completeness of data in a computer database (a transactional application). Each of these is critical to quality.

Measuring CTQs can be a major stumbling block for Black Belts. They may be assigned a Six Sigma project that looks easy enough from the outside, but due to the age of the measurement apparatus and budget constraints, they may find it difficult to measure and evaluate the necessary processes. It's important to realize that the Measure phase of the Breakthrough Strategy can take more time and resources than was originally anticipated.

Our point is simple: If a Black Belt cannot retrieve "good" data, it is doubtful that the data will help in the decision-making process. The crucial link between data, information, process metrics, and management decisions will be broken.

As discussed in Chapter 5, process metrics are vital to understanding process performance and capability. Metrics such as throughput yield, rolled throughput yield, defects per unit, and sigma are all measures of process capability.

ANALYZING THE DATA. In the Analyze phase, data are collected to determine the relationships between the variable factors in the process and to determine the direction of improvements. The Analyze phase determines how well (or, in many cases, how poorly) the process is currently performing, and identifies possible root causes of variation in quality. The data analyzed can reveal the basic nature and behavior of the process, and show how capable and stable the process is over an extended period of time. These performance metrics also tell what the physical limit of the process capability is if everything goes perfectly. If the inherent capability is poor, the Black Belt project should be terminated, because the Black Belt will not be able to sufficiently improve the process to warrant the time and expense. However, if the metrics show the potential for improvement, the project can progress to the next phase.

IMPROVING KEY CHARACTERISTICS. Once a business realizes that improving a product means improving the process, the central question becomes, How are the key factors in a process identified, defined, optimized, and controlled? It is the job of the Black Belt to focus on the critical-to-quality (CTQ) characteristics inherent in a product or service and then go about improving the capability of such characteristics by "screening" for variables that have the greatest impact on the processes.

As the average CTQ capability increases, the capability of the corresponding process increases. In other words, process capability is a function of CTQ capability. In order to improve any CTQ, Black Belts must isolate the key variables, establish the limits of acceptable variation, and then control the factors that affect these limits.

The capability of any given CTQ is the result of such things as machine capability, material capability, human capability, and management capability. For example, capability of any given machine is simply the sum of its mechanical and electrical capabilities. An individual's capability is a reflection of his or her intellectual, physical, emotional, and spiritual capabilities. Using this perspective, businesses should be better able to see how they are affected by the hierarchical nature of interrelationships.

The Six Sigma Breakthrough Strategy specifically trains Black Belts in this form of advanced problem solving, as well as in the art of "statistical reasoning." The improvement of CTQs requires more than just brains and experience. It requires "mind tools," which provide the "edge" in real life. When this kind of knowledge is paired with the Breakthrough Strategy, breakthrough can take place individually and collectively.

To improve the capability of any given CTQ, it's important to understand it and define its performance objectives. This means that Black Belts must (1) define the CTQ's scale of measure (inches, millimeters, grams, pounds, etc.); (2) identify and assess performance standards (also known as specification limits or "tolerance bands"); and (3) establish what parameters must change and the extent that they need to change in order to achieve the desired goal. These steps help Black Belts translate the practical problems of improving CTQ capability into a statistical problem. By doing this, a Black Belt can change the process and the CTQs by specific amounts.

Next, Black Belts identify the potential sources of variation in a process that can impact the CTQ's parameters. Following this, the Black Belt can begin to study the CTQ's mean and standard deviation over a limited period of time, looking for trends and patterns.

Black Belts next conduct a "variable search" to confirm or deny the original list of variables that they believed could exert influence, using statistical and "logic-based" tools such as Design of Experiments (DOE). In general, DOE guides the manipulation of the selected variables through a mathematically prescribed series of test conditions that measure the resulting data. Using the results of this statistical analysis, Black Belts are able to make certain "probability-based" statements as to (1) which variables exerted "leverage" over the CTQ's performance, and (2) which direction the key variables must be manipulated to create the desired change in the CTQ's parameters.

Once Black Belts have identified the key process variables and know which direction to twist their respective "knobs," they can set the "tolerances" for these variables. In other words, they can establish new "operating specifications."

CONTROLLING THE KEY PROCESS VARIABLES. Once the process has been improved, Black Belts must implement measures that will control the key variables within their operating limits over time. The idea of controlling processes has been around as long as the concept of a process. However, the way processes are improved and controlled has evolved in terms of thinking and technology. Unfortunately, many organizations think that they are controlling their processes when, in reality, they are actually only monitoring their process outcomes, as is the case with a commonly used monitoring system known as statistical process control (SPC). SPC was originally created to exploit the power of *a priori* control. Unfortunately, most organizations today confuse statistical process monitoring with statistical process control, inadvertently focusing on *a posteriori* control (after the fact) rather than *a priori* control (before the fact).

STANDARDIZE THE METHODS THAT PRODUCE BEST-IN-CLASS PROCESS PERFORMANCE. After Black Belts have improved the capability of the target CTQ(s), and achieved their Six Sigma project goals, they must also promote and standardize those Six Sigma methods which produced optimum results. We must also standardize the optimized processes that result in best-in-class performance.

Standardizing best-in-class performance is vital to many business goals and objectives. For example, twelve different ways of accomplishing a certain task may be effective, but not always efficient. By measuring and characterizing the twelve ways of completing a task, those that show "high capability" potential can be optimized, and then the "vital few" can be standardized. Doing this creates not only savings, but higher levels of efficiency.

INTEGRATE STANDARD METHODS AND PROCESSES INTO THE DESIGN CYCLE. Sometimes engineers feel that they need to create new processes for every new design or evolution of an existing design. Not only is this costly, but it's inefficient. Often it's easier and more productive to make changes to the design itself than to make equivalent changes in the processes. One of the key principles of Design for Six Sigma (DFSS) is that it makes use of existing components, processes, and practices that have proven to be best-in-class.

Understanding this makes it important for the executive leadership to reevaluate how they recognize and reward their design engineers. Often design engineers are rewarded on product performance rather than product producibility. Prior to Six Sigma's implantation at Motorola, for example, an electrical design engineer's performance was based on how well the product operated. If the design was "clever," and the proof-of-principle evaluation was good, the engineer was a hero. However, if there were problems manufacturing the product, the manufacturing manager was in the hot seat, not the engineering manager. Following the implementation of Six Sigma, Motorola's executive leadership began to understand that in order for any engineer to be a "hero," not only did the design need to be clever, but it had to have best-in-class performance, and it had to be "manufacturable" to the extent that production costs and manufacturing cycle time were minimized—all by virtue of the design configuration. This may seem like a tall order, but it is achievable when the expectation and the right leadership is present.

For any organization to achieve its goals and objectives, standardizing the performance of best-in-class processes is vital. This approach not only increases profitability, but promotes higher levels of overall efficiency.

Summary

The key to institutionalizing Six Sigma is having the right people in place at the businesses, operations, and process levels of an organization to implement and deploy the Breakthrough Strategy. Unless Six Sigma is structured so that it's interwoven up and down the organization, the initiative will never gain the velocity and strength it needs to sustain itself.

Companies that implement the Breakthrough Strategy at each level of the organization will see that as Black Belts improve processes, their efforts flow up to the operations level, where business unit managers see improvements in yield, which allows them to reduce labor and material costs. Improving the cost of quality at the operations level then flows up to the business level, where improvements in operating margins and overall profitability are seen.

The Six Sigma Breakthrough Strategy fundamentally changes the way every level of a business is managed on a daily basis. As Six Sigma flows up and down and across organizations, those at the business level communicate with those at operation and process levels in new ways. Six Sigma offers companies a way to step back and look at themselves holistically and see how the collective results of many smaller projects affect the large, high-level processes that run the day-to-day business. As companies learn what kinds of measures and metrics are needed to improve their processes, they are able to gain new insights and develop new practices. In turn, these "lessons learned" can be standardized and subsequently integrated into management's thinking and the organization's intellectual capital.

Measuring Performance on the Sigma Scale

Sporadic vs. Persistent Problems

Some defects that occur in the course of industrial processes, or commercial processes, are the result of sporadic or periodic flare-ups in a process that is otherwise maintained at some level of capability. While most processes function within an expected range, occasionally the production of a product or the execution of a commercial activity will depart from its usual performance and show up as a series of spikes on a defect chart. A process that is defective 2 percent of the time, but suddenly jumps to 5 percent at a given moment, can be considered sporadic and will undoubtedly trip a variety of alarms within the company. Managers will converge on the scene and assign a team to troubleshoot the problem until production or service returns to its normal 2 percent defect rate. Successfully troubleshooting sporadic problems, however, does not help to lower a company's defect average and raise its sigma level. While most companies respond capably to sporadic problems, it is the persistent, chronic, and "hidden" problems that evade attention and erode profits. The Breakthrough Strategy is designed specifically to tackle persistent problems.

Here is an example. Let's consider a persistent problem that is masked by its relatively low defect rate when compared with the overall rate of defects. Take an automobile manufacturing plant where engine blocks are built out of aluminum. By using aluminum rather than steel, the company is able to lower production costs and add less overall weight to the car, improving the consumer's gas mileage. Unfortunately, despite the aluminum engine's safety and durability, the company comes to realize that the aluminum blocks don't tolerate stress as well as the steel blocks did. Unbeknownst to the plant's engineers, microscopic fractures sometimes occur in the aluminum due to consistent contamination of trace elements. Over time, drivers who push their cars to the limit exacerbate the hidden flaws; temperature and pressure also work to damage the aluminum and cause parts to break or wear prematurely. The cars with damaged engines are returned to dealerships for repair, which the company repairs under warranty, significantly eroding profits. Meanwhile, the company's engineers scratch their heads, unable to determine whether the problem lies with the engine's design, the materials used, or in the processes developed to build the engine. Many companies feel they have no choice but to tolerate a certain number of defect problems, particularly when the defect rate associated with the problem is well below the overall rate of defects. In this sense, the defects become "hidden." Rather than redesign the product and/or process, they decide to treat the problem sporadically by fixing faulty products as they crop up. Six Sigma, on the other hand, helps companies strive to reduce the overall defect level so that virtually *every* problem buried within an industrial system or commercial system is exposed and corrected in a uniform manner.

The fact is, most defects are persistent in nature. They are tenacious and covert, making them hard to identify and correct. They do not raise any alarms or sound any whistles. As a result, they are often factored in as part of the cost of doing business. Companies compensate by raising the price of their products to cover the cost of materials and labor used, knowing that their competitors are probably suffering similar losses. By tackling persistent problems with the Breakthrough Strategy, companies such as General Electric, Allied-Signal, Polaroid, and Bombardier have achieved windfall savings totaling billions of dollars. What these companies discovered was that persistent problems were costing as much as 30 to 40 percent of annual sales and affecting the corporation's long-term viability. By applying the Breakthrough Strategy to persistent problems, they were able to reduce their annual costs by at least 6 percent, without increasing sales at all.

Persistent defects are usually caused by hidden design flaws, inadequate tolerances, inferior processes, poor vendor quality, lack of employee training, inadequate tool maintenance, employee careless-ness, insufficient inspection feedback, and so on. Moreover, persis-tent problems can exist in products and services that do well in the marketplace—making management reluctant to allocate the time and resources needed to redesign the product. Sometimes management, not recognizing the true cost of such defects, assumes that correcting or redesigning such processes would be uneconomical, or fails to see how it could make a profitable product even more profitable. In other instances, management isn't even aware that hidden persistent prob-lems exist.

Some companies believe that they can keep the lid on such per-sistent problems by simply holding materials, processes, and products to the company's specifications, and by keeping failure rates, cus-tomer complaints, warranty returns, and other external performance measures below preset levels. By maintaining the status quo on the cost of inspections, tests, scrap, rework, and other internal costs, they think they are doing the best that can be done. In other words, they tolerate persistent problems because they don't believe they can do better. But persistent problems are like a lingering cancer. Left alone, they can insidiously spread and potentially undermine an otherwise healthy company.

The Trivial Many and the Vital Few

Industrial and commercial problems rarely have equal impact. It's important to focus on processes that will simultaneously produce the greatest benefit to the bottom line and the customer. Companies that want to increase their quality and reduce defect levels should analyze performance patterns and trends to identify the few chronic processes that make up the bulk of a company's "avoidable" costs. The eighteenth-century Italian economist Vilfredo Pareto, in studying the distribution of wealth in Europe, found that 80 percent of the wealth was held by 20 percent of the population. He went on to discover that the same 80/20 principle applied to a host of other things, as well. Twenty percent of a company's employees, for example, tend to contribute 80 percent of a company's revenues; 20 percent of a company's customers generate over 80 percent of the profits. Today, Pareto's law tells us that 80 percent of defects will be traceable to 20 percent of the different types of defects that can occur. These types of defects that account for 80 percent of the defects produced are called the "vital few," while the others are referred to as the "trivial many." Given this, we can surely recognize that there is a Pareto distribution of sporadic problems; however, we must also realize there is a distribution of persistent problems. But, it is the vital few persistent problems that cause the greatest headaches. Companies need to be able to pinpoint the "vital few" factors that generate the highest costs, then separate them from the "trivial many," before deciding which processes would contribute the greatest savings from initiating the Breakthrough Strategy. By focusing on the "vital few," and avoiding those with lesser impact, companies can leverage this information to produce maximum results.

Long-Term vs. Short-term Capability

One strength of the Six Sigma approach is that it recognizes and accounts for the fact that processes vary over time. Inevitably, when data about a process are gathered over a period of time, observers will see that the process does not always perform on target, or within specified limits or boundaries.

When discussing a critical-to-quality characteristic (CTQ) such as the length of time it takes to respond to a customer's phone inquiry, the maximum acceptable time to answer an inquiry becomes the upper specification limit (USL). For some CTQs, there might also be a minimum response time, or lower specification limit (LSL). In the case of the telephone inquiry, an LSL may be specified to ensure that adequate research time is given to "getting the facts straight." In addition, there is usually a target time (T), a limit usually centered between the USL and LSL. The USL and LSL create a bandwidth of acceptable performance.

Owing to the natural sources of variation, we would expect a distribution within the design bandwidth of the length of time it takes to handle various calls. By comparing the actual process distribution spread (or process bandwidth) with the limits allowed by the USL and LSL (the design bandwidth), companies can quantitatively see how capable their processes are. As the process bandwidth narrows in relation to the design bandwidth, process capability increases. The reverse also holds true.

Over time, the process bandwidth will increase in size due to process centering errors. In other words, over an extended period of time, the process center (average) may be on target. However, during any given interval of time, the process average will be off target for one reason or another. The aggregate effect of shifts in the process center will widen the process bandwidth. When this happens, the probability of seeing a defect jumps radically. In a nutshell, process centering errors over time degrade capability, which, in turn, increases the likelihood of defects. Consequently, yield drops and costs go up.

The average time-to-time centering error for a "typical" process will average about 1.5 sigma. In other words, a four sigma process will normally shift and drift from its design target value (T) by about 1.5 sigma over an extended period of time. For a typical process, this means that factoring in the shift and drift factor of 1.5 sigma, divided by the existing sigma level—say, 4.5 sigma—will equal .375. In other words, 38 percent of the inherent short-term capability is "lost" due to normal process centering errors that occur over time. This means that a process that measures at four sigma short-term capability actually runs at about 2.5 sigma over repeated cycles of the process. Years of theoretical and empirical research on this subject have proven this to be true. This amount of shift and drift is inevitable, and has to be accounted for during the design cycle of the process, product, or service. So when companies claim that their processes are at six sigma, what they are really saying is that the short-term capability of their processes is six sigma; the long-term performance, however, is 4.5 sigma because of process centering errors.

To cope with the phenomenon of shifts and drifts, any given design (industrial or commercial) should be what we call "robust" to at least a 1.5 sigma shift in centering of all critical-to-quality characteristics so as not to show any practical change in performance or yield. The methods used to accomplish this are incorporated in Design for Six Sigma (DFSS) practices.

The Six Sigma Breakthrough Strategy recognizes the importance of "shift and drift" and makes it possible to account for them when assessing process capability.

In order to precisely represent the unknown distribution of a process and its output data, the total process variation is subdivided into short-term and long-term components. Sigma short-term is the metric for the effect of the trivial, while sigma long-term measures the effect of both the vital few and the trivial many.

Understanding the Shift and Drift Factor

Imagine that you have just hired an architect to build a single-car garage. As the plans are being drawn up, the architect will have to make a decision on the width of the garage door opening. Considering the variation among car widths—a Cadillac or Lincoln Continental needs more room than a small sports car—the architect will need to design an opening wide enough to accommodate any size car while still providing enough support to the structure of the garage. One approach our architect could take is to measure every model of automobile and truck manufactured, and take an average of vehicle widths. Or the architect could take into account only the widest vehicle manufactured and build the garage to accommodate that vehicle's width.

Now picture a line drawn down the center of the garage, starting at the garage door and ending at the back wall. If we were to line up the center of our car exactly to that centerline every time we drove into the garage, we would always have adequate room to get in and out of the garage. (In fact, we've probably all seen garages with a tennis ball hanging from the ceiling to help the driver properly position the car.) But regardless of how attentive our architect is in getting the garage door exactly the right width, no architect, regardless of experience and expertise, can control such factors as a sixteen-year-old boy who zips into the garage without giving much thought to the position of the car, or the time the driver pulls into a garage late at night after having had too much to drink. What the architect does know is that the driver will rarely drive the car exactly to the center of the garage. Therefore, the design must take into account operator (the driver of the car) error and create a wide enough margin so that neither the side of the car nor the walls of the garage are damaged. Essentially, what the architect is doing is allowing for shift and drift of the centering of the car as it is driven into and out of the garage.

This analogy illustrates the importance of being able to compensate for the consequences associated with process centering. By offsetting normal distribution by a 1.5 standard deviation on either side, the adjustment takes into account what happens to every process over many cycles of manufacturing—or, in the case of our garage and car illustration, the many times the car will be driven into the garage. Simply put, accommodating shift and drift is our "fudge factor," or a way to allow for unexpected errors or movement over time.

Using 1.5 sigma as a standard deviation gives us a strong advantage in improving quality not only in industrial processes and designs, but in commercial processes as well. It also allows us to design products and services that are relatively impervious, or "robust," to natural, unavoidable sources of variation in processes, components, and materials. The following table shows what the sigma shift means with regard to the number of nonconformities or defects per million opportunities.

SIGMA (σ) QUALITY LEVELS BEFORE AND AFTER A SHIFT IN THE AVERAGE		
	DPMO*	
SIGMA (σ) LEVELS	WITHOUT SHIFT	WITH SHIFT
1	317,4000	697,700
2	45,400	308,537
3	2,700	66,807
4	63	6210
5	0.57	233
6	0.002	3.4

To compensate for the inevitable consequences associated with process centering errors, the distribution mean is offset by 1.5 standard deviations. This adjustments provides a more realistic idea of what the process capability will be over repeated cycles.
* Defects per million opportunities

The carpet example we used in Chapter 1 illustrates the difference between sigma levels and quality. By taking this carpet example a step further, we can show what a "shift in the average" means, and how it relates to defects per million opportunities. Suppose the person cleaning the carpet showed up overly tired from a night of no sleep and as a result was weaving the machinery across the floor instead of pushing in it a straight line. How much of the carpet do you suppose might not be cleaned because of this? If our carpet cleaner normally performed to three sigma level when well rested, we would expect to see about 100 square feet of soiled carpet when the job was completed—an area about the size of a second bedroom, rather than the area beneath a recliner chair. If we had hired an overly tired cleaner who normally performed to a six sigma level when well rested, we would expect to see a soiled area about the size of the base of a chair, rather than an area the size of a pin. The six sigma process capability, in other words, allowed very good cleaning performance in spite of the fact that lack of sleep was causing the "process" to weave a little.

How Does Variation Come About?

There are three primary sources of variation. The first is inadequate design margins. Inadequate design margins are a fundamental problem at manufacturing plants in the United States and Europe. We are still learning how to establish tolerances, and determine how much range is permissible when designing a product or process that allows for natural variation. As a result, we are continually fighting inadequate design margins. The second source of variation is unstable parts and materials provided to us by vendors and suppliers. The third source of variation is insufficient process capability, or the inability of processes to meet specification limits of the critical-to-quality characteristics that customers demand.

One goal of Six Sigma is to attack the area of overlap among these three sources of variation.

Specification Limits

Specification limits express the customer's needs and, literally and figuratively, set the "goalposts" for determining defects. If a process does not function within a specified range, then a defect is quite likely to occur. In manufacturing, specification limits are determined by engineers, and employees creating the product ensure that it falls within those parameters. When the product—or the output of a process—falls below the lower specification limit (LSL) or above the upper specification limit (USL), a defect has been produced. Just because a "defect" has been produced, however, does not mean that the product will necessarily fail. Conversely, just because defects are not observed does not guarantee that the product will work. Specifications can be wrong or inadequate.

Here is an illustration of specification or performance limits at work. A Black Belt is asked to reduce the length of time it takes to ship out customer information packages. Through customer benchmarking, interviews, and other sources, the Black Belt learns that journalists, students, and stock analysts want computer-readable copies of major executive speeches, news releases, and financial reports. The volume of requests is too heavy to accommodate Internet access, making it necessary for the company to mail paper copies of requested materials.

Before the Black Belt can benchmark the current process and assign a sigma value to it, she has to relate the concept of defects to the request for information. The Black Belt knows that the process begins with the potential customer's request for information, and that the goal is to get that information into the customer's hands as quickly as possible. If delivery time should never exceed forty-eight hours, then forty-eight hours becomes the upper specification limit. (Since this process involves cycle time, there is no lower specification limit.) If the information does not reach the customer within forty-eight hours of the request, the delivery time is outside the specification limit and a defect has occurred.

Wanting to deliver this information to callers quickly, but in a cost-efficient manner, the Black Belt team defined their process.

DEFINING A NEW PROCESS		
PRODUCT CONCEPT	EARLY SERVICE CONCEPT	EARLY PROCESS CONCEPT
CD-ROM of key items in the last six months	1-800 phone number for requests	Answer phone request
Mailing envelope	Fast response via overnight mail	Build disk and prepare mailing list
Standard transmittal document	Free to requesters	Assemble, pack, and ship
	Low cost to company	Customer installs product
	All official releases from the past six months would be made available	
	Updated weekly	

After determining the customer's CTQs, the team developed four matrixes to rate the CTQs according to customer importance. The matrixes included: (1) Product and Service Attributes, (2) Features of the Parts of the Product and Service, (3) Process Attributes, and (4) Process Controls. As seen below, an analysis of each matrix revealed the customer's critical-to-quality characteristics.

QUALITY FUNCTION DEPLOYMENT				
CTQS	PRODUCT AND SERVICE ATTRIBUTES	FEATURES OF THE PARTS OF THE PRODUCT AND SERVICE	PROCESS ATTRIBUTES	PROCESS CONTROLS
Fast	Overnight	Twenty-four-hour phone service	Phones are answered quickly	Phones are answered within 8 seconds
Easy to use	Lightweight	Fits into envelope	Meets UPS deadline	Delivery by 5 P.M. next day
Cost-effective	Intuitive (to use)	Needs no directions	Assemble, pack, and ship for <35¢	Assembled for <20¢
Pleasant	Cheap	Fits into pocket	All information on one disk	Usable within 5 minutes of receipt
	Available			
	Small			

Once the process controls were implemented, account managers were better able to respond to customers. The end result was more complete and accurate orders, increased customer knowledge and satisfaction, improved productivity, and a streamlined, more efficient, and profitable way to meet or exceed customer expectations.

Moving Past the Five Sigma Wall

In Six Sigma, it is easy to see how process variation determines product quality. As a result of this domino relationship, optimum product reliability is directly tied to an organization's ability to take a design concept from development on through production with minimal variation. Organizations that have adopted Six Sigma have learned that once they have achieved quality levels of roughly five sigma, the only way to get beyond the five sigma wall is to redesign their products and services from scratch using Design for Six Sigma (DFSS). DFSS is a rigorous approach to designing products and services and their enabling processes from the very beginning to ensure that they meet customer expectations.

The primary aim of DFSS is quite simple. It's intended to create designs that are (1) resource efficient; (2) capable of very high yields regardless of complexity and volume; and (3) impervious or "robust" to process variations. Although this sounds intuitive, it is often elusive. DFSS is a system of Six Sigma principles and methods (statistical and nonstatistical) that allow a designer of products, processes, or services to:

1. Define robust configurations that incorporate mature activities, parts, components, and processes that have already been optimized and standardized. For example, a new service process is encouraged to incorporate a communications system that is currently available and already operating at a high sigma level. This principle ensures that all CTQs will reflect best-in-class capability. In turn, this has a positive impact on

throughput yield, as well as rolled throughput yield. For example, if a process consists of 20 steps and all steps are three sigma capable, the expected rolled throughput yield would be 25 percent. However, if through DFSS practices and methods we were able to increase the average capability per step to 3.5 sigma, the rolled throughput yield would be 63 percent. This half-sigma improvement in capability more than doubles the yield.

2. Minimize absolute complexity and its relative influence on system performance. Again, if a process consists of 20 steps and all steps are three sigma capable, the expected rolled throughput yield would be 25 percent. But, if the process *complexity* could be reduced to 15 steps, the rolled throughput yield would increase to 35 percent. In short, the company would achieve a 30 percent improvement in yield as a result of a 25 percent reduction in process complexity.

When the above principles are practiced concurrently, the results can be quite dramatic. Figure 1 shows the effect of process capability and complexity on rolled throughput yield. Figure 2 repeats the data, except that the process capability has been degraded by 1.5 sigma at each step in order to account for normal long-term variations in process centering. From these two graphs, we can see that a four sigma process with 1,000 steps is efficient in the short term (see "Capability Centered for Each Process Step"), but in the long term (see "Capability Shifted 1.50 for Each Process Step") its rolled yield is near zero. However, a *six sigma* process with 1,000 steps produces high rolled yield in both the short and long term, displaying high robustness to process centering error and requiring fewer controls and creating greater resilience to increases in complexity. As your organization evolves in Six Sigma, you will learn more about DFSS and the importance of it.

The classical or traditional approach to product and service process design generally involves several functional departments work-

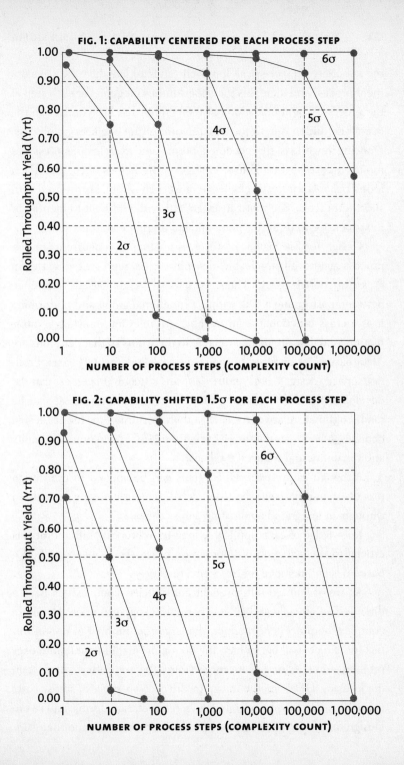

FIG. 1: CAPABILITY CENTERED FOR EACH PROCESS STEP

Rolled Throughput Yield (Y.rt)

6σ

5σ

4σ

3σ

2σ

NUMBER OF PROCESS STEPS (COMPLEXITY COUNT)

FIG. 2: CAPABILITY SHIFTED 1.5σ FOR EACH PROCESS STEP

Rolled Throughput Yield (Y.rt)

6σ

5σ

4σ

3σ

2σ

NUMBER OF PROCESS STEPS (COMPLEXITY COUNT)

ing in series. This classical approach tends to lengthen the development process and increases the opportunities for defect at each step of the process. Communication between groups has little impact on the overall definition due to the serial nature of the engineering process. Drawing rework is the accepted norm, and as schedule pressures mount industrial "firefighters" emerge as the heroes of the day. Each industrial or commercial challenge must then be quickly resolved with short-term fixes. The root causes are either too difficult to identify or too expensive to fix at this point and are therefore not pursued.

Design for Six Sigma, however, is a *parallel* (concurrent) design process where all applicable disciplines are represented within a cross-functional team. There is a vast psychological difference between performing a task within a functional group and performing it as a cross-functional team member. All relevant knowledge, information, and data are made available to the teams so that decisions are "data based," as opposed to the traditional "judgmental" basis. Product/service designs and industrial/transactional processes can be developed together—meaning that the product and process can be made optimal relative to each other, resulting in fewer design changes, lower manufacturing cycle times, enhanced product quality and reliability, and reduced total cost.

Although each of the DFSS tools can be applied to the design process in and of itself, the true "global" benefit can only be realized through an integrated application across the board.

Knowledge of each applicable long-term process shift and drift is crucial to the selection of appropriate processes to meet the CTQ-based design tolerance for Six Sigma quality.

As we've pointed out, product and process complexities have a direct effect on yield and defects per million opportunities. The more complex the process or product, the larger the number of opportunities for defects will be. In fact, the notion of "manufacturability" uses product simplification as its cornerstone. Rigorous efforts have been made using DFSS methodology to drive down process steps, parts count, fastener count, special tooling, reorientation, forms, and so on. Design for Six Sigma allows new products and services and their supporting processes to be designed in ways that ensure the outcomes remain as simple and cost-effective as possible, while serving the needs of the customer.

DFSS Leverage in Product

A Master Black Belt was asked: "Why is it so important to develop and adopt a Design for Six Sigma methodology?" The Master Black Belt used the following illustration to answer the question:

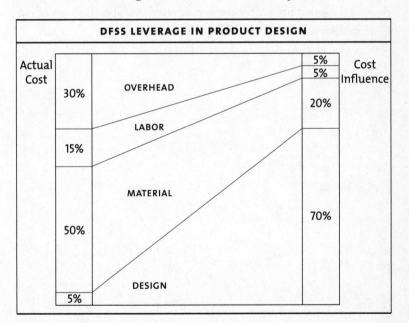

"While design typically represents the smallest actual cost element in products, it leverages the largest cost influence," the Master Black Belt replied. "If one were to identify the top item in the list of the vital few factors to address, Design for Six Sigma would surely be it." The Master Black Belt continued, "As you can see from this graph, an incremental improvement in the design, through the use of DFSS methodology, has a huge direct impact on actual costs. For example, a 30 percent savings through design simplification would translate into over 21 percent overall cost savings. The same 30 percent savings applied to labor or overhead alone results in a mere 1.5 percent savings overall."

While improving the quality of a process may reduce its costs and increase customer satisfaction, DFSS has the potential to eliminate the part or process altogether, or at least simplify it. This simplification often results in a reduction in material and labor costs, as a result of a reduction in the cost of overhead, and can greatly improve customer satisfaction.

The next case study illustrates how the Breakthrough Strategy, including Design for Six Sigma, was applied to a specific problem in General Electric's Medical Systems division.

How General Electric Used Six Sigma to Design a Multimillion-Dollar Product

> A lot of companies preach Six Sigma, but they don't have the vehicle to get there. The Breakthrough Strategy is the vehicle to achieve Six Sigma.

Perhaps no corporation has integrated Six Sigma in its operations as widely and thoroughly as General Electric. GE uses Six Sigma to identify and carry out projects that "focus on improving our customers' productivity and reducing their capital outlays, while increasing the quality, speed and efficiency of our operations," according to GE's 1997 Annual Report. In its first twenty-four months, Six Sigma produced dramatic results in productivity in many of GE's divisions, as discussed earlier. In this chapter, we will follow the Breakthrough Strategy in solving a difficult problem at GE's Medical Systems division (GEMS), to better illustrate how the Breakthrough

Strategy is applied to a specific problem in improving a key product.

One of Medical Systems' key products is a high-speed computed tomography scanner (or computed axial tomography scanner), commonly known as a CAT scanner. An expensive piece of equipment, costing approximately $1.2 million, it is able to generate X-ray images from computerized cross-section views of soft tissue like the brain, lungs, and liver. It works by emitting electromagnetic waves through a patient's body and reading the amount of energy different tissues absorb. Since various tissues and organs absorb the electromagnetic waves differently, the waves that emerge from the body after passing through a target area can offer a reliable image of soft-tissue structures. In an age when the cost of medical technology is a major factor in health care economics, a CAT scanner is a necessary but costly investment for hospitals and other medical institutions. In order for an institution to amortize the large investment represented by a CAT scanner, the machine must have a very high use rate, and minimal maintenance and operating costs. The hospital suffers significant lost income during any downtime due to a malfunction.

In 1995, GEMS decided it wanted to completely revamp its scanner, which was the market leader at the time, in order to increase its speed, reliability, and imaging. The new GE CAT scan would be named the LightSpeed, a reference to its planned speed of operation. It would be the first project GE designed from start to finish using Six Sigma methodology.

Although GEMS led the field with its scanner, the company knew that several competitors were working on more advanced, faster CAT scanners, as well. GE felt it could leapfrog the competition with a scanner that was even faster, get FDA approval, and take its product to market in time to present it at the major trade show at which the manufacturers of medical apparatus display their latest wares to health care customers—the 1998 Radiology Society of North America show, held in December.

Because multiple cross sections of the body are required for the imaging created by this noninvasive diagnostic process, speed is essential. (It's also easier on the patient, since he or she has to remain absolutely still in the claustrophobic tunnel-like center of the machine while the X rays are being taken and processed.)

After defining the critical-to-quality (CTQ) characteristics most desired by their customers (who had given them ample, if not vociferous, feedback), GEMS used Six Sigma to identify the key internal processes in its operation that determined the CTQs. Then they applied the Breakthrough Strategy to specific targeted processes to bring the product's performance quality up to the standards identified by Six Sigma that would satisfy GEMS' customers. "Six Sigma," Carol Deutsch reported in an article about the scanner in *The New York Times,* "enabled GE Medical to anticipate which compromises doctors would accept."

GE, which controlled 30 percent of the $1.6 billion global market for scanners at the beginning of the project in 1995, committed some 200 engineers to work on the scanner. They divided the engineers into three teams, and "spent nearly three years and almost $50 million to run 250 Six Sigma analyses," according to *The New York Times.* While one team investigated the reliability of the measurements used in calibrating and producing the scanner, another explored what factors affected the useful life of the scanner, and yet another analyzed the factors that affected image quality and speed. In the course of working through the measurement phase of the Breakthrough Strategy, a Product Tree was created to better understand relationships between process and materials so that the performance variables could be clearly identified. GEMS created a process map and measured the performance variables. Finally, the teams established performance capability.

Measuring the Elephant

Anyone who recalls the story of the blind men measuring an elephant can appreciate the grief GEMS would have been in for if such an enormous, complex undertaking had been run along the old, pre–Six Sigma lines of random, hit-or-miss approaches to problem solving.

The outcome might well have been as distorted as the descriptions given by the blind men measuring the elephant—to one, the elephant seemed "very much like a wall," and to another, grasping the elephant's trunk, it felt very much like a snake. GEMS might well have grabbed hold of the elephant—but it never would have been able to figure out the elephant's full dimensions.

To have their scanner ready in time for the 1998 launch, GEMS would have to go way out on a limb. In the Analyze phase of Six Sigma, they got a pretty good idea of the odds against them. The performance variable they were striving to achieve required what Vivek Paul, the general manager of GEMS' CT business, would later describe as a "quantum leap" in technology.

Because GEMS was the market leader at the inception of the project, their product was already best-in-class. But the benchmark they wanted to establish for the new scanner was for tomorrow's best-in-class scanner.

The Improvement phase in GE's high-stakes race against time was fraught with difficulties. The most important components in LightSpeed, as reported in *The New York Times,* were the tubes that focus the X rays and the detectors, which converts them into pictures after the radiation travels through the patient's body. Both of these components had been identified as the things on which the Breakthrough Strategy had to focus.

The tubes in service on the GEMS scanner now on the market cost $59,000 to replace. Given that, customers wanted a much longer life span than the current tubes were capable of—"at least twelve hours a day, for six months" was the major customer critical-to-quality target. The operating life of the current tubes was only half that. Moreover, GEMS was scrapping "some 20 million in tubes each year because they failed preshipping performance tests." And even with such preshipping performance tests, a good many scanners arrived at hospitals "DOA"—dead on arrival, to use GE's nomenclature. So another key to producing a lower-cost, more dependable scanner was to improve the manufacturing variable.

The Six Sigma methodology called for either major modification of the tubes or a complete redesign. The team working on extending the operating life of the tubes literally took the tubes apart. An analysis of how the tubes were fabricated—every step in the process taken into account—alerted them to a persistent and significant defect. Like all radiation-emitting CRTs (cathode ray tubes), the GEMS scanner required that the positively charged anode and the negatively charged cathode be bathed in a petroleum-based oil to prevent short-circuits.

Using Six Sigma tools and methodology, the team discovered that for some reason this oil was breaking down. As a result, the life span of the tubes was dramatically shortened. Was it a supplier problem? Could there be some design defect responsible for the oil breaking down? Were there environmental factors involved in contaminating the oil during the manufacturing of the tube?

Ultimately, the team identified the lead-based paint that coated the inside of the tube as the factor responsible for contaminating the oil. The paint brought about a chemical reaction that broke down the oil and resulted in its failure as an electrical insulator. By using a different paint, the defect was eliminated.

CRT scanners create images by bombarding the metal element that generates the actual X rays with electrons. For the scanner to work effectively, it must function in a vacuum. Even a few molecules of air would interfere with the imaging. Failure of the tube to seal in that vacuum would allow ambient air to enter, destroying the functionality of the tube. Six Sigma's Breakthrough Strategy revealed that a significant number of tubes in the final inspection had tiny "beads," or openings that admitted ambient air, at the crucial seam of the metal and glass used to fabricate the tube.

In the Analyze phase, GEMS engineers were able to statistically analyze all of the factors that might contribute to the tube's failure to preserve a vacuum. Among the possible causes were the length and type of glass used. Six Sigma analysis, however, eliminated this as an element contributing to the defect. Eventually, the Analyze phase revealed that the metal connector through which current flows into the tube had a tendency to oxidize, which contributed to the imperfections in the seal. The team also found other process variations, as a result of the gas used as part of fabricating the tube, and strains created in the annealing of the glass (the speed with which the glass cooled down after going through a heat-treating furnace).

Now that the causes of defects in the tube had been identified, the team applied Six Sigma tools in the Analyze and Improve phases to determine which steps in the production process, interacting with all other possible factors, needed to be changed. They decided to pre-oxidize the metal pin, helping it to adhere to the glass. They also replaced the hydrogen gas with nitrogen gas, and revamped the tube heating process. "Six Sigma gave us a methodical way to test how changes in one factor would interact with changes in others," says Beth Hulse, the engineer who led the project. There was still room for further quality improvement, but time was growing short. The team had to decide how to preserve critical-to-quality characteristics while determining which variations or defects could be tolerated in order to bring the scanner to market on time and within budget. In order to achieve its schedule and avoid running over budget, GEMS, according to *The New York Times,* "settled for a process that cut the preshipment scrap rate by 40 percent" and eliminated scanners that arrived DOA—those that didn't work when first installed. While the new tubes would be priced at $85,000, or 40 percent more than the previous scanner, they would carry a full one-year warranty, six months more than customers had demanded.

It's Never "Just One Thing"

The "fix" for the fabrication of the scanner tube, materials, and design was made by one of the three Six Sigma teams. The other two teams worked on other aspects of the scanner, analyzing the complex interdependent factors that affected product variability. LightSpeed, like all CAT scanners, generated a good deal of heat during operation. Only a small amount of the energy is used to produce the desired imaging after the X rays pass through the body; most of the energy is converted to heat, which can impair the quality of the imaging.

The Six Sigma Breakthrough Strategy showed that the addition of a $100,000 resistor would control the temperature and improve the quality of the imaging. But the process also showed that changing a few inexpensive capacitors elsewhere in the tube, and redesigning how the wires are insulated, would yield a similar result, according to *The New York Times*.

Another way to reduce inaccurate or inconclusive diagnostic readings, the team discovered, would be to redesign the tube entirely, at considerable expense, so that it was able to target smaller areas of the body more accurately. But in redesigning the tube there would be no way to meet the deadline GE had set for itself. Then, in April 1997, a Six Sigma team discovered that "widening the tungsten wires that cover many of the [X-ray] wave-receptor cells in the detector plate would create a bigger target, thereby compensating for any tiny inaccuracies in the beam's trajectory," reported *The New York Times*. The change meant that patients would receive a slightly higher dose of radiation, but one that was still well within acceptable medical limits. "By making the data collection process less efficient, we made the scanner as a whole more efficient," said Gary Strong, a LightSpeed designer.

The image quality could have been improved further, but it would have involved redesigning parts in the detector plate—and there was simply no time left to do that and roll out the new product on schedule. Was there another way to make the new GEMS scanner achieve what GEMS had set out to do—create a best-in-class scanner? Using Six Sigma analyses, the GEMS engineers discovered that the critical-to-quality characteristics they were striving to achieve could be realized through reprogramming the scanner's computer software to compensate for the energy emitted by the preamp chips, which caused shadows to the image.

Six Sigma analysis resulted in a staggering range of choices for manufacturing changes. The sheer quantity of the options and the ways the various processes interacted could not have been identified or weighed against one another without the powerful tools of Six Sigma, and the computer technology that makes it possible to deal with a huge

number of combinations and permutations. By using Six Sigma to analyze which factors in the manufacturing process were critical to quality, GEMS was ultimately able to enter the market with LightSpeed on
schedule. Thanks to Six Sigma, GEMS was able to produce "a 10-fold
increase in the life of CT scanner X-ray tubes—increasing the 'uptime'
of these machines and the profitability and level of patient care given
by hospitals and other health care providers," according to GE. GE's
LightSpeed, when introduced on the market in September 1998, was
capable of generating a number of images simultaneously, "requiring
only 20 seconds to do full-body scans that once took three minutes,"
according to *The New York Times*. LightSpeed is also able to handle the
heat generated in operating the machine more efficiently than competitive scanners from other companies; as a result, it requires less
time for the equipment to cool down between the end of one operating cycle and the beginning of another. Six Sigma not only delivered
the critical-to-quality characteristics demanded by customers, it had
also increased the life span of the scanner, reduced the scrap rate, and
improved the scanner's quality. Although the new scanner cost more,
customers were willing to pay more for the increased speed and
dependability. Improved quality compensated for the price increase
that had resulted from changes in materials and manufacturing
processes. While unit sales remained roughly the same, gross income
from sales rose to meet GEMS' margins.

The Control Phase: Completing the Sequence
Before Initiating New Six Sigma Breakthroughs

Having managed to roll out the new, faster scanner with less downtime and a longer life span, GEMS took steps that would ensure its
position as a market leader. Yet the control phase itself generated data
that, added to what had been learned in the Analyze and Improve
phases, allowed GE's Black Belts to continue to improve quality. No
sooner had they won the race than they geared themselves up to apply
the entire Six Sigma Breakthrough Strategy again to guarantee that

HOW DOES SIX SIGMA WORK?

SELECT KEY PROBLEM AREAS	SELECT AND TRAIN THE RIGHT PEOPLE	DEVELOP AND IMPLEMENT IMPROVEMENTS	MANAGE SIX SIGMA PROJECTS	SUSTAIN THE GAINS
• High customer impact • Critical to success • Fastest or largest return	• Champions • Master Black Belts • Black Belts • Green Belts • Strong analytical skills • Strong problem-solving skills • People and leadership skills	• Define • Measure Processes –Select CTQ characteristic –Define performance standards –Validate measurement system • Analyze Processes –Establish product capability –Define performance objectives –Identify variation sources • Improve Processes –Screen potential causes –Discover variable relationship –Establish operating tolerances • Control Processes –Validate measurement system –Determine process capability –Implement process controls	• Lead a focused effort • Frequently review process and remove barriers • Check real business impact • Continuously communicate progress to executive leadership and those involved in projects	• Implement effective control plans • Conduct regular Six Sigma training to reinforce the initiative throughout the company • Review the project's effectiveness at regularly scheduled intervals • Continually identify and launch new Six Sigma projects

GEMS products would retain their status as best-in-class and dominate the market in the twenty-first century.

Although completing projects is necessary to achieving Six Sigma, GE understands that the Breakthrough Strategy is more than just reaching a goal. It's a never-ending journey that leads companies down the path of continual self-discovery and allows employees endless opportunities for individual growth and learning. GE also knows that projects with the magnitude of the LightSpeed need commitment and involvement from top management, to ensure not only that projects succeed but that the results are incorporated into the future of the business. At GE, Six Sigma has become, in the words of Jack Welch, "part of the genetic code of our future leadership." The redesign and manufacturing improvements in LightSpeed show why.

CHAPTER NINE

Implementation and Deployment

To achieve Six Sigma, companies must determine how to focus and deploy the Six Sigma Breakthrough Strategy so that key business priorities and strategy issues are addressed. One company may decide to focus on short-term cost reductions because of recent and substantial losses—losses due to high labor costs caused by elevated defect levels and rework that diverts industrial capacity; delays in how quickly a company can get its products to market; shrinking market share due to customer dissatisfaction; or a sales force consumed with warranty and customer complaints rather than generating new sales. A company that is enjoying strong profits may decide to focus on long-term projects that will strengthen its business by improving overall quality and customer satisfaction. Still another company may decide to innovate and improve the quality of its product designs. Another company might want to reduce costs by focusing on reducing its cycle time.

None of these choices conflict. In fact, reducing defects not only improves reliability but also helps to reduce cycle time and increase capacity. Service or information-intensive processes can be optimized with Six Sigma tools in the same way that an industrial process can be improved. Focusing on one or two areas to unroll Six Sigma doesn't exclude making other areas of the business the focus of a later Six Sigma project. All it means is that for the purposes of an initial rollout, companies have chosen to focus their efforts on one specific product, process, or division, knowing that over time they can expand Six Sigma to include additional processes and projects critical to customer satisfaction. Other companies might choose to decentralize their rollout by allowing each business unit to define the focus of Six Sigma while maintaining an overall corporate theme. We have had success with a range of rollout schemes; however, all implementation and deployment strategies must flow down from the executive leadership. *Six Sigma is not a grassroots initiative.* It simply will not "bubble up" to the surface.

Successful implementation depends on an interaction among the following principles:

- Highly visible top-down management commitment to the initiatives. Employees must perceive active leadership during implementation.

- A measurement system (metrics) to track the progress. This weaves accountability into the initiatives and provides a tangible picture of the organization's efforts.

- Internal and external benchmarking of the organization's products, services, and processes. This information inevitably leads to a "significant emotional event" when the organization understands and begins to discuss its "real" market position. This experience leads the organization to gravitate toward a breakthrough philosophy.

- Stretch goals to focus people on changing the processes by which the work gets done, rather than "tweaking" the existing processes. This leads to exponential rates of improvement.

- Educating all levels of the organization. Without the necessary training, people cannot bring about breakthrough improvement.

- Success stories to demonstrate how the Breakthrough Strategy is applied and the results.

- Champions and Black Belts to promote the initiatives and provide the necessary planning, teaching, coaching, and consulting at all levels of the organization.

Creating a Six Sigma Focus

How a company decides to focus its Six Sigma projects heavily influences the way Six Sigma is deployed. Here are some of the ways a company might choose to focus its Six Sigma efforts:

- **FOCUS ON PROJECT COST SAVINGS.** By focusing on project cost savings, a company can determine the number of projects it needs to complete to save a specific dollar amount. (Even with this focus, it is essential that companies track the reductions in cost of poor-quality projects, as well.) Projects are selected for potential reductions in fixed and/or variable costs, and not necessarily for their effect on the root drivers of process capability. Companies need to be aware of the limitations of this approach when trying to establish a new mind-set about quality within the company. This is a more limited approach, and will likely do less to spread Six Sigma throughout the organization.

- **FOCUS ON THE DELIVERABLES.** Another way to focus the Breakthrough Strategy's efforts is to identify the product family or system that is the greatest cause of poor customer satisfaction in a product or service that is important to a company's overall strategy. High warranty costs, for example, can signal products that might benefit from the Breakthrough Strategy. This kind of focus requires that companies examine a number of processes that contribute to the product or service. Companies should be wary of selecting projects that focus solely on products. Focusing on problems such as high warranty returns and customer complaints will highlight a product's symptoms but not the processes that create the symptoms. It is shortsighted to focus on the defects rather than the processes or systems that go into creating the product.

■ **FOCUS ON THE PROCESSES.** Focusing the Breakthrough Strategy on process capability is the best way to attack the root causes of defects and customer-satisfaction concerns. The key in applying the strategy is to identify processes that are critical to value and that are operating at low sigma levels. This approach requires strong cross-functional coordination, since many of the processes cross traditional departmental boundaries. *Companies that focus on processes over product will find that correcting a process in one division will almost always have applications for other divisions within the company.* Bombardier learned that Six Sigma was most profitable when it targeted processes that influenced the greatest number of products. After Bombardier applied the Breakthrough Strategy to fixing a reoccurring defect in the heaters within the Ski-Doo's handlebars, it found that the results could be applied to other product lines. The Breakthrough Strategy kept Bombardier from having to reinvent the wheel, eliminating customer complaints and rework in other areas of the company.

■ **FOCUS ON THE PROBLEMS.** Although Six Sigma is designed to focus on "inputs" rather than "outputs," or root causes rather than problems or symptoms, one of Bombardier's initial Six Sigma projects provides a good example of a problem-focused project. Profits and customer surveys showed that consumers, while satisfied with the Sea-Doo personal watercraft and the Ski-Doo snowmobiles' high-performance engines, wanted a more modern, sleeker look. A Six Sigma team was put together to redesign the products, focusing on design innovation to create machines that were sleeker and more sophisticated in appearance. Although this project did not focus on processes, it did address a problem that was affecting sales and customer satisfaction.

Additional Ways to Focus Six Sigma
Breakthrough Strategy Projects

There is a certain amount of crossover in terms of project focus. A project that focuses on process quality will also initially focus on a certain key product line. Here are five additional ways to deploy Six Sigma:

- **BY GEOGRAPHIC LOCATION.** A company may want to deploy Six Sigma in stages based on a division's or plant's geography. For example, it might focus its efforts on its Canadian division or at a specific plant site. This approach works well when there are many small operations that individually could not support a Six Sigma initiative. For example, if a business has ten facilities and each facility has only a hundred employees, creating a pool of Champions and Black Belts to service the geographic region for those ten facilities would be a successful approach.

- **USING DESIGN FOR SIX SIGMA.** Achieving Six Sigma levels of quality requires a combination of *process characterization* (Measure and Analyze) and *process optimization* (Improve and Control), as well as efforts to improve the design of products so that they can be made error-free. An organization may decide to use Design for Six Sigma to focus its initial efforts on improving the design of certain key processes, products, systems, or components. If redesigning a process, product, system, or component is to be part of a Six Sigma initiative, companies should also consider focusing on their product development and design processes.

- **FOCUSING ON INTERNAL PROCESSES.** An organization may decide to focus its initial efforts on optimizing its internal processes, using the information gathered to define future Design for Six Sigma projects.

- **FOCUSING ON SUPPLIER PROCESSES.** We feel strongly that companies need to improve their own processes before they require outside suppliers to launch Six Sigma initiatives. A company attempting to require outside suppliers to implement Six Sigma will need to be prepared to devote considerable resources to the effort and manage its supplier relationships carefully. First, however, companies must determine which supplier processes are critical to their products or services. Focusing on suppliers is by far the most difficult choice and requires a high degree of experience with Six Sigma.

- **FOCUSING ON CUSTOMERS.** The heart of Six Sigma lies in improving products and services that will benefit the customer. Companies need to understand how their customers measure quality and to create products and services that meet their expectations. Six Sigma translates issues critical to customers' satisfaction to what is critical to a products or service's quality. Companies that improve their ability to consistently meet their customers' needs will produce positive bottom-line business results.

The Elements of an Organization's Structure

Most companies deploy Six Sigma in increments or in "waves," training employees from four or five business units or factories during each deployment cycle. Over time, Black Belts within a factory or division can expand the use of Six Sigma to other processes within the factory or division and reinforce the initiative. Six Sigma begins to reach a critical mass as employees are trained to apply the Breakthrough Strategy simultaneously across the organization. Momentum of the initiative is sustained as organizations standardize and integrate Six Sigma into all its day-to-day operations by incorporating Six Sigma practices into its policies and procedures.

How a company organizes the people working on Six Sigma projects depends on: (1) how the company focuses its deployment—does it begin in a particular geographic location or focus on design and engineering processes? and (2) how Six Sigma is integrated into the organization so that Six Sigma resources don't get lost in the concerns of "business as usual," or the latest firefighting endeavor. There are a number of concerns that must be discussed and decided on prior to launching Six Sigma projects. Among them:

- Who will oversee Black Belt selection? What selection criteria will be used? What will be the company's policy on pay, recognition, and rewards linked to Six Sigma performance? Taking into consideration the current state of product and process quality, and the company's strategic goals, how many Black Belts will the company need and in what areas?

- What should the project selection process look like, and what criteria must be met to engage or terminate a project? Who within the company will sign off on projects? What guidelines will the company use? How will the company track savings? How will it treat the various categories of savings?

- What quality metrics will be used? Which metrics will be standard across the company? What improvement goals will the company set? Should learning curves be used to establish a standardized rate of improvement?

- How will the company orient and coordinate Six Sigma with its other major initiatives and systems, such as new-product development, materials requirement planning (MRP), or just-in-time inventory control (JIT), to name a few?

- How will the company handle budget issues, such as whether the salaries of Black Belts are categorized as direct or indirect costs?

- How will the company train its Master Black Belts to deliver Black Belt training? What is a realistic lead time for training given the backgrounds and skill levels of the Master Black Belts selected?

Six Sigma Roles and Responsibilities

A clear definition of roles and responsibilities is vital to the deployment of Six Sigma. While all employees need to understand the vision of Six Sigma and eventually be able to apply some of the Six Sigma tools to improving their work, there are ten distinctive roles that are prevalent during initialization, implementation, and deployment.

- **EXECUTIVE MANAGEMENT.** As a group, executive management must inspire, own, fund, and drive the Six Sigma initiative. This group establishes the corporate-level goals and targets and determines the time frame of performance expectations. They establish how the Six Sigma initiative will initially be focused. Their initial steps can significantly add to the likelihood of success or detract from it. It must be remembered that nothing is more disappointing or frustrating than a "hard restart." Getting it right up front is the ticket to overall success.

- **SENIOR CHAMPION.** This is a strategic corporate-level position. It requires a strong business executive selected from the executive group, most often on a direct report to the Office of the President. This person is fully responsible for the day-to-day corporate-level management of Six Sigma. He or she must be a strong leader, capable of "doing the right thing—now." The Senior Champion is accountable to the president, as well as to the business unit leader, for the projected Six Sigma results. Often the Senior Champion is required to get business unit leaders on board and to get the executive leadership to commit to specific financial goals and performance targets. A Senior Champion typically remains in this position indefinitely. However, as the Six Sigma deployment progresses, the Senior Champion will move from a full-time position to a less dedicated role.

- **DEPLOYMENT CHAMPION.** This is a strategic business unit–level position. These individuals are responsible for the development and execution of Six Sigma implementation and deployment plans for their respective business unit or defined area of responsibility. They are also responsible for the effectiveness and efficiency of the Six Sigma support systems. Deployment Champions most often report to the Senior Champion, as well as their business-unit president or area vice president. Initially, the position is fully dedicated. However, as the Six Sigma deployment progresses, the Deployment Champion will move to a less dedicated role.

- **PROJECT CHAMPION.** This is a tactical business unit–level position that is most often dedicated for a period of two years. This person is responsible for the identification, selection, execution, and follow-on of Six Sigma Black Belt projects. Project Champions are the "trail bosses" that drive the Six Sigma initiative. Their leadership must be sound, strong, consistent, and prevail when guiding Black Belts. In addition, they develop and oversee many of the details associated with the implementation and deployment plan.

- **DEPLOYMENT MASTER BLACK BELTS.** This is a dedicated and strategic position with a highly technical orientation, normally posted at the business-unit level. These people are responsible for the long-range technical vision of Six Sigma. They are responsible for the development of technology road maps and work technically across functional areas and businesses. They also seek out and transfer new and advanced Six Sigma technologies, methods, procedures, and tools, and ensure that this knowledge is translated into training materials, manuals, and

operational documents. The "tour of duty" for this position
varies from organization to organization. They are Six Sigma's
"Johnny Appleseeds." They spread the seeds of Six Sigma,
while the project Master Black Belts plant and water the
seeds so that Black Belts can harvest the fruit.

- **PROJECT MASTER BLACK BELTS.** This is a dedicated and
tactical position with a highly technical orientation. Project
Master Black Belts usually serve in this position at the
business-unit level for two years. They are responsible for the
transfer of Six Sigma knowledge to the Black Belts. They are
the teachers of Six Sigma and mentor their students on the job.
They need sound technical skills, a strong stage presence, and
credible leadership ability. If Black Belts are where the rubber
meets the road, Project Master Black Belts are where the tire
meets the rim—if the tire slips on the rim, it's likely that the
rubber on the road will do little for acceleration and braking.

- **PROJECT BLACK BELT.** This is a two-year dedicated technical application position within a business unit. This person is
responsible for executing his or her application project and
realizing the targeted benefits. Black Belts are developed and
implanted on-site as Six Sigma experts within each business
unit of a corporation. These on-site experts are referred to as
"Six Sigma Black Belts." Black belts have the ability to (1)
effectively develop and lead line-of-sight or cross-functional
process-improvement teams; (2) work with, mentor, and
advise middle management on the formulation and subsequent implementation of process-improvement plans; (3) utilize and disseminate the Six Sigma tools and methods; and (4)
network with other Black Belts around the world for the benefit of their business. The aim is to produce highly credible
process breakthrough success stories using the four-phase
Breakthrough Strategy and then transfer the application
methods, techniques, procedures, and tools to their peers and
process-improvement teams. The central focus is on develop-

ing an in-depth application-based knowledge of the Six Sigma philosophy, theory, tactics, Breakthrough Strategy, and tools. Particular emphasis is placed on the tools of the Breakthrough Strategy—statistics, quantitative benchmarking, process-control techniques, process diagnostic methods, and experiment design. Throughout the Plan-Train-Apply-Review (P-T-A-R) learning cycle, Black Belts learn how the key tools are blended and sequenced to form a scientific and repeatable process for solving critical manufacturing, engineering, service, and administrative problems.

■ **PROCESS OWNERS.** Line managers "own" specific business processes and are in the position of ensuring that process improvements are captured and sustained. In cases where a process cuts across organizational boundaries, several line managers may need to work together to coordinate resources.

■ **SIX SIGMA GREEN BELTS.** These individuals work part-time in their specific areas, extending the reach of Black Belts on Six Sigma projects, and take on mini-projects of their own.

■ **PROJECT TEAM MEMBERS.** Project team members should have fundamental Six Sigma training so that they can provide project-specific, part-time process and cross-functional support. Under the guidance of Black Belts, they can gather and analyze data, as well as help sustain the gains created by Six Sigma projects. Project team members work part time on projects and can provide expertise on areas directly or indirectly involved in the process. In the case of larger projects, team members may dedicate themselves full time to the project.

Monitoring Financial Gains

Companies that are in the process of implementing purchasing, materials planning systems, financial accounting systems, inventory planning, and other multisystems, such as Oracle, SAP, and Bahn, should put these programs on hold until Six Sigma is firmly rooted in the company. There is no leveraged benefit in systemizing a three or four sigma company. Once organizations start to see Six Sigma cost improvements, they will find that many of the programs and systems they have implemented are no longer necessary; companies that postpone implementing major systems until their processes are functioning at better than four sigma will find that the time it takes to implement these systems is cut by 50 percent and the cost of implementation drops by 60 percent.

Organizations should also consider postponing additional capital outlays, such as building a new plant to meet production requirements. Each sigma shift increases an organization's capacity anywhere from 12 to 18 percent, and eliminates costly capital outlays.

An independent assessment of each project's financial benefit to the company must be made by a finance representative assigned to follow Six Sigma projects. Actual financial benefits should be tallied against project estimates and be reported to the executive leadership. Each Six Sigma project must be financially audited and supported by a written report. We have been in companies where managers allocate profits from a Six Sigma project to compensate for other process inadequacies. Although senior management and the finance department may agree to use the money in this way, Six Sigma improvements need to be reflected in the bottom line so that companies can gauge the profitability of their Six Sigma efforts.

We recommend that the financial representative charged with tracking Six Sigma project savings be responsible for:

- working with Black Belts to identify each project's financial metrics and potential financial impact

- working with Project Champions to formally approve the projected savings of each project

- working with Black Belts to adjust the project financial savings as the project evolves and assumptions change

- taking over the financial responsibility from the Black Belt as a project nears completion, and then tracking the actual financial savings of that project for one year

- working with Champions to prioritize Six Sigma projects

A Deployment Case Study

The following deployment plan, taken from an organization that implemented Six Sigma, illustrates how the deployment principles and guidelines are used to initiate Six Sigma. The steps outlined can be applied to any kind of business and can serve as a model for other companies.

At Company X, after the company's leadership decided to implement Six Sigma, management scheduled an executive briefing to explain to senior management how Six Sigma would improve their particular business. Business unit leaders then attended a one-day "Six Sigma Executive Briefing," where project-selection criteria were defined and a discussion took place describing what Six Sigma could accomplish in individual business units—what it would cost, how it should be implemented, how long it would take to implement, and how to sustain the gains that would come about. This briefing:

- explored the nature of Six Sigma and Design for Six Sigma (DFSS)

- established a Six Sigma leadership team and defined responsibilities

- defined key business and organizational values

- identified key business issues and noted their value intersects

- set aggressive Six Sigma goals and rates of improvement

- established implementation and deployment guidelines

The executive leadership realized that they were responsible for allocating the time, funds, and human resources for Black Belts and employees to apply the Breakthrough Strategy, and that those individuals involved needed their Six Sigma participation acknowledged through rewards and increased compensation. The executive leadership also grasped the importance of involving the finance department to track Six Sigma returns, and held the finance department responsible for making sure that those profits were returned to the company's bottom line.

It is not enough for senior management to attend a Six Sigma training session and then assign Black Belts to projects. While not every executive needs to dedicate 100 percent of his or her time to Six Sigma (after all, someone still needs to run the existing business), a senior manager (or managers, depending on the size and scope of the business) is needed to lead the deployment and provide day-to-day support to the effort.

Next, by appointing a key executive as a Six Sigma "Senior Champion," the executive board sent the company a clear and unmistakable message that Six Sigma was an important goal supported by the executive leadership. This Senior Six Sigma Champion and the appointed "Deployment Champions" received intensive training and became certified in the Breakthrough Strategy. This group oversaw and guided the overall Six Sigma initiative. Each of the Champions was trained in all of the implementation and application details associated with Six Sigma. During training at the Six Sigma Academy, the group developed a comprehensive deployment plan that spelled out the details of how Six Sigma would be implemented. They developed a metrics plan, training plan, human resources plan, finance plan, and communications plan. The executive leadership of the organization then reviewed the plans and agreed to support the effort.

Site deployment was done in clusters, with a designated number of employees moved into dedicated Six Sigma positions. This was done according to a documented deployment plan prepared by the Senior Champion that identified sites, dates, and the number of individuals dedicated to each Six Sigma role. Initial launch sites were chosen based on business need and the likelihood of success.

At this point, each business unit designated "Project Champions"

THE STAGES OF SIX SIGMA IMPLEMENTATION

DISCOVER	DECIDE	ORGANIZE	INITIALIZE	DEPLOY	SUSTAIN
Recognize the need for Six Sigma and explore its potential impact on your company	Executive leadership approves the Six Sigma initiative, and then defines the purpose and scope of Six Sigma	Establish financial targets, set time lines, and train senior executive team and Deployment Champions	Create deployment plans for metrics, communications, human resources, Black Belt training, and Black Belt project funding	Train Project Champions and Black Belts	Train Six Sigma Green Belts and Process-Improvement Team Leaders

who acted as conduits for making sure that the implementation process flowed smoothly and Black Belt projects were fully supported. During the two five-day training sessions, Project Champions learned the strategies, tactics, and tools associated with implementing and applying Six Sigma. They also learned how to manage Six Sigma projects and how to "keep the Six Sigma machine running."

Learning and applying the Breakthrough Strategy was a synergistic process, allowing Champions from different business units to interact with each other. They discovered how to pool their resources to streamline the costs and time associated with implementation. Following training, Champions returned to their respective business units and began executing their customized plans. Master Black Belts established a schedule for conducting Six Sigma implementation reviews to ensure that there was a "parallel rate of progress" among the participating business units. "Lessons learned" were shared in a real-time environment. Black Belt training was coordinated among business units, creating shorter implementation times across the company, greater economy of scale, and more efficient use of training resources. The Master Black Belts provided application and implementation guidance and feedback to their respective business-unit Champions during these reviews. On occasion, additional time was devoted for specialized training, as well as for inviting guest speakers from partnering organizations.

Six Sigma Compensation

Business-unit leaders will find that, on average, Six Sigma will increase their profitability by 6 to 8 percent beyond what was planned. Unless the executive leadership compensates these individuals for exceeding their annual business targets, they will lose these employees to companies willing to compensate them. Shareholders and the executive leadership cannot be the only beneficiaries of the financial gains achieved through Six Sigma. Corporate vice presidents and business-unit leaders need financial incentives to push beyond the projected earnings. Those who bring a significant improvement to their business unit's profit margins deserve a salary compensation that rewards their achievement. Similarly, Black Belts who return $1 million or more each year to the bottom line need to be rewarded for their effort.

Six Sigma compensation can be addressed in different ways. We recommend that CEOs and those at the executive level have a minimum of 30 percent of their incentive compensation tied to Six Sigma. Business-unit leaders expected to double their annual profit margins need to be compensated for their effort as well. Regardless of the incentive package, those business leaders who do not achieve their Six Sigma targets must be penalized in such a way that they know Six Sigma is to be taken seriously. In this sense, Six Sigma is very Darwinian—only the strong survive. Therefore, only the best should be tapped for leadership positions. While very rewarding, the Six Sigma effort is a veritable gauntlet of challenges and experiences that requires innovation and an adaptive mind-set.

Black Belt Compensation

Black Belt compensation is an important consideration when implementing and deploying Six Sigma. Black Belts' salaries must be standardized in a way that recognizes their roles within the company and competitive position within the market. In addition, companies have to create an incentive plan that includes receiving a specified number of corporate stock options each year over a three-year time period vesting forward; for example, a Black Belt may receive 20 percent of the stock options at the end of the first year, 40 percent at the end of year two, and 40 percent at the end of the third year. This ensures that those companies spending time and money on Black Belt training will preserve their knowledge base long enough for a company to benefit.

Companies that don't have stock options, or are not able to make stock options available to their Black Belts, can reward Black Belts with "dummy" stock. This stock has no value except to those Black Belts who return a predetermined amount to the bottom line and are compensated with cash equivalent of dummy stock based on the savings they generate.

In companies where the success of Six Sigma projects are heavily dependent on the Black Belt's team members, not only should Black Belts be rewarded in the ways discussed above, but 20 percent of the total project savings could be distributed among the team members.

Companies that do not have a competitive financial compensation package in place when they implement Six Sigma will not just lose Black Belts—they will not see Six Sigma reach its full potential.

Choosing a Six Sigma Consultant

In 1995, only two companies were teaching the Six Sigma methodology. While Motorola University was providing executives with an overview on how Six Sigma worked at a corporate level, the Six Sigma Academy was offering more comprehensive training that included executive orientation and Black Belt training. Since then, largely due to Wall Street's strong interest in how Six Sigma increases profitability and the media attention given to companies like General Electric and AlliedSignal, an entire cottage industry has been spawned that offers a range of Six Sigma training.

Successfully implementing and deploying Six Sigma depends heavily on engaging the right consulting firm. The following checklist suggests what qualities or experience any company should look for when hiring a Six Sigma consultant.

The answers to the questions on the following chart fall into one of four categories:

- Recognized in a third-party publication

- Fully experienced

- Some experience

- No experience

A Six Sigma consulting firm should be highly experienced at doing a corporationwide Six Sigma implementation and deployment. It should be comfortable working with an organization's executive leadership and have a command presence during meetings. Above all, it should speak the language of management—time and money. Black Belt training is easy to come by, but finding a consulting firm that

				GUIDELINES FOR CHOOSING A SIX SIGMA CONSULTANT
				Have members of the consulting firm ever functioned in the role of senior executives within Fortune 100 companies?
				How many Fortune 100 CEOs can the consulting firm list as references?
				Have members of the consulting firm ever functioned as corporate officers?
				Have members of the consulting firm ever functioned as first-line managers?
				Have members of the consulting firm ever been involved in a business changeover?
				How many corporationwide Six Sigma implementations and deployments have members of the consulting firm successfully guided?
				Have members of the consulting firm ever consulted for the federal government?
				Have members of the consulting firm facilitated or implemented a corporate strategic direction?
				How extensively have members of the consulting firm been recognized by professional societies for substantial contributions to the profession?
				How extensively have members of the consulting firm been published in recognized technical journals?
				How extensively have members of the consulting firm been published in recognized management journals and business periodicals?
				Are the consultants recognized worldwide as quality leaders?
				Have members of the consulting firm been involved in developing or acted as examiners for quality awards, such as the Malcolm Baldrige Award?
				Is the consulting firm officially recognized by the American Society for Quality, and/or do they have the endorsement of the American Society for Quality?

understands the depth and scope of Six Sigma is more difficult. Choosing the right consulting firm is much like selecting a surgeon for open-heart surgery—most can use a scalpel, but some are significantly more skilled than others. Seasoned consultants know that implementing and deploying Six Sigma involves much more than training Black Belts.

Six Sigma and Suppliers

One of the perennial problems associated with raising an organization's sigma level are suppliers. Companies think of themselves as producing goods or services. Yet most companies don't make all the components themselves; rather, they assemble products or deliver services created from many different parts or processes generated by other companies. As a result, the quality of a company's products or services is dependent on companies outside their control.

Suppliers can not only erode an organization's profitability, but they can also waste time and manpower through inspection, returns, rework, and inventory-carrying costs. Many organizations believe they can improve supplier quality by riding them a little harder or threatening penalties for delays or low quality. But while threatening suppliers with the potential loss of business may cause them to raise their sigma level half a point, that is about all. A better answer may be undertaking the training of key suppliers.

Since it takes companies about two years to get their own processes under control, we do not recommend that companies begin training key suppliers before then. A large percentage of supplier error is caused by poor drawings and specifications provided to them. Organizations that haven't applied the Breakthrough Strategy to their own processes, products, and services can't expect suppliers to improve their processes, products, and services without being given more accurate data and information. However, companies *can* create five or six sigma products from four sigma components using

DFSS methods and tools. For example, not every part in a product with 1,200 parts affects overall quality. By raising only the sigma level of those parts that are critical to quality, companies can still raise the overall sigma level of the product. By expanding the limits of noncritical parts, costs can be greatly reduced. Remember, not everything has to reach a six sigma performance level through variation reduction. Often, we can achieve Six Sigma by opening the bandwidth of noncritical parts and operations.

Traditionally, organizations select suppliers on the basis of their pricing competitiveness. This tradition runs counter to the Six Sigma philosophy that the lowest-cost producer is also the highest-quality producer. When companies and suppliers communicate in the language of Six Sigma, suppliers become partners in the quest for Six Sigma and breakthrough profitability. Good suppliers are as concerned about the product as their customers, and are willing to dedicate their own employees to training and allowing them to function as Black Belts or Green Belts. Suppliers are usually anxious to implement the Six Sigma philosophy, strategy, and tools. Supplier-trained Black Belts also understand that their products and services center on customer satisfaction.

Only key suppliers need to be trained in the Six Sigma methodology. Some suppliers are not—and probably never will be—integral to your organization's day-to-day operations. Nevertheless, they do have a certain impact on your products and services. Often a supplier will realize that your company is measuring the performance of its products and begin to start correcting its problems itself. Once a supplier sees the benefits of having a steady supplier-customer relationship, it may become interested on its own in having key personnel trained as Black Belts. Should the supplier undertake such training, your organization's Black Belts can offer to mentor supplier-trained Black Belts to ensure that products and services maintain the highest levels of quality and performance.

It is important to appreciate the effort and commitment suppliers are willing to make to satisfy their customers. Their willingness to closely examine their business processes, train key personnel in the Six Sigma methodology, and implement the changes needed to deliver quality goods and services to customers can help forge a strong bond between suppliers and their customers.

Again, companies cannot expect a supplier to improve its processes until they reach a certain level of understanding and improvement of their own processes. But as we saw earlier, when companies improve their own processes to a certain level, they can begin to require the same of their suppliers.

The initial steps a company takes to implement and deploy Six Sigma might look like this:

STEP ONE Generate executive leadership interest in Six Sigma

STEP TWO Conduct Six Sigma executive briefing

STEP THREE Decide to move forward with Six Sigma implementation

STEP FOUR Conduct Six Sigma Champion training

STEP FIVE Select the first cluster of businesses for Six Sigma implementation

STEP SIX Identify Black Belt candidates for training

STEP SEVEN Conduct Six Sigma Black Belt training

STEP EIGHT Conduct standard Six Sigma process review

STEP NINE Make second assessment of implementation

STEP TEN Make decision to expand the initiative

STEP ELEVEN Revise Six Sigma deployment schedule

STEP TWELVE Integrate lessons learned into strategy

The actual Six Sigma implementation within a single business unit takes approximately six months, with a schedule that looks similar to the following:

A SIX SIGMA DEPLOYMENT SCHEDULE	
Week 1	Orientation and planning
Weeks 2 to 5	Champion training
Week 6	Champion review
Week 7	The first wave of Black Belts begins the first five-day training session and covers the Measure phase of the Breakthrough Strategy.
Weeks 8 to 10	Black Belts apply knowledge learned in the Measure phase training to their designated training projects.
Week 11	The first wave of Black Belts returns for the second five-day training session to review the Measure phase and learn the Analyze phase of the Breakthrough Strategy.
Weeks 12 to 14	Black Belts apply knowledge learned in the Analyze phase to their designated learning projects.
Week 15	The first wave of Black Belts returns for the third five-day training session to review the Analyze phase and learn the Improve phase of the Breakthrough Strategy.
Weeks 16 to 18	Black Belts apply knowledge learned in the Improve phase to their designated training projects.
Week 19	The first wave of Black Belts returns for the fourth, and final, five-day training session to review the Improve phase and learn the Control phase of the Breakthrough Strategy.
Weeks 20 to 22	Black Belts apply knowledge learned in the Control phase to their designated training projects.
Weeks 23 and 24	The first wave of Black Belts returns for a review of the Control phase and reviews the overall Breakthrough Strategy.
Weeks 22 to 24	A contingency plan is developed to identify and replace Black Belt trainees who can't successfully manage a Six Sigma project. Experience shows that fewer than 8 percent of those who participate in training do not succeed as Black Belts.

The Six Sigma Players: Champions, Master Black Belts, Black Belts, and Green Belts

■ ■ ■ ■ ■ ■

> The best executive is the one who has sense enough to pick good men to do what he wants done, and self-restraint enough to keep from meddling with them while they do it.
>
> —THEODORE ROOSEVELT

Six Sigma quality is built around the customer. Everything starts and ends with the customer. They define quality and set expectations. They rightfully expect performance, reliability, competitive prices, on-time delivery, service, clear and accurate transaction processing, and so on. Customers expect excellence, and will take their business to where they can get it. They control the votes on satisfaction and value.

Customers are why companies implement Six Sigma Breakthrough Strategy. But customers don't want to just hear or read that companies have implemented Six Sigma. They want to see and feel the results. Training employees in Six Sigma Breakthrough Strategy is the only way companies can dramatically improve their processes that reach the customer.

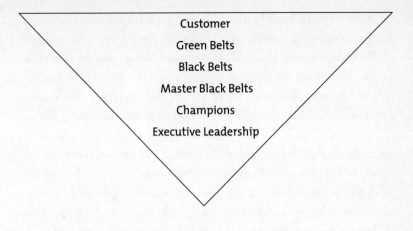

Customer

Green Belts

Black Belts

Master Black Belts

Champions

Executive Leadership

Do Your Employees Know Your Company's Values and Vision?

The inverted pyramid is a powerful metaphor for the support Six Sigma needs to succeed. The inverted relationships that result from this triangle have strong implications for the way Six Sigma infiltrates an organization. At the bottom of the pyramid, supporting and balancing the structure, is the executive leadership. Although few in number, their internal will and executive commitment lays the foundation for success. Without commitment from the executive leadership, Six Sigma will not have the support of senior management, middle management, and so on. If support is broken at any juncture, the structure will fall and Six Sigma will fail.

Successful companies are driven by the vision and values of their leaders. Six Sigma is driven by a desire to achieve a vision—a vision of where a company wants to be. The executive leadership must create a vision clearly understood by the entire organization. That vision must be so ingrained in the minds of employees that everyone understands what it means and how it drives the direction of the company.

With a strong vision of what Six Sigma can do for a company, a CEO is able to give employees the freedom to explore new ideas and concepts, and the power and resources to make decisions and implement the changes brought about by Six Sigma. As a result, employees will be 100 percent committed to following Six Sigma.

Bombardier, GE, Polaroid, and Seagate designated an executive leader in a full-time position to oversee and drive their Six Sigma initiatives forward. This executive plants the flag of change. The executive responsible for Six Sigma develops a comprehensive plan for rolling out the initiative, and organizes and leads the deployment of Six Sigma across the company. Following extensive training in the details of implementation and application associated with Six Sigma, he or she works with senior management and Champions to communicate the company's objectives, goals, milestones, and progress. He or she also tracks the financial benefits from Six Sigma projects.

Champions

The executive leader, or Senior Champion, selects individuals who will "champion" Six Sigma within specific businesses across the organization and can ensure that all the key functions of an organization are connected to Six Sigma. There are two types of Champions: Deployment Champions and Project Champions. Both must have key executive leadership roles in the business. In industry vernacular, they are typically strategic business unit leaders (SBUs), site management team leaders, or heads of major functional organizations. A Champion may be anyone from an executive vice president to a vice president in charge of a functional group at an operating site.

Deployment Champions play a role similar to the CEO, president, and executive vice presidents in terms of leadership and commitment, but take on the additional responsibilities necessary to nurture the success of Six Sigma. Deployment Champions work to implement Six Sigma throughout their respective businesses. We recommend that Deployment Champions have solid business experience at the strategic and tactical level, be experienced in leading a major change initiative, be experienced in leading cross-functional teams, and be able to develop businesswide financial targets for Six Sigma results.

Project Champions function at the business unit level as they oversee Black Belts and focus on Six Sigma at the project level. They break down corporate cultural barriers, create support systems, make sure financial resources are available, and identify improvement projects. Project Champions perform assessments of the organization's capabilities, benchmark the organization's products and services, conduct detailed gap analyses, create an operational vision, develop a cross-functional Six Sigma deployment plan, and provide managerial and technical leadership to Master Black Belts and Black Belts. Project Champions must integrate the methodologies and tools of Six Sigma into their existing jobs. They have to be knowledgeable in the underlying philosophy, supporting theory, practice, and implementation of Six Sigma strategies, tactics, and tools. Project Champions focus on changes in operation and functional results, and directly support the Master Black Belts as they implement Six Sigma methodology. These Champions select, review, and nurture Black Belts as they come up with solutions to key problems in their projects. They are usually functional group vice presidents or directors, and select projects that will provide substantial benefit to *their* business unit.

Deployment and Project Champions organize and lead the initialization, deployment, and implementation of Six Sigma across organizations. It is they who choose specific projects and begin the task of implementing Six Sigma strategies and tactics. They understand the underlying theories, principles, and practices of Six Sigma from a management perspective, but also have a technical understanding that allows for effective and efficient communication. They are able to pave the way for change and integrate the results. These Champions are the grounding force in making the strategy work and supporting the triangle. They are the "glue" that keeps the initiative moving forward.

How much statistical knowledge do the executive leadership and Champions need? Here is what Bombardier Senior Champion Bruce Miyashita says:

Managers don't need to be statisticians, any more than managers need to be accountants, but they need to be adept at using and

A HIGH-LEVEL COMPARISON OF ROLES

	CHAMPIONS	MASTER BLACK BELTS	BLACK BELTS	GREEN BELTS
QUALIFICATIONS	Senior executives and managers, such as a vice president or director of manufacturing or marketing Familiarity with basic and advanced statistical tools	Technical degree. Master Black Belt might be a chief engineer or head of customer service. Mastery of basic and advanced statistical tools	Technical degree or orientation. Black Belt might be an engineer or billing administrator with five years or more of experience. Mastery of basic statistical tools	Technical and support background. Their current positions are associated with the problem needing to be solved. Familiarity with basic statistical tools
TRAINING	One week of Champion training	Two one-week training sessions Black Belt training is highly recommended.	Four one-week sessions with three weeks between sessions to apply strategy to assigned projects Project review in second, third, and fourth sessions	Two three-day sessions with three weeks between sessions to apply strategy to assigned projects Project review in second session
NUMBER OF EMPLOYEES TRAINED	One Champion per business group or manufacturing site	One Master Black per 30 Black Belts. Master Blacks do not have to be on-site. They can represent a division.	One Black Belt per 100 employees. 100,000 employees would require 1,000 Black Belts.	One Green Belt per 20 employees

interpreting the concepts and tools of Six Sigma. Just as we would expect managers to understand the basics of cash flow, managers should know how to calculate Sigma, understand the concepts of rolled throughput yield, the essentials of factorial experiments, and the practical implications of hypothesis testing. While these activities don't need to be part of their job, they need enough familiarity with the terms and concepts that they can ask the right questions, provide proper support to their Black Belts, and make sure that the Six Sigma initiative is properly rolled out across the organization.

Master Black Belts

Master Black Belts—individuals selected by Champions to act as in-house experts for disseminating the Breakthrough Strategy knowledge throughout the organization—work with Champions to coordinate project selection and training. Master Black Belts devote 100 percent of their time to Six Sigma, assisting Champions in identifying improvement projects. They train and coach Black Belts and Green Belts, and communicate the overall progress and status of projects within their areas or business. Master Black Belt training is extensive, and includes Champion training as well as training in statistical problem solving. However, 90 percent of the Master Black Belt's work has nothing to do with statistics. Master Black Belts spend a significant amount of time using what we call "soft skills"—organizing people, designing cross-functional experiments, structuring and coordinating projects and meetings, teaching, coaching, and collecting and organizing information. They help inculcate Six Sigma into an organization's culture, and are responsible for creating lasting changes in an organization, getting all employees to think in terms of the Six Sigma vision. They negotiate for resources and clear the path to apply the Breakthrough Strategy to targeted Black Belt projects, particularly those that cut across the organization's boundaries.

Black Belts

Black Belts, working under a Master Black Belt, apply the Six Sigma Breakthrough Strategy's tools and knowledge to specific projects. Black Belts dedicate 100 percent of their time to working on Six Sigma projects.

Unlike the executive leadership and Champions, who decide *what gets done*, Master Black Belts and Black Belts work full time figuring out *how to get it done*. Like Master Black Belts, Project Black Belts undergo extensive training in statistics and problem-solving techniques, and should train 100 Green Belts a year. Although there is less focus on developing people skills, Black Belts are clearly seen as leaders and must possess both management and technical skills.

Since the bulk of executing the Breakthrough Strategy falls upon Black Belts, we have devoted the chapter that follows to discussing their roles and responsibilities in greater detail.

Green Belts

Green Belts are employees throughout the organization who execute Six Sigma as a part of their overall jobs. They have less Six Sigma responsibility and their energies are focused on projects that tie directly to their day-to-day work. Green Belts receive a more simplified version of Black Belt training, although they are still required to enter training after being assigned to a sanctioned project important to their operation's success. Green Belts have two primary tasks: first, to help deploy the success of Six Sigma techniques, and second, to lead small-scale improvement projects within their respective areas, much as a Black Belt does. Green Belts can do much of the legwork in gathering data and executing experiments in support of a Black Belt project. As they become more proficient, they can increase the Black Belt's effectiveness. By working with Black Belts, Green Belts gain experience in the practical application of the Six Sigma tools that help support line management's efforts to capture and sustain Six Sigma gains.

While Green Belts dedicate only part of their overall jobs to Six Sigma projects, there is no one formula for how their time should be divided. Some Green Belts work full time with a Black Belt in order to thoroughly learn the Breakthrough Strategy's tools, and work projects on a part-time (two to three days each week) basis thereafter. Other Green Belts might limit their Six Sigma involvement to collecting and analyzing certain types of data to help speed up the Measure phase. Others help run designed experiments during the Improvement phase. Today, many companies will not consider for promotion full-time, salaried employees who don't have at least Green Belt training.

Many hourly workers are trained in the fundamentals of Six Sigma, which typically involves two to four days of rudimentary training in the use of basic tools to apply the Measure, Analyze, Improve, and Control phases of Six Sigma. This gives them a stronger understanding of the process so that they can assist Black Belts and Green Belts on their projects. In this sense, they can be thought of as "White Belts"—newcomers to the Six Sigma infrastructure.

The long-term objective of any company wanting to successfully implement the Breakthrough Strategy is to train all employees in such a way that they make the methodology integral to improving everything they do.

Green Belts at General Electric

General Electric employs Carlson-Wagonlit Travel to handle its company travel. To effectively meet General Electric's travel demands, Carlson-Wagonlit Travel selected one of its senior managers to be trained as a Champion at GE's training center; this manager could then work closely with General Electric's own Master Black Belt at the Travel Center. The Carlson-Wagonlit Black Belts each function as a travel process expert, helping to identify travel tools, reports, and processes General Electric employees may not be familiar with. Carlson-Wagonlit Travel has trained a dozen employees within General Electric's Travel Center as Green Belts. These Green

Belts are now leading projects, as well as working in project teams. By applying the Breakthrough Strategy to other accounts as well, Carlson-Wagonlit Travel has increased its customer-satisfaction level and increased corporate sales.

General Electric also provided Green Belt training to the national account manager for Doubletree Hotels. Since Doubletree Hotels is one of GE's preferred hotels for employee travel, Doubletree has appointed an account manager expressly to handle all General Electric business. By assigning a Black Belt and several Green Belts to its GE account, Doubletree has improved its internal processes and made the company easier for GE employees to work with. Doubletree has saved hundreds of thousands of dollars by streamlining its processes, and has applied the tools and skills learned through its GE experience to its other corporate accounts.

GE also provided Green Belt training to Coldwell Banker employees who handle GE's employee relocation services. Prior to Coldwell Banker receiving supplier training, GE had been receiving an increasing number of complaints from employees saying that personal items had been damaged during a job relocation move. After training and mentoring of Coldwell Banker employees, relocation complaints from GE employees have dropped dramatically.

Summary

For Six Sigma implementation to be successful, the tip of the upside-down pyramid must be firmly grounded on the values and behaviors of the organization's executive leadership. If the executive leadership gives only lip service to the initiative, the program will falter at the first wave of resistance. But when the leaders of an organization insist that Six Sigma values become a part of the culture, then the pyramid will not sway.

HIGH LEVEL ROLL-OUT GUIDELINES		
Phase One	Business units select Champions and Master Black Belts. The number identified depends on the business priorities, but the rule of thumb is 1 Champion per business group and 1 Master Black Belt for every 30 Black Belts.	
Phase Two	Champions and Master Black Belts are trained in Six Sigma Breakthrough Strategy. A deployment plan is developed and presented by each business group.	General Awareness Training and Communication
Phase Three	Champions and Master Black Belts identify the first "wave" of projects, and select Black Belts and cross-functional teams.	
Phase Four	Master Blacks Belts receive additional training. They are "trained to train" Black Belts and others who will be applying the Breakthrough Strategy.	
Phase Five	Black Belts begin training and the first wave of projects is launched.	
Phase Six	Experienced Black Belts being training Green Belts.	

THE ROLES OF SIX SIGMA BREAKTHROUGH STRATEGY PLAYERS

CHAMPIONS	MASTER BLACK BELTS
Create the vision of Six Sigma for the company.	Understand the big business picture.
Define the path to implement Six Sigma across the organization.	Partner with the Champions.
Develop a comprehensive training plan for implementing the Breakthrough Strategy.	Get certified as Master Black Belts.
Carefully select high-impact projects.	Develop and deliver training to various levels of the organization.
Support development of "statistical thinking."	Assist in the identification of projects.
Ask Black Belts many questions to ensure that they are properly focused.	Coach and support Black Belts in project work.
Realize the gains by supporting Six Sigma projects through allocation of resources and removal of roadblocks.	Participate in project reviews to offer technical expertise.
Hold the ground by implementing Black Belt recommendations.	Help train and certify Black Belts.
Make sure that project opportunities are acted upon by the organization's leadership and the finance department.	Take on leadership of major programs.
Recognize people for their efforts.	Facilitate sharing of best practices across the corporation.
Champion training is one week.	Master Black Belt training consists of two one-week sessions.

THE ROLES OF SIX SIGMA BREAKTHROUGH STRATEGY PLAYERS

BLACK BELTS	GREEN BELTS
Act as Breakthrough Strategy experts and be Breakthrough Strategy enthusiasts.	Function as Green Belts on a part-time basis, while performing their regular duties.
Stimulate Champion thinking.	Participate on Black Belt project teams in the context of their existing responsibilities.
Identify the barriers.	
Lead and direct teams in project execution.	Learn the Six Sigma methodology as it applies to a particular project.
Report progress to appropriate leadership levels.	Continue to learn and practice the Six Sigma methods and tools after project completion.
Solicit help from Champions when needed.	
Influence without direct authority.	Green Belt training consists of two three-day sessions with three weeks in between.
Determine the most effective tools to apply.	
Prepare a detailed project assessment during the Measurement phase.	
Get input from knowledgeable operators, first-line supervisors, and team leaders.	
Teach and coach Breakthrough Strategy methods and tools.	
Manage project risk.	
Ensure that the results are sustained.	

CHAPTER ELEVEN

Six Sigma Black Belts

We will select from among our best people, give them four months of intense problem-solving training, and assign them full time to lead teams to solve our toughest problems. The result of this activity will enhance customer satisfaction and dramatically improve the operational and financial performance of our company.

—SEAGATE

Every company faces the issue of finding the right people to help grow the business. Six Sigma creates opportunities for people to learn new skills and try new things that they might not otherwise have the opportunity to do. Black Belts develop a very unique and valuable skill set as they work their projects. Not only do they hone their analytical skills and tactics, but they also develop practical, real-life leadership skills. They become change agents.

—BRUCE MIYASHITA, DIRECTOR, STRATEGIC INITIATIVES, BOMBARDIER

Organizations are built around individuals and their knowledge, not just around philosophies or programs. So it stands to reason that successfully implementing the Breakthrough Strategy depends on people. Strategy alone cannot make a better company, but strategy coupled with the right people will. In the end, it's people that increase profitability. Few choices are more important than selecting and developing the right people to lead your organization through the Breakthrough Strategy at all levels—business, operations, and process.

While the Six Sigma methodology trains individuals as Champions, Master Black Belts, Black Belts, and Green Belts, the bulk of implementing the Breakthrough Strategy rests on Black Belts. Black Belts possess the Six Sigma knowledge and skills necessary to implement, sustain, and lead a highly focused Six Sigma initiative within a target business area or unit. Training employees in the Breakthrough Strategy ensures that Six Sigma methodology and philosophy are disseminated throughout the company, and that the technical expertise to implement the Breakthrough Strategy is available to help companies achieve Six Sigma. Because Black Belts are so pivotal to Six Sigma's success, we will discuss their roles in greater detail.

What Does a Black Belt Do?

Black Belts characterize and optimize key processes that exert undue influence on the business landscape. They identify and execute projects that will reduce errors and defects in industrial and commercial processes, and in products and services. Black Belts can help do such things as reduce labor, material, cycle time, and inventory. These improvements are then accounted for by the finance department, in order to validate the extent of the Six Sigma returns. By applying each phase of the Breakthrough Strategy's Measure, Analyze, Improve, and Control phases (M-A-I-C), Black Belts can solve problems by identifying and focusing on the key factors at the root of causation.

Why the Name "Black Belts"?

The term "Black Belts" was coined by Mike in the mid-1980s, while consulting to the printed circuit board operation at Unisys Corpora-

BLACK BELTS PERFORM THE FOLLOWING TASKS	
MENTOR	Cultivate a network of Six Sigma individuals at the local organization or site
TEACH	Provide formal training of local personnel in new strategies and tools
COACH	Provide one-on-one support to local personnel
TRANSFER	Pass on new strategies and tools in the form of training, workshops, case studies, and local symposia
DISCOVER	Find application opportunities for Six Sigma strategies and tools, both internal and external (e.g., suppliers and customers)
IDENTIFY	Highlight/surface business opportunities through partnerships with other organizations
INFLUENCE	Sell the organization on the use of Six Sigma strategies and tools

tion in Salt Lake City. It was there that the first Black Belts were trained and deployed. The term designated project leaders trained in statistical problem solving. Its roots lie in the parallels between the physical sport of karate and the implementation of the Six Sigma Breakthrough Strategy. Both karate and the Six Sigma Breakthrough Strategy depend on mental discipline and systematic, intensive training. Just as Black Belts in karate depend on power, speed, and decisiveness, Six Sigma Black Belts depend on the resources of their company behind them, and their own personal mental concentration and agility to juggle multiple projects and complete them quickly. And similar to karate Black Belts, who must continually reposition their bodies quickly as their center of gravity changes, Black Belts must be able to physically and mentally reposition themselves as they move from project to project.

Why Are Black Belts Important?

Black Belts can dramatically raise an organization's sigma level while delivering financial gains to the bottom line. They stimulate management thinking by posing new ways of doing things, challenge conventional wisdom by demonstrating successful applications of new methodologies, seek out and pilot new tools, create innovative strategies, and train others to follow in their footsteps. They have to be patient, persuasive, imaginative, and creative. They need the respect of front-line employees, those in supervisory positions, and middle and senior management if they are to manage risk, set direction, and pave the way to breakthrough profitability. Most important, they translate intention into reality and help to sustain it. They clarify an organization's purpose and funnel that clarity into specific Black Belt projects.

Becoming a successful Black Belt requires not only intellectual ability and drive, but the desire and tenacity to rethink and relearn the business. Most organizations have a reservoir of talented people open to new challenges who would welcome the opportunity to be part of something that will make a difference. Giving people the opportunity to become Black Belts allows them the opportunity to satisfy their ambition and shine within the company.

The Breakthrough Strategy requires that Black Belts do more than successfully manage a project. It also means taking responsibility for achieving financial targets set at considerably higher levels. They have to know that the coming weeks and months will require them to continuously measure their project's performance so that they can spot unexpected variances and anticipate appropriate actions. They have to use "radar" to detect potential bottlenecks. They have to know when to spend money, what to spend it on, and not be afraid to spend it. As stated in Chapter 10, executives and Champions worry about *what* gets done, and Master Black Belts and Black Belts worry about *how* things get done. Similarly, while executives measure Black Belt projects solely in terms of money and customer satisfaction, Black Belts measure not only money but defects, process capability, and variation.

Building the skills to apply the Six Sigma methodology within an organization requires that those selected for Black Belt training want not only to *learn* the Breakthrough Strategy but to *practice* it.

What Kinds of Results Can Black Belts Return to the Bottom Line?

Companies can expect to reap at least $150,000 to $175,000 per Black Belt project, although we see many Black Belts average closer to a savings of $230,000 per project. A fully trained Black Belt will deliver a minimum of $600,000 to well over $1,000,000 in direct cost savings and productivity improvements to the bottom line each year by completing, in succession, an average of four to six projects annually, or approximately one project every two to three months. The length of time it takes for a Black Belt to complete a project depends on the scope and complexity of the project, the availability of the proper measurement equipment, and how much money has been budgeted for the project. Even a Black Belt's training project is designed to return cash to the bottom line. As Black Belts become more experienced, they can take on projects in parallel by leveraging Green Belts and thus dramatically increase bottom-line results.

Crane Co. implemented the Six Sigma Breakthrough Strategy in 1997, training twenty Crane employees from various companies. Crane estimate that each of these new Black Belts will save his or her company $400,000 per year, adding to the overall bottom line and strengthening the competitive position of the respective businesses.

As Black Belts bolster their company's financial position, the message of Six Sigma self-propagates within the organization. A healthy form of competitiveness sets in, and as individuals begin to see that others can achieve success and be rewarded for it, they will want the opportunity to strive for these results as well.

Black Belt Training

Black Belt training is divided into four instructional sessions; each session is organized around one of the four core phases (Measure-Analyze-Improve-Control) contained within the Breakthrough Strategy. Black Belt training takes place over a four-month period, with one week devoted to classroom instruction for each phase of the Breakthrough Strategy, followed by three weeks devoted to applying that knowledge to an assigned project. After three weeks of hands-on work, Black Belt trainees and their respective projects are reviewed before the trainees return to the classroom to learn about the next phase of the strategy and how it applies to their project. This process continues until Black Belt trainees have completed each of the four phases and have successfully applied their knowledge to a specific project. A traditional proverb has it that an ounce of practice is worth a pound of preaching. Even with proper training, it will take Black Belts two or three projects before they become truly adept at using the Breakthrough Strategy tools and understanding how the concepts link together. Black Belts need about twelve months of practice to become fully proficient in the Breakthrough Strategy. Once Black Belts are certified, they can guide others in applying the Breakthrough Strategy to selected projects.

A Black Belt's program of study follows the Six Sigma Plan-Train-Apply-Review (P-T-A-R) model, and works as a closed-loop feedback system.

After Champions select potential Black Belts and assign them their initial projects, training can begin. Black Belts spend one week learning each phase of the Breakthrough Strategy with three weeks between each of the four weeklong sessions to apply their knowledge of the phase they have just learned to their assigned project. Training extends over a four-month period, with project reviews in Week Two, Week Three, and Week Four.

The Black Belt's program of study focuses on an understanding of the Six Sigma philosophy, theory, tactics, Breakthrough Strategy, and

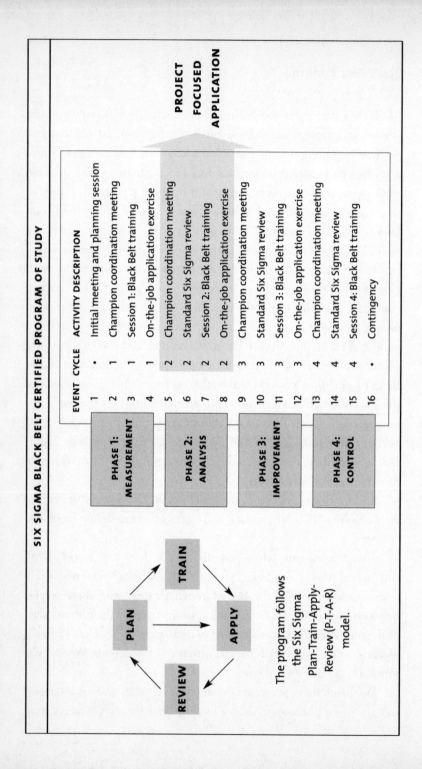

SIX SIGMA BLACK BELT CERTIFIED PROGRAM OF STUDY

EVENT	CYCLE	ACTIVITY DESCRIPTION
1	•	Initial meeting and planning session
2	1	Champion coordination meeting
3	1	Session 1: Black Belt training
4	1	On-the-job application exercise
5	2	Champion coordination meeting
6	2	Standard Six Sigma review
7	2	Session 2: Black Belt training
8	2	On-the-job application exercise
9	3	Champion coordination meeting
10	3	Standard Six Sigma review
11	3	Session 3: Black Belt training
12	3	On-the-job application exercise
13	4	Champion coordination meeting
14	4	Standard Six Sigma review
15	4	Session 4: Black Belt training
16	•	Contingency

PROJECT FOCUSED APPLICATION

PHASE 1: MEASUREMENT

PHASE 2: ANALYSIS

PHASE 3: IMPROVEMENT

PHASE 4: CONTROL

PLAN

TRAIN

APPLY

REVIEW

The program follows the Six Sigma Plan-Train-Apply-Review (P-T-A-R) model.

application tools. Particular emphasis is placed on the breakthrough tools—statistics, quantitative benchmarking, process-control techniques, Design of Experiments, and so on. As Black Belts go through the training process, they discover how the key tools are blended and sequenced to form a scientific and repeatable process for solving any industrial or commercial problem.

A BLACK BELT'S COURSE OF STUDY	
THE TWELVE M-A-I-C OBJECTIVES	
MEASURE the Frequency of Defects	Select critical-to-quality characteristics (CTQs) Define performance standards Validate measurement systems
ANALYZE When and Where Defects Occur	Establish product capability Define performance objectives Identify variation sources
IMPROVE the Process	Screen potential causes Discover variable relationship Establish operating tolerances
CONTROL the Process So That It Stays Fixed	Validate measurement system Determine process capability Implement process controls

Security Is for Insecure People

Being a Black Belt requires being a risk taker. Black Belts also need leadership skills. One of the Black Belt's greatest challenges is to get others to practice new behaviors. Although leadership skills are crucial to a successful Black Belt, their roles have little to do with that of a traditional manager.* Black Belts focus on teaching and coaching employees to analyze and control the processes they work on. Time

---

*Learning leadership skills should be part of the Black Belt certification program.

that was once spent expediting production, responding to crises, or micromanagement of processes is now devoted to studying, thinking, and learning about applying bold new innovations to solving problems and increasing profitability, as well as coaching others to think and act in the same way. Black Belt leadership means applying the Breakthrough Strategy and teaching it to others, hour after hour, day after day—in other words, living it.

It takes an exceptional individual to be an effective Black Belt and to sponsor and implement a venture as powerful as the Breakthrough Strategy. Black Belts must sustain extraordinary levels of energy and focus. Many find the process of developing the necessary critical thinking skills to be a life-altering experience; they no longer evaluate situations, address problems, or communicate potential solutions the way they did before their training. As Black Belts move from project to project and the results of their efforts compound, the way they approach and solve problems is permanently transformed.

Over time, Black Belts either become Master Black Belts and eventually move into management or leadership positions, or they transfer their skills to another area while moving up in the organization. Typically, a Black Belt serves a two-year tour of duty. Given the intensity of their roles, this approach has proven to work very well.

Black Belt Selection

Identifying and selecting Black Belts is a challenging process. A great many are unable to perform at the level of intensity necessary for the Black Belt role. Managers and technically oriented people who understand the potential of Six Sigma and are frustrated by past management practices may be good candidates for Black Belt training. In general, we have found that the best Black Belt candidates are those already oriented in their organization's products, services, and processes. When adequately trained and technically supported, they can serve as change agents, internal consultants, and mentors, and they can assist the Six

Sigma Champions. However, newcomers to an organization who lack corporate experience and historical knowledge of the organization often bring fresh perspectives and the drive needed to overcome a company's history. Knowing when and how to create the right mix of old and new employees is the role of the Champion.

To bring about cultural changes and make sizable improvements using Six Sigma, we have found Black Belts should remain in their positions for a minimum of two years, and generally not more than three years. Here are some of the characteristics that we have found make an effective Black Belt leader:

CHARACTERISTICS OF SIX SIGMA BLACK BELTS
• Highly respected by superiors, peers, and subordinates
• Understands the "big picture" of the business
• Focuses on results and understands the importance of the bottom line
• Speaks the language of management (money, time, organizational dynamics, etc.)
• Committed to doing whatever it takes to excel
• Sponsored by a vice president, director, or business unit manager
• Is an expert in his or her specific field
• Possesses excellent communication skills, both written and verbal
• Inspires others to excel
• Challenges others to be creative
• Capable of consulting, mentoring, and coaching
• Drives change by challenging conventional wisdom, developing and applying new methodologies, and creating innovative strategies
• Possesses a creative, critical, out-of-box intellect
• Allows room for failures and mistakes with a recovery plan
• Accepts responsibility for choices
• Views criticism as a kick in the caboose that moves you a step forward

CHARACTERISTICS OF SIX SIGMA BLACK BELTS (cont.)
• Encourages commitment, dedication, and teamwork
• Unites and inspires a team to a core purpose
• Able to communicate all sides of an issue
• Solicits diverse ideas and viewpoints
• Empathizes
• Promotes win-win solutions
• Disagrees tactfully and does not overreact
• Acts decisively under pressure
• Anticipates and confronts problems early and corrects causes
• Effectively identifies priorities from a business standpoint
• Manages limited resources in a highly efficient and effective manner
• Careful not to assign an unrealistic number of tasks to any team member
• Understands and respects that people have limitations
• Displays a genuine concern and sensitivity toward others
• More concerned about business success than personal gain
• Does not lord his or her expertise over others
• Recognizes that results count more than fancy titles and silk nightshirts

The above criteria represent a set of guidelines few Black Belts can meet. The guidelines, however, are intended to idealize the position and indicate the general traits a Champion should look for when selecting Black Belts.

How Many Black Belts Does an Organization Need?

There are several ways to answer this question. But since different factors apply to different companies, the answer requires some sort of organizational assessment. Invariably, when people think of sending trained individuals into an organization for any type of improvement, they think of a group the size of a SWAT team. Once they start to assess what they need, they begin to find that they will need to muster a legion more the size of a small army.

A company's financial goals also influence the number of Black Belts needed. Although there is no single equation for success, experience has shown the rule of thumb to be roughly one Black Belt per one hundred employees in industrial sectors and one Black Belt per fifty employees in commercial sectors. One Master Black Belt is needed per business unit and/or site, or approximately one Master Black Belt per one thousand employees. Although Master Black Belts can train one hundred Black Belts a year, they should never have more than thirty Black Belts reporting to them at a single time. Another way to determine the number of Black Belts and Master Black Belts an organization needs is through a simple calculation.

REVENUES ÷ 1,000,000 = NUMBER OF BLACK BELTS
NUMBER OF BLACK BELTS ÷ 10 = NUMBER OF MASTER BLACK BELTS

Using the above calculation, a company with $1 billion in annual revenues would need one hundred full-time Black Belts and ten Master Black Belts. Of course, the number of Champions depends on how an organization chooses to deploy Six Sigma—is it by geographic location, a particular product line, and so on.

Another way to calculate how many Black Belts an organization needs is to determine what the organization wants its level of dollar savings to be. For example, a company with $1.5 billion in annual revenues may decide it wants to show a Six Sigma savings of $250 million over a five-year period, or a savings of $50 million per year. Assuming that *each* Black Belt project will save the company $175,000, 286 Black Belt projects would have to be completed *each year* to generate a five-year savings of $250 million. Keeping in mind that a Black Belt can complete five projects a year, a company would need fifty-seven full-time Black Belts to meet its annual savings goal of $50 million.

There are other factors that determine the number of Black Belts needed. If the business, for example, is composed of small factories within the same geographic location, fewer Black Belts may be needed. On the other hand, if the business is composed of many small factories spread across a geographically diverse area, additional Black Belts may be needed. Answering the following key questions can provide additional insights:

- Why is your company implementing Six Sigma?

- Is it to remove defects? Is it to improve customer satisfaction?

- Is it to improve delivery time? Is it to extract costs from the organization?

- How is your company laid out?

- Are you divided by product or by location?

- How does your product mix vary from one geographical location to another?

- Is English the organization's principal language?

Companies with strong-willed, knowledgeable people trained as Black Belts will find that such people can work Black Belt projects faster and take them to a greater depth than can Black Belts in other companies. Companies whose Black Belts aren't as aggressive, who lack the support of their management, who become mired in corporate politics, or who are weak in technical knowledge will need more Black Belts to reap the same rate of return in the same period of time, or will have to wait longer to get the same benefits from implementing Six Sigma. Although each Black Belt project will have different levels of return, most companies can plan on seeing positive cumulative financial results from their Six Sigma investment by the end of the second year of implementation.

Should Companies Train Black Belts
or Hire from the Outside?

It is unlikely that a large company will be able to find enough Black Belts on the outside to hire. And even when a Black Belt from outside the company is hired, there is a risk that the person, although a certified Black Belt, will not fit in with the corporate culture. New to the organization, and under pressure to succeed in the Black Belt projects, the person also has to familiarize himself with the company's culture and history.

In a number of companies, Six Sigma is now part of the genetic code for future leadership, and in some cases, as we have shown, is an ironclad prerequisite for promotion to any professional or managerial position and a requirement for stock option awards. In such organizations Master Black Belts and Black Belts who have completed Six Sigma assignments have become the most sought-after candidates for senior leadership jobs.

Summary

Since people, not programs, achieve results, it takes people trained in the Breakthrough Strategy to implement the methodology. Black Belts must be allowed to dedicate 100 percent of their time to tackling Six Sigma projects. Less than 100 percent dedication of a Black Belt's time will result in lower financial returns over longer periods of time. Whereas training in the Breakthrough Strategy tools is fundamental to Black Belts' success, they also need the time and human and financial resources to allow them to work effectively to improve the industrial or commercial processes within a corporation. Only by unleashing the power of trained Six Sigma Black Belts can a company hope to move forward quickly and with the greatest possible impact.

ONE COMPANY'S EXPERIENCE:

AlliedSignal's Journey to Six Sigma

We've taken the difficult but basic Six Sigma skill of reducing defects and applied it to every business process, from inventing and commercializing a new product all the way to billing and collections after the product is delivered. Just as we think we've generated the last dollar of profit out of a business, we uncover new ways to harvest cash as we reduce cycle times, lower inventories, increase output, and reduce scrap. The results are better and more competitively priced products, more satisfied customers who give us more business—and improved cash flow.

—LAWRENCE A. BOSSIDY,
1998 ALLIEDSIGNAL ANNUAL REPORT

AlliedSignal was the first corporation to implement the Breakthrough Strategy as we know it today. In the process of working toward Six Sigma it learned some powerful lessons about training employees and applying Breakthrough Strategy principles to achieve Six Sigma quality.

A Brief History of AlliedSignal's Journey Toward Quality

AlliedSignal's 70,000 employees manufacture and design a steady stream of highly profitable products, including chemicals, fibers, plastics, and aerospace and automotive products. Like many organizations implementing Six Sigma, AlliedSignal had already attempted quality initiatives, with mixed results. Its pursuit of quality was accelerated when Lawrence A. Bossidy left General Electric in 1991 to take over an ailing AlliedSignal as CEO. He immediately set about paring corporate fat, motivating employees, and setting formidable financial targets. In the course of achieving those targets, AlliedSignal went from having a market value of $4 billion in 1991 to a market value of $29 billion by the end of 1998, and expects this figure to surpass $38 billion by the year 2000, largely as a result of Six Sigma initiatives. Allied's goals today are equally ambitious:

- 6%+ productivity

- 99.8% on-time delivery

- Reduced inventory

- Full-capacity utilization

- Little or no overtime

- Reliable products

- Five sigma manufacturing

- Five sigma designs

- Predictable cash flow

- Five sigma suppliers

By the end of 1998, the total impact of Six Sigma within Allied Signal reached the $2 billion mark. Today, AlliedSignal is realizing Six

Sigma profits in its service areas as well, including order processing, shipping, procurement, and product innovation.

"Innovation is the underpinning of perpetuating an organization," says Bossidy. At the end of 1998, the CEO began pushing the company to achieve $3 billion to $4 billion in new products by the year 2000, boosting the company's revenues to $18.5 billion. As a result, Six Sigma has become increasingly crucial to AlliedSignal's new-product development. (1) It allows the company to increase its success rate in new-product development. (2) It has helped the company reduce cycle time and get new products to market faster. (3) Reduced cycle time has reduced overhead, making Allied more productive with fewer resources. Overall, Six Sigma has saved AlliedSignal $1.5 billion since the program was implemented. Savings in 1998 alone were $500 million, and are expected to reach $600 million in 1999.

With Six Sigma as AlliedSignal's standard of excellence, the company has improved its performance, efficiency, and quality. During the summer of 1997, for example, a mysterious shutdown of the Boeing 777 air supply control system manufactured by AlliedSignal occurred four times within six weeks—each time on a different airline. In each case, loss of cabin pressure forced the pilot to perform an emergency descent. With AlliedSignal's reputation on the line, a cross-functional team of more than 85 employees, customers, and suppliers, led by Aerospace Equipment Systems, used the Six Sigma Breakthrough Strategy to diagnose the problem and develop an innovative, cost-effective software solution in 90 days. Not only did AlliedSignal please Boeing, its customer, but it also helped Boeing's customers avoid tens of millions of dollars in potential lost revenue. Moreover, AlliedSignal avoided spending hundreds of thousands of dollars in development and retrofit costs.

We can't tell other organizations how to do Six Sigma, but we can tell them how not to do it. Allied has made mistakes along the way and, in the process, learned some tremendous lessons.

Lessons Learned

LESSON ONE: THE ORGANIZATION'S
LEADERSHIP MUST OWN SIX SIGMA

Although AlliedSignal's upper management supported Six Sigma upon its introduction, and understood that by training employees in the Breakthrough Strategy they could create a common purpose throughout the organization, managers below top management didn't understand how the Breakthrough Strategy worked. They viewed Six Sigma as the new flavor-of-the-month initiative foisted on them from on high, and they saw Black Belts as nuisances.

Many AlliedSignal sites complained that they were being inundated with initiatives, starting with Total Quality in 1991, and following with Materials Management, Customer Excellence, and other programs. The first thing AlliedSignal did was to make Six Sigma Breakthrough Strategy the foundation for everything it did, and used the other "initiatives" to enhance the Six Sigma. Even so, AlliedSignal discovered initially that its project management teams did not have a clear understanding of how individual initiatives can be used to enhance the Six Sigma foundation. The problem was compounded by the fact that Black Belts began talking to managers using Six Sigma terminology, confusing those they were trying to make part of the team.

AlliedSignal realized that *all* levels of management needed to be introduced to Six Sigma so that they understood the methods of the Breakthrough Strategy and understood how to utilize the experience and training of the Black Belts effectively. To get their managers on the same page, AlliedSignal began holding weeklong managers' training sessions so that leaders could reach an agreement on key business issues and decide how Six Sigma, in conjunction with other initiatives, could help them achieve their goals.

For the Six Sigma Breakthrough Strategy to take off within an organization, it must have upper management's full support. Senior management must have a clear idea of what the Breakthrough Strategy is and a guiding vision of how to pass that vision down through the organization. When an organization aligns its employees behind a clearly defined vision or purpose, that can have a powerful effect. AlliedSignal found that what the Black Belts trained at Six Sigma Academy needed most from senior management was direction, trust, and hope.

As AlliedSignal puzzled over how to get midlevel executives to change the way they looked at and solved problems, it found that getting people to think out of the box was difficult. Employees tended to ask traditional questions that focused on the symptoms—questions that concentrated on development and production schedules, meeting cost targets, and quality. As employees began to internalize the Six Sigma Breakthrough Strategy, they focused on questioning the root causes that drove costs, created defects, and affected customer satisfaction. Rather than reacting emotionally to a problem, they would focus immediately on data that would identify the problem so that they could come up with concrete solutions. Their questions invariably drove new behaviors in the organization.

As AlliedSignal Master Black Belts gradually were promoted to positions as vice presidents and directors, the company began to see these Black Belt standard-bearers help the company adopt new ways of thinking about and solving problems. The "new guard"'s innate understanding and support of the Six Sigma initiative helped to keep it moving forward. As AlliedSignal executives and managers became more knowledgeable about Six Sigma Breakthrough Strategy, performance expectations increased accordingly. Those autocrats who refused to change were gradually weeded out.

Focusing on Processes, Not People

AlliedSignal found that its managers and employees were better able to correct problems when they had a plan of action rather than just a blanket order to make something happen. Employees simply ordered to find a solution would leave meetings in a cold sweat, worried that their job was on the line, wondering how they were going to solve the problem. But when given the tools to ask the right questions, measure the right things, correlate a problem with a solution, and plan a course of action, they could find solutions to problems more easily. The Breakthrough Strategy creates an entirely different environment for problem solving. Using the tools provided by Breakthrough Strategy, problems are met with enthusiasm rather than fear and frustration. Because they have the tools necessary to fix whatever problems arise, employees are motivated by the thrill of learning to do their work in new and challenging ways, rather than the fear of finding that their skills have become obsolete.

In addition to generating dramatic financial results for Allied-Signal, Six Sigma has also changed the entire company culture, and the behavior of everyone from senior management to line workers.

> One of the flaws at Allied is that we had too much vertical mobility. Managers inch up the same smokestack, learning more and more about less and less. But companies that train promising individuals as Black Belts circumvent the vertical flow and move people around horizontally, having them serve time in as many major businesses or divisions as possible to give them a kaleidoscopic view of the organization and the benefit of being mentored by a variety of new blood.

Today, Allied feels that it has created a strong link between its goals, its vision of the company, and the activities that take place throughout the organization. By correlating processes throughout the organization to a specific sigma level, AlliedSignal has helped the company chart its course.

LESSON TWO: A BEGINNING WITHOUT AN END

Once AlliedSignal realized that all senior management needed some form of training in the Breakthrough Strategy, it dedicated the next year to training 1,000 leaders in the organization in how Six Sigma worked, and in its potential financial impact. Training sessions lasted for three and a half days and emphasized Six Sigma's impact on profitability through improved processes, as well as the crucial role of

Black Belts, rather than teaching statistical processes involved in achieving Six Sigma. They initially trained top management at each of AlliedSignal's eleven Strategic Business Units, and gradually worked their way down the organization to middle management, line supervisors, and so on. At the end of that first year, the company had been successfully educated about Six Sigma, and the Six Sigma training staff could move on to handling the grittier problems of training Black Belts and assigning the right number of Black Belts to individual projects, ensuring that each project's financial goals were achieved.

Six months later, however, those responsible for driving Six Sigma within AlliedSignal started to receive calls from Black Belts expressing familiar complaints: "My manager is not supportive." "I'm being asked the wrong questions." "I'm not getting any financial or team support." "My manager is firefighting instead of placing the problem in the context of a Black Belt project." When AlliedSignal's Six Sigma coordinators investigated, they found that many of the leaders they had trained were no longer in their previous positions; the Six Sigma coordinators were dealing with a sea of new faces.

Success had made AlliedSignal's management a target for other companies. Promotions, too, had resulted in a good deal of management turnover. It was at that point that AlliedSignal recognized that management training is never done. As one manager leaves, another must be trained to keep the Breakthrough Strategy vibrant and alive. Black Belt training, too, is an ongoing process, as Black Belts over time move on to other positions within the company, or leave the company altogether.

As Richard A. Johnson, director of Six Sigma, says, "We don't look at Six Sigma as a business process, but as a means to improve our business process. We've seen too many companies use TQM, Kaizen, and lean manufacturing as marketing ploys, allowing the initiatives to become business processes unto themselves. People started counting the number of Kaizen events, the number of quality teams or quality circles within a plant as the measure of their success. No one was looking at effectiveness or performance improvement and tying them to business performance measurements. Allied is not in the business of measuring activity. We are in the business of measuring results. If something doesn't have a positive impact on customer satisfaction, our shareholders, and employees, and in the process makes us lots of money, then we just flat out aren't going to do it."

LESSON THREE: BLACK BELT RETENTION

Three years ago I would compare a Black Belt's job to conducting a symphony. But as Allied has become more sophisticated in its use of the methodology, I now compare it to a jazz ensemble. Like an eclectic piece of jazz, there is more improvisation and almost an element of surprise in how our people use the tools to squeeze more dollars out of a project. In the process, I've also seen our Black Belts transition from a macho-like attitude to becoming maestros of innovation, finessing people to achieve their goals.

—RICHARD A. JOHNSON, DIRECTOR OF SIX SIGMA

AlliedSignal made significant investments in training its Black Belts, its best and brightest employees, and making them even better through Black Belt training. AlliedSignal's goal was to send Black Belts with a minimum of 18 to 24 months' experience mastering the Breakthrough Strategy back into the organization to re-create Six Sigma behavior and thinking throughout the company.

But the strategy started to backfire. Managers began to view Black Belts as white knights who, by brandishing their statistical swords, could increase production levels and profitability overnight. Despite the fact that Black Belts were recognized as one of their most valuable resources, they were prematurely pulled out of their Black Belt roles and placed in environments where there were fewer opportunities to encourage Six Sigma.

Black Belt attrition at AlliedSignal was the result of several causes. Forty percent of the Black Belts were promoted to positions as departmental and plant managers; others were enticed into higher-paying jobs by suppliers. In some instances, Black Belts completed only one or two projects before they were returned to their original, pre–Black Belt jobs. The reason came back to leadership's involvement. Leadership was not taking the time to review projects and act upon the financial opportunities created by Black Belts. As a result, managers felt that Six Sigma wasn't all that important.

AlliedSignal realized that without a significant time commitment, Six Sigma's success would falter and the company wouldn't reap the financial returns it expected. When AlliedSignal realized that an astonishing 50 percent of its Black Belts were being absorbed back into the organization within six months—long before their Six Sigma training had become profitable to the organization—it established a companywide policy that stipulated that Black Belts were required to dedicate a year and a half to two years to their new roles in spreading Six Sigma methodology before being transferred or promoted out of their assignment. Today, AlliedSignal reinforces the two-year commitment of Black Belts with stock awards, withholding promotions until Black Belts have completed their "tour of duty" and their projects have been reviewed by an assigned Champion.

AlliedSignal's director of Six Sigma, Richard Johnson, describes newly trained Black Belts as saplings who have not yet developed strong roots. Intellectually, they may understand the purpose of Six Sigma and the Breakthrough Strategy, but only after a series of implementations does the strategy reshape the way they interpret problems and do the tools become part of their thinking and practice. Today he sees AlliedSignal as a company blanketed with saplings and oak trees.

We wholeheartedly endorse AlliedSignal's decision to require Black Belts to work at least 18 to 24 months on a series of Six Sigma projects to give them a mature perspective on the Breakthrough Strategy. Like young medical doctors working their way through a surgical residency, Black Belts build speed and finesse as they continue to work on Six Sigma projects. AlliedSignal discovered that Black Belts need to go through several cycles of learning and applying the Breakthrough Strategy tools until the methodology becomes second nature. Only time and experience can develop their skills and expose them to a wide variety of problems, making them more efficient. Repeated learning experiences give Black Belts increased confidence in the Breakthrough Strategy's effectiveness. Moreover, the stories of their success tend to self-propagate across the organization.

AlliedSignal's Champions and Master Black Belts

Initially, AlliedSignal's Six Sigma Champions functioned as pseudo-management, working as translators and providing the link between the Black Belt community and the organization to ensure that the Six Sigma initiative was kept alive. As Champions worked full time to create cultural change, they also created an infrastructure to support the initiative until deployment was well under way.

The role of Champions at AlliedSignal is critical. AlliedSignal requires candidates to attend three and a half days of Six Sigma executive overview and participate in the traditional four-month Black Belt training process.

Master Black Belts are selected from the best of the Black Belts. Each Master Black Belt, in turn, is required to train and mentor ten Black Belts. Those ten Black Belts are then asked to train and mentor ten Green Belts. This domino effect has helped to achieve a rapid deployment of Six Sigma within the company. Until 1998, Green Belt training was not a company requirement; it was an optional program available to anyone interested. But the company has since indicated that it expects all salaried employees to undergo the 26 hours of training required for Green Belt certification by the year 2000.

ALLIEDSIGNAL EMPLOYEES TRAINED IN THE BREAKTHROUGH STRATEGY	
Champions	20
Master Black Belts	70
Black Belts	2,000+
Green Belts	18,000
Total number of employees	70,000 worldwide

LESSON FOUR: SUPPLIER CAPABILITY IS CRITICAL
TO THE SUCCESS OF THE BREAKTHROUGH STRATEGY

Like other companies, AlliedSignal has turned more and more to independent suppliers to provide many of the critical components contained in its products. Many companies' products are an amalgamation of goods made by a wide range of companies. Yet the quality of a product is no greater than the sum of its parts. While AlliedSignal allowed its suppliers more responsibility for the design and manufacture of critical components, it recognized that AlliedSignal's quality could suffer because of the increased variability in each supplier's manufacturing process. Regardless of how much AlliedSignal improved its own processes, lesser-quality components from a supplier could undermine the overall quality of a product.

AlliedSignal found that the majority of its suppliers operated at a three sigma capability, or well below the level AlliedSignal needed to reap the full benefits of a Six Sigma implementation. The company recognized that it needed to view its suppliers as partners in pursuing Six Sigma quality. Since a large percentage of suppliers are small businesses and lack the resources for Six Sigma training, AlliedSignal began training suppliers itself, and offering other technical assistance in order to ensure higher levels of quality and reliability in their operations.

The traditional management approach is to use as many suppliers as possible to hold down costs. To achieve Six Sigma, however, the only way to bring down costs is to use fewer suppliers, and limit them to those who have been trained in the Breakthrough Strategy's methodology. AlliedSignal not only trains suppliers in the Breakthrough Strategy, but it then follows up by dedicating its own Black Belts to mentor and work on a specific part or process with critical suppliers. Today, AlliedSignal estimates that for every 300 Black Belts it trains, 100 are either customers or suppliers. By training suppliers to apply the Breakthrough Strategy to problems rooted in their own factories, AlliedSignal has increased its savings from Six Sigma, and has eliminated many supplier-based problems that would create dissatisfied customers.

LESSON FIVE: THERE IS NO SUCH THING AS OPERATOR ERROR

Six Sigma is based on the belief that it is *processes,* rather than people, that fail. Traditional quality programs focus on correcting human error rather than process error. The Breakthrough Strategy is designed to change the process, not the person. Here is how Richard Johnson describes it:

> *You can see the "before" and "after" of an organization when Six Sigma grabs hold and takes place. Problem-solving meetings take on a different tone. Accusations are replaced with a palpable enthusiasm for finding the right solution. Problems become opportunities rather than obstacles that can't be overcome. An abatement of fear allows people to communicate differently. Problems no longer mean that people failed to perform, but that the process failed to perform.*
>
> *Focusing on defects rather than people required AlliedSignal to undergo a culture change. In the early 1990s, the Allied-Signal culture promoted the idea that defects were caused by people. Our response was to reprimand the operator, subject the operator to more training, or, in some cases, replace the operator. In 1994, as our culture began to shift so that processes, not people, were blamed, we began to give people the tools and opportunities to make improvements.*

When employees are able to accept that there are only faulty processes, rather than faulty people, the floodgates open for the exchange of more information. People no longer try to hide their perceived shortcomings or mistakes. When people realize excuses aren't necessary, and they have the leeway to ask new questions, as well as the tools to identify causes and create solutions, individual defenses break down. "If you look at the entire philosophy of Six Sigma—questions drive behavior, measure the Xs, and focus on processes rather than people—management can't help but change the culture of an organization," notes Richard Johnson. "Our goal is to allow great people the opportunity to use Six Sigma, thus creating continual profitability and growth. We want to continue to be the hallmark of quality by which our competitors worldwide benchmark themselves."

LESSON SIX: FOCUS ON BOTTOM-LINE IMPROVEMENT

The number-one failure in deploying Six Sigma, AlliedSignal discovered, is not due to poor training or selecting the wrong candidates for Black Belt training. It is the result of a lack of commitment from the organization's leadership. Bottom-line results are 100 percent contingent on leadership's involvement. In Lesson One, we discussed the importance of an organization's leadership in understanding Six Sigma. But upper management must also involve the finance department in such a way that opportunities created by Black Belts return a profit to the bottom line. If an organization's leadership is unaware of the improvements being made, if they do not act upon the opportunities created for the organization by their Black Belts, if they fail to involve the organization's financial operations, the initiative will fail. Regardless of how savings from Black Belt projects are used, the finance department needs to be involved to ensure that cost savings are actually being reflected in the bottom line, and perhaps being reallocated.

Black Belts, the finance department, and the executive leadership of an organization can work in tandem to ensure that Six Sigma is a profitable endeavor. While Black Belts create opportunities for cost reduction and increased profitability, the company's leadership must make sure that Black Belts focus on the right projects and take action on the savings opportunities they generate. Finance provides closure to the effort by ensuring that the savings are returned to the organization's bottom line.

In 1994, AlliedSignal emphasized the technical side of Black Belt training. Today, it trains Black Belts to be much broader in their outlook. A large part of a Black Belt's role is to create improvement opportunities. But AlliedSignal does not hold Black Belts responsible for creating financial savings. Although the Breakthrough Strategy will produce opportunities for savings (reduced scrap, reduced rework, and reduced cycle time), these cost savings are effective only when returned to the bottom line. A Black Belt may generate a project cost savings of $1 million in materials and find that the job can be done with fewer people. But unless management takes corrective action by reducing material purchases accordingly and decreasing employee head-count, the project's net savings will be zero. Again, the role of the Black Belt is to create the opportunity for the company to save money, not to change purchasing requirements or lay off employees. It is management's responsibility to act upon the opportunities created by the Black Belts.

LESSON SEVEN: INITIATIVE OVERLOAD

> One of the things I have trouble with is . . . nonfinancial objectives. Often they're just as obscure and vacuous as they sound.
>
> —LAWRENCE A. BOSSIDY

AlliedSignal CEO Larry Bossidy has two mantras: "Total quality" and "Make the numbers." Yet he describes quality improvement programs as a way to survive, not a way to prosper. Bossidy's aversion to "refinement" programs supports his fear that people can too easily get caught up in form rather than substance. Although Bossidy sees nothing inherently wrong with quality programs, he quickly grows impatient with those that focus on customer satisfaction and continuous improvement while ignoring the end results—making the numbers. Six Sigma has provided substantial cost savings for AlliedSignal, but more important, it set the stage for even greater improvements in the future.

Although organizations can achieve powerful results from Six Sigma Breakthrough Strategy, renewal is the key to sustaining long-term results. AlliedSignal has identified five actions that it believes are critical to perpetuating Six Sigma within the organization.

- **Training.** AlliedSignal's employee base changes enough every nine to ten months, as employees are lost through attrition, promotion,

or retirement, that new employees need training in the Breakthrough Strategy to maintain the Six Sigma culture.

- Senior management involvement.

- Continued on-site leadership training, and alignment of goals
  among divisions to reinforce Breakthrough Strategy thinking and
  goals.

- Requiring Black Belts to dedicate a minimum of two years to working Six Sigma projects.

- Supplier improvement in Six Sigma initiatives.

Since Six Sigma was kicked off in November 1994, no one at
AlliedSignal has preached Six Sigma with more fervor or passion than
Larry Bossidy himself. The AlliedSignal CEO has been known to
postpone business trips to speak to Black Belt candidates during their
training sessions at the company's Morristown headquarters.

What nuggets of wisdom does this physically imposing CEO,
whose intellect and business instincts closely match Jack Welch's,
share with Black Belt candidates during closed-door sessions? While
reiterating that the Black Belt's role is ultimately to help maintain
AlliedSignal's position as the premier manufacturer of auto parts, aerospace equipment, and chemicals, he emphasizes that Black Belts are
not the company's silver bullet. He drives home the message that the
company can never stop listening to its customer. Improving products
and processes is not an end unto itself, he warns. The greatest strength
of Six Sigma, he claims, lies in its ability to develop critical thinking
among management at all levels. Products and services should be
improved *only* to the degree that customer value is increased. Over the
course of an hourlong speech, Bossidy's message is beat home like a
drumbeat: Six Sigma is a program designed to generate money for the
company, either through savings resulting from reduced costs, or from
boosting sales by increasing customer satisfaction.

Today executives at AlliedSignal spend a great deal of their time
thinking about new sources of earnings growth for their company, and

Six Sigma has been an important factor in their drive for higher profits. Larry Bossidy's goal is to see the company reach a five sigma level
before his retirement in the year 2000.

Summary

We believe that AlliedSignal's lessons are applicable to any organization implementing Six Sigma. There are obstacles that can hinder or
prevent organizations from achieving the kind of substantial and lasting business performance improvements they should expect from Six
Sigma Breakthrough Strategy. The most common are:

- working on too many improvements at the same time
- not having someone accountable for the problem
- not being a process-based company
- a lack of trained and experienced people
- middle managers who fear uncertainty about future roles
- a lack of metrics focused on customer value-added processes
- a lack of integrated information and financial systems
- fragmented, staff-driven approaches—"alphabet stew"

By avoiding these potential pitfalls that can slow or impede the
successful implementation of Six Sigma, and by following the guidelines AlliedSignal has identified that help sustain and perpetuate Six
Sigma quality, companies adopting Six Sigma should see dramatic
improvements in their long-term profitability.

CHAPTER TWELVE

Six Sigma and the Service Industry

■　　■　　■　　■　　■　　■

How often have you dealt with a company that has high-quality products, but its service is so poor that you've considered taking your business elsewhere? According to Robert W. Galvin, former Motorola CEO and COB, failing to implement Six Sigma in commercial areas with the same force that the company implemented it in its industrial sectors cost $5 billion over a four-year period. Today, companies such as General Electric, AlliedSignal, and Sony realize that they consist of complex operations containing many processes—some processes produce products sold to the customer and other processes create services. As a result, these companies and others are applying the Breakthrough Strategy to the commercial sides of their businesses, with enormous improvements to the bottom line.

A Quick History of Service Quality

Most commercial processes have developed from a company's need to facilitate the production of manufactured goods. Industrial companies developed their commercial processes quickly, almost as a knee-jerk reaction to customer demands or a growing employee population. They were relegated to the back offices, and rarely the target of quality programs. But as companies grew, more commercial processes and services were needed, and additional checks and balances were put in place. Employees did not understand how their work overlapped or how it affected internal and external customers. Service departments became inefficient, labor-intensive, time-consuming, and costly.

Their fundamental purpose—to effectively and efficiently service internal and external customers—was not recognized, and the fact that their processes were subject to variation at enormous costs to the company was not measured and, consequently, not understood.

Today, more than 79 percent of the U.S. workforce is employed by commercial businesses, and 90 percent of those employed in manufacturing are actually doing service work, such as finance, marketing, sales, distribution, and purchasing within their industrial divisions. Despite the high number of service employees, some companies still believe that improving commercial processes is less important than improving industrial processes, or that seemingly intangible commercial processes cannot be controlled. Both beliefs are wrong. First, customers are more likely to take their business elsewhere because of poor service than a poor product, and, second, companies like GE and AlliedSignal have shown that improving internal and external commercial processes adds significantly to the bottom line and customer satisfaction.

Service constitutes a large portion of any industrial company's costs. Industrial organizations will find that by applying the Breakthrough Strategy to all processes—whether they are design, engineering, industrial, or service—they create an opportunity to increase market share. Since commercial processes such as sales, human resources, field service, and so on have relied less on science and technology to improve performance than have design divisions or sectors focused on engineering and manufacturing, the need for the Breakthrough Strategy in these sectors is even stronger.

The service industry contains many invisible processes. That is because its "products" are not as tangible as those that come off a factory line. Accounts receivable transactions, for example, can have over twenty process steps. The Six Sigma methodology breaks service transactions into individual process steps in order to create greater efficiency at lower costs. Smooth and efficient transactions translate into faster response time to inquiries, greater speed and accuracy in the ways inventory and materials are supplied, and foolproof support processes so that errors, inaccuracies, and inefficiencies are eliminated.

As we read about in the section on General Electric, General Electric's Capital Services Group has applied the Six Sigma methodology to reduce the backroom costs of selling consumer loans, credit card insurance, and payment protection. "Although Six Sigma was originally designed for manufacturing," says Denis Nayden, president and COO of GE Capital, "it can be applied to transactional services. One obvious example is in making sure the millions of credit card and other bills GE sends to customers are correct, which drives down our costs of making adjustments. One of our biggest costs in the financial business is winning new customers. If we treat them well, they will stay with us, reducing our customer-origination costs."

Cycle time and customer satisfaction are two important components in determining the level of service quality and associated costs. A hospital, for example, can determine commercial quality costs by measuring the cycle time of admitting a patient into the hospital. By measuring the total cycle time for filling out paperwork, taking the patient's medical history, preliminary testing, and room assignment, a cost can be attached to it. In doing so, the cost of errors associated with the process can be identified, as well. Incorrect or incomplete paperwork, transposition errors, and patient retesting are all examples of commercial quality costs in hospital environments.

Surgical procedures in an outpatient surgery center could be evaluated to determine the number of successful operations and number of operations performed without complications. Customer satisfaction (the patient's and the patient's family) could be measured by degree of comfort and lack of pain experienced by the patient, the length of time it takes hospital staff to respond to the patient's call button, the accuracy of diagnosis and prognosis, and billing errors.

Finding the right performance metrics and indices of capability and then learning what commercial defects to track is traditionally a tricky area for commercial businesses only because "they don't know what they don't know." However, the application of Six Sigma to transactional processes is even more straightforward than it is for manufacturing and engineering processes. The misunderstanding often results because commercial businesses are not accustomed to thinking of their "work" as being accomplished through a series of "processes" producing a "unit" output.

Critical-to-quality (CTQ) characteristics in service transactions share two similarities to CTQs in manufactured products—customers still expect reliability and consistency. The Six Sigma Breakthrough Strategy provides a way to statistically view customer requirements and then quantitatively evaluate how well the customer's expectations are being met. A national hotel chain found that cycle time could be applied to something as simple as room-service coffee orders. Orders that took an average of twelve minutes to fill were reduced to five minutes through process mapping and the Pareto chart to show which problems offered the greatest potential for improvement. Not surprisingly, as cycle time improved, customer and employee satisfaction increased. When cycle time is at its optimum, there is no time to create defects. Improved cycle time results in improved quality. Again, focusing on the "process" naturally led to an improved outcome, which, in turn, led to increased customer satisfaction.

In calculating the number of defect opportunities in customer service, we substitute the word "transaction" for the traditional manufacturing notion of "parts." In the hotel industry, any contact between a hotel guest and an employee counts as a transaction. A transaction can include the efficiency with which a room reservation was made, the competency of the hotel staff at the time of the guest's check-in, cleanliness of room at arrival time and for the duration of the guest's stay, and, in the case of a hotel-based conference, whether meeting rooms are properly equipped and staffed.

In thinking of the service world through the concept of transactions, the "unit of product" can be virtually anything—a line of code in software, a guest registration form, a cash register receipt, even the traffic-violation ticket issued by a law-enforcement officer. If a traffic cop put the wrong license number on a ticket or forgets to take his copy of the citation, he has created a defect that results in lost revenue for local governments. Companies can create categories to be measured, collect data, and analyze the data with statistical tools to establish a baseline capability. As a result, the defects that occur most often can be pinpointed. Knowing this can provide managers with critical leverage points. Black Belts may conduct a cause-and-effect analysis to establish which processes are flawed and at the root of the problem, and then implement a mistake-proof process that prevents the defect from occurring again. The following case study shows how the Breakthrough Strategy can be applied to a transactional problem.

Applying the Breakthrough Strategy to a Commercial Process

For fifteen months, from April 1996 through May 1997, Foxboro, a process automation control company, was finding that its domestic delinquent accounts were costing the company over $7 million each month—a process calculated to be operating at roughly two sigma. Not only was Foxboro slow to collect the money it was owed, it was using significant manpower trying to resolve disputes that often antagonized the customer further. Moreover, 65 percent of delinquent accounts could be attributed to administrative errors that generated inaccurate bills. As a result, customers withheld payment because the sales order information did not match the purchase order or contract information. There were inconsistencies in how policies and procedures were followed by the company's 175 employees, who were spread out over several locations. Human error and a lack of accountability for the delinquent accounts added to the $7 million lost each month.

Because many service-oriented businesses—hotels, restaurants, department stores—are decentralized, the quest for Six Sigma is even more valuable as companies try to communicate and implement common goals and values among their various sites.

Putting together a Black Belt team, employees at Foxboro began to work through each phase of the Breakthrough Strategy. In the Measure phase, the Black Belt team identified what metrics should be used and designed graphs to track their progress. The team decided to focus on the cost of delinquent accounts with receivables over thirty days due. The baseline was $7 million per month. The secondary metric they decided on focused on yield, defined by measuring delinquent accounts receivable invoice dollars against the month-end accounts receivable balances. The baseline was a 15 percent "defect rate" and an 85 percent accounts receivable yield.

Next, the Black Belt team created two detailed process maps. The first map, called the "Order Quotation Process," showed each step employees made from the time a customer requested a quote to the time the customer received a price quote. The second map, called the "Order Through Invoice Process," showed the movement of orders from receipt of the purchase order, through the warehouse and shipping departments, and eventually on to accounts receivables and possibly credit and collections.

Then the team developed a database that reflected twelve months (from April 1996 through March 1997) of disputed and delinquent invoices over $10,000. Ninety percent of the delinquent invoices represented amounts of $10,000 or more. Working with the credit department, the team next implemented a two-digit coding system to streamline future reporting and analysis. The first digit identified a major category of dispute; the second digit indicated minor causes within the major category.

A two-level Pareto chart identified the root causes for the disputed invoices. The first level on the chart showed that commercial delinquencies were tied to 65 percent of all defects. The second level showed that 80 percent of commercial account disputes were tied to one of four key factors:

1. The purchase order/contract value did not equal the order value.

2. The invoice didn't agree with the purchase order or the terms and conditions of the contract.

3. The customer needed one invoice per purchase order.

4. The customer needed an itemized bill.

At this point, the Black Belt team felt they had properly measured the right information and were ready to move into the Analyze phase. After more detailed information about sales orders was obtained— such as the kinds of products ordered, information on the sales personnel, and the areas of the country they worked in—other Breakthrough Strategy tools such as Pareto charts, cause-and-effect matrixes, and a Failure Modes and Effects Analysis (FMEA) were systematically applied to the data collected. What they showed was that delinquent accounts could not be correlated to specific types of orders, individual salespeople, or specific regions in the country:

Analyses did, however, reveal several root causes for delinquent payments.

1.   Employees were not verifying purchase orders against the sales order information that was keyed into their system.

2.   No one was held accountable for reviewing customer purchase orders against the sales orders.

3.   Hard-copy confirmation of verbal purchase orders or letters of intent were sent late or not at all.

4.   There was inadequate monitoring of monthly billings.

5.   Payment terms were not properly established during the quotation process.

Once the Black Belt team realized that each of the above causes resulted in purchase order or contract information inconsistent with what eventually appeared on the sales order forms, they verified these root causes generated at the point of the order's origination with a statistically designed experiment.

The Improvement phase began with brainstorming sessions that identified ways to combat the root causes identified in the Analyze phase. A new corporate policy was issued that penalized each region with a one-percent-per-month interest charge for their delinquent accounts receivables. The penalty was reflected as an interest expense on the regional profit-and-loss statement.

The team also issued several recommendations. The first, addressing the issue of accountability, required sales personnel to indicate they had reviewed the purchase order before the order could be transmitted. The second, addressing the issue of efficiency, involved enhancing the current computer system so that purchase orders were no longer manually updated. The third, addressing company auditing of delinquent accounts, created a follow-up tool for sales and regional finance managers to identify and resolve billing discrepancies, and provided a vehicle to track repeat delinquent accounts. Finally, the team recommended use of a confirmation stamp designed to provide a uniform approach to purchase order data collection, identifying the nature of the order (new, confirmation of an existing order, or a revised order) and indicating the date and person responsible for completing the purchase order review.

The delinquent accounts receivable reporting process was streamlined so that regional managers could receive an e-mail file with the details of the delinquent accounts. The Black Belt team's goal was to reduce delinquent account receivables from $7 million to $2.45 million using a time series graph to measure the decrease in delinquent accounts. A $3.55 million reduction in delinquent accounts would raise the sigma level from 2.4 to 2.5. While the increase in the sigma level may not seem significant, the reduction in dollar delinquencies was significant. True to Pareto's law, the majority of the $3.6 million reduction in delinquent accounts receivable was achieved by eliminating the same defects. The Black Belts and credit and collections manager shared responsibility for updating the time series chart each month until the savings goal was achieved.

It took one Black Belt, supported by nine team members from a range of departments across the company, three months to execute the project and begin returning financial results to the division's bottom line. Since the project involved many different departments from several divisions, the support of senior management was critical to its success. By taking on the role of Senior Champion, the company's chief financial officer virtually guaranteed the project's success. As a result, new corporate policies were implemented and funds were made available for better computer systems. Without the support of the Senior Champion, the Black Belt project would not have been nearly as successful—in such a short period of time—as it was.

Summary

Nontechnical processes within an organization, such as in the purchasing or finance departments, are considered invisible processes because their elements are not physical or tangible like those in manufacturing. However, Six Sigma has a rightful place in the overall organization, and can mean delivering top-quality services while virtually eliminating all internal inefficiencies. A true Six Sigma organization not only produces excellent products but also maintains highly efficient production and administrative systems that work effectively with the company's other commercial processes.

CHAPTER THIRTEEN

Project Selection Guidelines

Clarify the Big Picture

Project selection takes on different faces in different corporations. While the overall goal of any Six Sigma breakthrough project is to improve customer satisfaction and profitability, some projects will focus on industrial processes, and others will focus on commercial processes. Six Sigma breakthrough projects must be linked to the highest levels of strategy in the organization and be in direct support of specific business objectives. The projects selected to improve business productivity must be agreed upon by both business and operational leadership, and someone must be assigned to "own" or be accountable for the project, as well as someone to execute it.

Strategic Alignment Through Projects

At the business level, projects should be selected based on the company's strategic goals and direction. Black Belt projects should be aimed at improving such things as customer satisfaction, cost, capacity, and top-end growth. At the operations level, Six Sigma projects obviously will have a greater local impact than they will have at the corporate level. However, plant projects should still tie to the overall strategic goals and direction and directly involve the plant leadership. Projects at this level should focus on key operational and technical problems that link to strategic goals and objectives.

When it comes to selecting Black Belt projects, some of the questions we hear most often include the following:

- What is the nature of a Six Sigma project?

- What is the scope of a Six Sigma project?

- How many Six Sigma projects should be identified?

- What are the criteria for selecting Six Sigma projects?

- What types of results should be expected from a Six Sigma project?

Project selection can rely on a "top-down" or "bottom-up" approach. The top-down approach considers a company's major business issues and objectives and then assigns a Senior Champion—a senior manager—most affected by these business issues to broadly define the improvement objectives, establish performance measures, and propose strategic improvement projects with specific and measurable goals that can be met in a given time period. Following this, teams (led by a Six Sigma Champion) identify processes and critical-to-quality characteristics, conduct process baselining, and identify opportunities for improvement. This is the favored approach and the best way to align localized business needs with corporate goals.

The bottom-up approach often results in projects being selected by production managers under pressure to make budget reductions, resolve specific quality problems, or improve process flow. These projects should be considered "targets of opportunity," and don't always mesh well with the company's strategic business goals. For example, managers may be asked to identify specific areas of waste, part-shortage problems, supplier quality issues, or unclear or impractical engineering requirements, and then a Black Belt is assigned to solve a specific problem. With this approach, it is easy for the operations-level focus to become diffused and disjointed in relationship to the higher strategic aims and directions of the business.

During deployment planning, an organization should consider how it will allocate resources between the two types of approaches. While the top-down approach has structural and managerial appeal, the bottom-up approach can ensure that key opportunities at lower levels of the organization are not lost. Usually, the optimal approach is a rational combination of the two.

At the process level, Six Sigma projects should focus on those processes and critical-to-quality characteristics that offer the greatest financial and customer-satisfaction leverage. Each project should address at least one element of the organization's key business objectives, and be properly planned. As discussed earlier, it's the Champion's responsibility to gain the executive leadership's support so that roadblocks are cleared and projects are successfully aligned and completed, regardless of the approach. A staunch proponent of Six Sigma, Polaroid's Six Sigma team leader and program manager Ken Pickering, underscores the importance of the executive leadership's support.

In its early days at Polaroid, Six Sigma could have easily been derailed without the support of our executive leadership. As we went through the process of project selection and began applying the Breakthrough Strategy, we realized that single projects could involve several business units, and that projects with the highest potential for financial windfalls required us to cross organizational boundaries.

Black Belts in our Chemical and Coating Manufacturing unit, for example, expected to return between $250,000 and $500,000 per project to the bottom line—but at a cost to other units. Plant A, providing materials to Plant B, might suffer annual losses, while Plant B generated tremendous savings and boosted their profitability. Even though Polaroid as a whole *would see increased profits, individual plant managers would suffer financial losses. These units needed the blessing of Polaroid's executive leadership before they were willing to make greater expenditures with lower profits.*

Individual business units handled this dilemma by making sure that their projects retained strong visibility within Polaroid. Our executive leadership wanted to know, and we continually reminded them of a project's overall savings. They understood that a plant spending $150,000 to save $500,000 in another plant needed to have the cause of their internal losses recognized. Although one plant working a Six Sigma project may not show a profit, or may even lose money, plants working in tandem on a single project can significantly boost the overall bottom line. In terms of Six Sigma, Polaroid would not be where it is today if our executive leadership did not understand and make allowances for this.

Six Sigma Project Criteria

The company's leadership needs to identify the primary business objectives of the company, identify the primary operational objectives for each business unit, and baseline the key processes before the right projects can be selected. Hidden factories need to be identified and analyzed to pinpoint sources of waste and inefficiency. Every Six Sigma project is designed to ultimately benefit the customer and improve the company's profitability. But projects also need to improve rolled throughput yield, scrap reduction, downtime, and overall capacity. Industrial businesses should focus on high-volume and high-revenue product lines, while commercial businesses should streamline transactional processes that directly impact the customer. Successful projects, once completed, should each add at least $175,000 to the division's bottom line. Readers of this book can probably identify several potential Six Sigma projects in their own operations and plants today that hierarchically connect to the strategic goals of the business.

Breakthrough projects should be selected based on the potential dollar amount they can return to the company, the amount and types of resources they will require, and the length of time it will take to complete the project. Companies may choose to dedicate time and money to a series of smaller projects rather than a few large projects that would require the same investment in money, time, and resources.

Measuring Six Sigma Projects

The key to good project selection is to identify and improve those performance metrics that will best boost a company's financial success and impact the customer base. Projects can be measured through the following key metrics:

- Defects Per Million Opportunities—the total number of defects per unit divided by the total number of opportunities for defects per unit multiplied by 1,000,000. This number can be directly converted into a sigma value. (See Chapter 1.)

- Net Cost Savings—verifiable reductions in fixed or variable costs.

- Cost of Poor Quality—the cost of failing to produce 100 percent quality the first time through.

- Capacity—the number of good units a process is able to produce in a given period of time.

- Cycle time—the length of time it takes to produce a product or service.

By analyzing the performance of these five key metrics and placing the data in a single database, companies better understand their operations. They can create a baseline to (1) show how well a current process is working; (2) determine theoretically how well a process should work; (3) determine how much processes can be improved; (4) determine how much a process improvement will affect customer satisfaction; and (5) establish how much impact will be realized in costs.

The theoretical view of how well a process should work is also known as "entitlement." For some companies, entitlement is "best possible performance" and usually occurs intermittently and for very short periods of time. The logic behind entitlement is that if something functions well for even a short period of time, by using simple process improvements, it should be able to function at the "best possible performance" level all the time. Entitlement does not involve creating new technologies or significantly redesigning current processes.

Polaroid, for example, breaks its project-selection criteria into three primary categories:

1. Low Yield Rate. When a company's current processes produce low yield on a continual or unpredictable basis. This can be characterized by lower-than-expected production numbers or slower-than-planned-for line speeds or production rates.

2. Cost of Poor Quality. Products and processes that require continuous and unusually high levels of inspection or quality-related intervention in order to deliver products or services satisfactory to the consumer. The cost of poor quality affects internal inspection, scrap and rework costs, and warranties and repairs. The cost of poor quality can be compared against revenues to determine whether or not a business needs to implement a Six Sigma project.

3. Capacity. Undercapacity means that a company does not have the facilities, tools, or human resources to produce products on time. While capacity has not been a problem for Polaroid, the company feels it is an appropriate criterion for selecting a Six Sigma project.

Other criteria for project selection can include:

1. Customer Satisfaction. Businesses can survey customers to determine their level of satisfaction with a product or service. A Six Sigma project could result from customers identi-

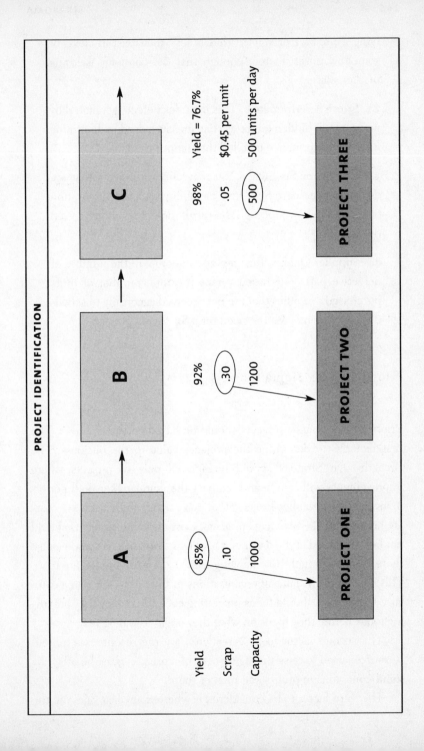

PROJECT IDENTIFICATION

A → B → C →

	A	B	C	
Yield	85%	92%	98%	Yield = 76.7%
Scrap	.10	.30	.05	$0.45 per unit
Capacity	1000	1200	500	500 units per day

PROJECT ONE

PROJECT TWO

PROJECT THREE

fying a product or service that is less than best-in-class, or somehow unsatisfactory enough that the company is losing market share.

2.   Internal Performance. This includes defects generated by processes in hidden factories. The measure used to determine internal performance is rolled throughput yield.

3.   Design for Six Sigma. You may choose projects that are designed to achieve Six Sigma capability via a reconfiguration of the product or process. As a result, defect levels are driven down.

4.   Supplier Quality. Businesses can compare the number of defective parts purchased versus the total number of units purchased. Supplies that are not received according to schedule can also indicate the need for a Six Sigma project.

Prioritizing Six Sigma Projects

Prioritizing Six Sigma projects should be based on three factors. The first factor is to determine the project's value to the business. The Breakthrough Strategy should be applied only to projects where improvements will significantly impact the company's overall performance and profitability. Projects that don't significantly decrease costs are not worthwhile Six Sigma projects. Cost-avoidance projects should not be considered at the onset of a Six Sigma initiative, simply because there is far too much "low-hanging fruit" to provide immediate cash. This applies to virtually all organizations in the 3.5 to 4.5 sigma category. Companies should focus on getting back the money they are losing today before they focus on what they *might* lose next year.

The second factor to be considered are the resources required. Resources used to raise the sigma level of a process must be offset by significant gains in profits and market share.

The third factor to be considered is whether any lost sales are the result of the length of time it takes to get new products to market, or whether there is an eroding customer base because of specific problems with a product or service—and whether or not a Six Sigma project meshes with the overall goals of the business.

Not all Six Sigma projects need to have a direct impact on the customer. For example, a company's finance department believed that their role was to track the dollar savings generated by Six Sigma projects and see that the money was returned to the company's overall bottom line. Although the finance department claimed they were different because they generated pieces of paper instead of electronic parts, they finally realized that their profitability was also influenced by such factors as productivity, defect rates, and cycle time. By using Six Sigma methodology, the finance department reduced the amount of time it took to close its books each month from twelve working days to two. Decreasing defects and cycle time in the finance department alone saved the company $20 million each year.

This same company's legal department has also benefited by applying Six Sigma to the length of time it took to file patent applications. Through process mapping, measuring performance, and identifying sources of errors and unnecessary variations, the company streamlined the process so that a patent application went through a chain of lawyers assigned to handle one aspect of the process, rather than a single lawyer handling the entire patent application. The outcome was that, without adding more lawyers, this company's legal department files more patents in shorter periods of time.

In both cases, this company recognized that even a small improvement would produce great savings for the company. And although neither Six Sigma project was chosen for its impact on customer dissatisfaction, both supported the company's goal of becoming more efficient and profitable in all its processes, both those that are internal and those that affect the customer.

Polaroid learned that, particularly in manufacturing, product designs need to have advanced to an appropriate point before the Breakthrough Strategy should be applied. After Polaroid identified a Six Sigma project in the company's Chemical and Coating Manufacturing unit, a significant amount of money and a team of Black Belt engineers were dedicated to creating a more sophisticated and economical reagent (the liquid that spreads over instant imaging film immediately after exposure and causes the photo to emerge). After devoting six months to making a higher-quality product at a lower cost to the company, the Black Belt team learned that the film itself had been redesigned and that the reagent formula developed in their Six Sigma project was not compatible with the new film. Today Polaroid recalls a valuable lesson—the process for building the final product needs to be advanced enough so that if changes are made, individual components in the process aren't affected.

Potential Six Sigma projects should undergo three screening levels, tiered in order of their importance. The first level focuses on its potential impact on the business and the customer. The second level focuses on how well the project will meet operational initiatives and enhance quality goals. The third level has to do with organizational and technical feasibility. Organizational feasibility includes internal resources such as the number of qualified employees available to work on Six Sigma projects, while technical feasibility can involve large expenditures for things such as equipment upgrades. Companies need to weigh the costs of investing in human and physical capital against the potential profits generated by Six Sigma projects.

Low-Hanging Fruit

Most organizations have low-hanging fruit—those processes that can be easily fixed with an immediate impact on profits. As Bombardier discovered when it purchased low sigma companies, Six Sigma provided an easy avenue to almost immediately increase profitability by focusing the Breakthrough Strategy on those "cost problems" that would produce immediate results in the form of cash. Rework, scrap, and warranty costs dropped, quickly taking the newly acquired companies up to about three sigma. But it's at the top of the tree where the bulk of the fruit is hidden, and where Black Belts need apply the Breakthrough Strategy in full strength.

AlliedSignal found that in its first two years of applying Six Sigma nearly 80 percent of its projects fell into the category of low-hanging fruit—processes that could be easily improved with simple tools such as scatter plots, fish bone diagrams, process maps, cause-and-effect diagrams, histograms, FMEA, Pareto charts, and elementary statistics. As a result, Allied was able to move quickly through a series of projects that returned significant sums to the bottom line. However, as the relatively simpler processes were improved, Allied began to select projects that focused on harvesting what we call the sweet fruit—the fruit found at the top of the tree, and the hardest to reach—and it required more sophisticated tools such as Design of Experiments and Design for Six Sigma.

Over ten years of guiding companies through the implementation of Six Sigma and the Breakthrough Strategy, it has been shown that the Black Belt's first Six Sigma project is especially important. Projects selected for the training phase should not be those with the biggest and most difficult return potential, but ones that are straightforward and manageable. Management cannot expect Black Belts to immediately solve persistent problems that have been entrenched and tolerated for long periods of time. Despite the effectiveness of the Breakthrough Strategy, it takes training and practice to gain speed and finesse.

Finally, Six Sigma is far more than completing projects. Over time, companies will discover what kinds of measures and metrics are needed to improve quality. Each new insight needs to be integrated into management's knowledge base, strategies, and goals. Ultimately, Six Sigma requires a company to transform how it does business, which, in turn, transforms the essence of its culture. It learns how to focus its energy on specific targets rather than random and nebulous goals.

A Process-Level Case Study

The following discussion of the Breakthrough Strategy applies to the process level or Black Belt level and represents how "low-hanging fruit" can be gathered using the Breakthrough Strategy. Our story takes place within General Electric's Plastics Division. GE Plastics, by applying the Breakthrough Strategy to over 3,000 projects, saved $137 million in 1997. One of these projects took place in Polymerland—a division within GE Plastics that distributes thermoplastic resins. Polymerland ships plastic products to a variety of customers, including manufacturers of computers, CD-ROMs, compact discs, digital videodiscs, and automobiles.

Polymerland employees had already pulled together a Black Belt team to focus on a suspected problem. The team was in the midst of the Define phase of what they called their "Damage-Free Delivery Project" when one of their largest and most lucrative customers came to their sales force and said, "Look, we are ready to take our business elsewhere. Too many of the products you are sending us have been contaminated." The customer was frustrated by the fact that it was constantly receiving damaged products, and that it then had to use its own time and manpower to ship the defective product back to Polymerland for replacement. Between January 1, 1997, and June 30, 1997, Polymerland delivered 275,501,855 pounds of product to its customers. During this period, 176,381 pounds of product was contaminated—meaning that the packaging had been damaged during shipping—and thus a damaged product was delivered to the customer. This resulted in a damage-free reported sigma of 4.72 and a DPMO (Defects Per Million Opportunities) of 640.

Realizing that one unhappy customer probably meant there were many more who were not voicing their unhappiness, and that lost customers meant lost sales, employees at Polymerland told the customer that they were aware of the problem and that they were pulling out every stop to find a solution.

In the Measure phase, Polymerland's Black Belt team decided to take a closer look at each of their ten warehouses from which the product was shipped, in an attempt to determine where the damages were occurring. Of the ten warehouses, two warehouses (Maumee and Piedmont) produced the highest number of defects; one warehouse (Brampton, Ontario), on the other hand, was operating at six sigma. The Black Belt team calculated that, between the 10 warehouse locations,

POLYMERLAND'S DEFINE PHASE	
	• Select process critical-to-quality characteristics.
	• Define performance standards.
	• Define performance objective.
	• Benchmark.
Customer:	End customer is whoever purchases Polymerland products.
CTQ:	Damage-free delivery.
Defect:	Product damage reported by customer or damage identified in warehouse.
Unit:	Each pound of product delivered.
Cost of Quality:	Rework costs and write-off and warehousing of damaged product.

the 50 different product lines, the 14 different types of packaging used, and the 100 transportation carriers used, there were nearly 700,000 combinations of variations that could be the source of the problem.

In the Analyze phase, the Black Belt team focused on the Maumee and Piedmont warehouses. They found that 95 percent of the damaged boxes had two punctures at the base of one side of the box, causing the product to leak. The Black Belts also found that 87 percent of the damage occurred when the boxes were moved by forklift onto stacks or into trucks. It didn't take long for the Black Belt team to decide that there was a strong correlation between the number of

POLYMERLAND'S MEASURE PHASE
• Establish process capability.
• Validate measurement system.
• Take initial data.
• What is influencing the CTQs?
• What is the frequency of defects?
• Understand/describe the process.

boxes damaged in-house—as opposed to being damaged during shipping—and the number of damaged products received by customers. The team also discovered a relationship between how the product was packaged and the type of damage done. Bags were more likely to be damaged if they were scraped across the floor, whereas boxes were more likely to be damaged when being handled by a forklift operator.

Why, they asked, were the boxes handled by forklifts damaged while the bags were not? The answer turned out to be fairly simple. The forks on the forklift protruded six to nine inches out from under the box, so that as the fork was fully inserted under the box being retrieved, the box behind it was punctured. But if this was the case, why was the Brampton, Ontario, warehouse able to operate at six sigma using the same forklift?

Several answers were offered, but the most tenable seemed to be the drivers' experience and the control they wielded over the forklift operation. When a box was lifted, the forks were tilted back for load stabilization. But if the driver did not lower the fork tilt, the protruding fork, instead of sliding under the first box, would puncture the second box as the first box was placed next to it. Because drivers could not see over the lift, they were forced to blindly place the boxes onto the pallets.

FORKLIFT DRIVER EXPERIENCE AND SKILL LEVEL			
AVERAGE YEARS OF EXPERIENCE		IN-HOUSE BOX DAMAGE (DPMO)	
BRAMPTON	20 YEARS	BRAMPTON	0
MAUMEE	5.8 YEARS	MAUMEE	995
PIEDMONT	4 YEARS	PIEDMONT	4,628

Now that the problem had been thoroughly analyzed, the Black Belt team was ready to begin the Improve phase. There were several possible solutions to this problem. More-experienced forklift operators could be hired into the Maumee and Piedmont plants at a significant cost to the company, assuming it was possible to find forklift operators with nearly twenty years of experience. A second option was more extensive training for the forklift operators in the Maumee and

POLYMERLAND'S ANALYZE PHASE
• When and where do the defects occur?
• Translate the practical problem into a statistical problem.
• Use quality tools to identify sources of variation.
• Identify the "vital few" factors that will have the greatest impact on the CTQs.
• Are defects technology or process related?

Piedmont warehouses—another expensive solution without a guaranteed outcome. In the end, however, the team decided to install shorter forks, eliminating the fork protrusion altogether. In December 1997, the Piedmont plant replaced the forty-two-inch forks with thirty-six-inch forks at a relatively nominal cost of $350 per forklift truck. Within a short period of time, thirty-six-inch forks had replaced the forty-two-inch forks not only at the Piedmont warehouse but at the Maumee warehouse and other warehouses as well.

POLYMERLAND'S IMPROVE PHASE
• How can we fix the problem?
• Define statistical solutions to the problem.
• Determine which "vital few" variables need modification, and how they should be modified.

Now the Black Belt team was ready to move into the final phase, the Control phase, where steps are implemented to make sure the process stays fixed. GE has a mandate that before any Six Sigma project is completed, it must pass through data points. A data point shows intervals and can reflect how often an event occurs within a given time period. A data point might be weight, inches, the number of hospital deaths that fall within a specific time period, and so on. In Polymerland's case, a data point was a period of time, anywhere from two weeks to two months, during which Black Belts must show beyond a doubt that their projects have a workable and permanent solution.

POLYMERLAND'S CONTROL PHASE
• Did the solution work?
• Future performance must be monitored.
• Did the improvement process cause a problem elsewhere?

Inspect the Process, Not the Product

In summary, the Breakthrough Strategy helps businesses understand and *characterize* their processes and *optimize* these processes (make them more consistent through new approaches and practices). This new knowledge must be systemically organized and communicated throughout the organization. Consistently applying the Measure, Analyze, Improve, and Control (M-A-I-C) approach across diverse businesses and processes is the only way companies can leverage the power of the Breakthrough Strategy's tools to achieve significant financial results. The rigorous, systematic, disciplined approach to problem solving that forms the basis of the Breakthrough Strategy provides a common language different business units can use to talk to one another, share lessons learned, and compare the effectiveness of their processes and levels of quality with those of companies with dissimilar products.

A sample project chart used in project selection:

Product or Service Impacted:		Projected Project Savings:	
Black Belt:		Telephone Number:	
Champion:		Business Unit:	
Start Date:		Expected Completion Date:	

ELEMENT	DESCRIPTION	PROJECT GOALS	
1. Process	The production process where an opportunity exists.		
2. Project Description	Describe the project's purpose and scope.		
3. Objective		Baseline Theoretical	
		Entitlement Units	
		Yield	%
		Scrap	S/A
		Capacity	Units/A

Item	Description	(blank)
4. Dollar Savings	What are the anticipated savings?	
5. Team Members	Name of Black Belt and team members with their titles.	
6. Project Scope	Which part of the processes will be investigated?	
7. Benefit to External Customers	Who are the final customers, what are their CTQs, and what benefits will they see?	
8. Schedule	Give key milestones. Project Start Date: M - Measure Phase Complete: A - Analyze Phase Complete: I - Improve Phase Complete: C - Control Phase Complete: Project Completion:	
9. Support Required	Will the team need any special capabilities, hardware, trials, etc?	
10. Potential Barriers		

CHAPTER FOURTEEN

The Psychology of Six Sigma

Larry Bossidy claims that one of corporate America's most egregious errors is not telling people what we think of them. Reward and recognition are an important part of the process in supporting Black Belts and others who deploy the Breakthrough Strategy, and, in many instances, *costs nothing more than time on the part of senior leadership*. Employee motivation is a complex science, but it rests upon the principle that people need recognition for their successes—particularly people implementing Six Sigma, where they step outside of established roles to take on assignments beyond the scope and structure of their existing jobs.

The nature of being a Champion, Master Black Belt, or Black Belt allows employees the authority to make and execute important decisions without top-down interference. Successful Six Sigma organizations encourage autonomy and trust, and expect people at all levels to take full responsibility for their work and for the organization's performance. In other words, they take the success of Six Sigma personally. However, those involved in the daily grind of implementing and moving the initiative forward need to be recognized and rewarded in three distinct areas if they are to sustain the intensity of the job a Black Belt demands. In a sense, Black Belts are no different from customers: They need to be asked what kinds of rewards are meaningful to them. The answers range from money to recognition, promotion, and increased corporate autonomy.

Black Belts Need Financial Compensation

While money isn't always at the top of their reward list, most Black Belts expect and need to be acknowledged and compensated for their work. Reward and recognition are an organization's guide to encouraging or reinforcing desired behavior among employees. Compensation and reward mechanisms send messages. Jack Welch, who nearly left GE in 1961 after receiving a meager, but standard, salary raise of $1,000, believes that rewards drive behavior. Welch demands that the bonuses disbursed by managers be highly differentiated and based on performance rather than some preset formula. To emphasize the importance of the Six Sigma initiative, Welch weights 40 percent of the bonus compensation for managers on the intensity of their efforts and their measurable progress toward Six Sigma quality in their operations. The result of Welch's attention on people is that GE employees know that their boss is a fierce believer in the power and potential of his employees.

One of the central challenges is finding a way to align rewards with the key drivers behind an organization's success. Management has the power to create financial outcomes for Black Belt performance that reinforce the importance of the Breakthrough Strategy initiative. The reward strategy and resulting performance should create an overall link between strategy and action. Linking rewards to strategy lets employees better understand the organization's strategy, and is critical to achieving Six Sigma levels of quality. When employees better understand an organization's reward strategy, organizations are better able to change cultures and behaviors.

Watson Wyatt Worldwide, a global human resources consulting firm, in a 1998 study of 1,000 publicly traded North American companies, found that 61 percent of top-performing companies link their rewards to their business strategies, while lower-performing companies create minimal linkage. Watson Wyatt also found that 56 percent of top-performing companies link employee compensation to employee performance, while only 38 percent of lower-performing companies do. Watson Wyatt defines "top performers" as those companies whose performance ratings can be verified by an independent source that tracks financial data on publicly traded companies.

As discussed in Chapter 9, financial compensation is a powerful reinforcement tool in helping organizations implement the Breakthrough Strategy and retain their Six Sigma players. Compensation levels tell employees what management considers important, and is a way for senior management to reinforce their words and show commitment to a vision. When the Breakthrough Strategy is implemented, financial compensation should encourage commitment to the organization's goals and priorities and underscore only those actions, attitudes, and accomplishments that help move an organization toward Six Sigma. The needs of the individual are aligned to the needs of the organization.

Black Belts Need the Promise of Promotion

Black Belts, driving scores of Six Sigma projects throughout a company, epitomize the best that people can be, and companies that treat Black Belts as heroes create the stage for these individuals to redefine how the work of the organization gets done. At GE, pioneers of the Six Sigma Black Belt movement have been rewarded with leadership positions in various divisions of the business. These promotions include positions such as general manager, director of finance, vice president of sales, vice president of the audit staff, and president of GE Mexico. As GE puts it, these Six Sigma leaders have moved into the "big jobs." Not all high performers, however, want management positions. The best situations occur when a Black Belt is promoted and still remains an individual contributor. Those companies postured with a technical ladder that complements the management ladder are in excellent positions to allow Black Belts this opportunity.

Black Belts Need Written and Verbal Recognition

Too often, companies underestimate the power of recognition. Recognition isn't solely *what* employers reward their employees with, but *how* they reward them. People want their accomplishments to be recognized. Verbal and written recognition is inexpensive and simple, whether done privately or in an open and public way. Jack Welch never sends form letters when acknowledging accomplishments—whether to directors in the GE boardroom, executives, managers, or employees. Personalized notes, accompanied by a phone call, are his favorite form of communicating a job well done. His handwritten notes to everyone from senior executives to hourly workers carry enormous impact because they are heartfelt and spontaneous. They are written to inspire and motivate as often as they are to stir and demand action.

Motivation is highest when success is acknowledged. When major contributions to an organization are ignored, disillusionment sets in. People flourish when their accomplishments are celebrated in ways that are personal. Ritual recognition is not nearly as meaningful as a thirty-second phone call from the company president acknowledging the value of someone's work. Sometimes recognition can be something as simple as being mentioned in the company newspaper. People need to feel that what they are doing is important and making a difference. Another Watson Wyatt Worldwide study revealed that although 50 percent of employees felt satisfied with their compensation programs, only 34 percent thought their companies did a good job recognizing performance. After presidential speechwriter Peggy Noonan received a draft of one of her speeches back from President Reagan with the words "very good" scrawled across the top of the first page, she claims that she cut the words off and taped the paper to her blouse. Like a second-grader given a gold star for a book report well done, she wore the note for the rest of the day.

Understanding Human Motivation

Psychologist Abraham Maslow published his pioneering theory of human motivation in 1943. Maslow believed that actualization is the driving force of human personality. One of Maslow's greatest insights was to place actualization into a hierarchy of motivation. Maslow believed that self-actualization is a fundamental need, but before that need can be met, other needs—such as hunger, safety, and belonging—must be filled.

Maslow pointed out that the hierarchy is dynamic, and that the dominant need is always shifting. For example, artists may become lost in the self-actualization of their art, but will eventually become tired and hungry enough that they have to stop to eat and sleep.

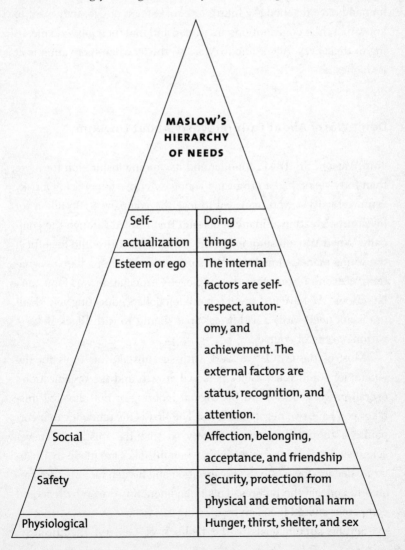

MASLOW'S HIERARCHY OF NEEDS

Self-actualization	Doing things
Esteem or ego	The internal factors are self-respect, autonomy, and achievement. The external factors are status, recognition, and attention.
Social	Affection, belonging, acceptance, and friendship
Safety	Security, protection from physical and emotional harm
Physiological	Hunger, thirst, shelter, and sex

Moreover, a single behavior may combine several levels. Eating dinner can fulfill both physiological and social needs. The hierarchy does not exist by itself but is affected by the situation and the general culture. Satisfaction is relative. A satisfied need no longer motivates. For example, a hungry man may be desperate for food, but once he eats a good meal, the promise of food no longer motivates him. The point is that once Black Belts have had the first three needs on Maslow's chart met and have reached the fourth level of esteem or ego, they want to know that their contributions are valued and that their jobs add meaning to their lives. According to Maslow, this is when motivation is at its highest.

Don't Worry About Failure; Worry About Low Aim

Tom Watson, Sr., IBM's founder and its guiding inspiration for more than forty years, had a promising young executive supervising a risky venture for IBM who managed to lose the company $10 million for his efforts, creating a financial disaster that rippled through the company. When Watson summoned the nervous executive into his office, the young man assumed that Watson wanted his immediate resignation. Watson's response to the employee's expectation was "You can't be serious. We have just spent ten million dollars educating you!" Failure is not necessarily a bad thing. So it should go with Black Belts—within reason, of course.

Most of the CEOs we work with see mistakes as tools for the Champion's and Black Belt's personal growth and the organization's overall progression toward Six Sigma. Ignoring or not allowing mistakes can have two negative effects. The first is the tendency to incorporate a form of revisionist history so that the mistake is never acknowledged. The second occurs when mistakes are made that penetrate deeper down into the organization and hidden factories are created to conceal the failures. This phenomenon is driven by fear, and companies should focus on eradicating this fear.

Setting stretch goals is the bedrock of General Electric's Six

Sigma culture. For General Electric, "stretch" means that employees commit to huge gains before having any idea of how they will get there. Though workers at General Electric often hit their stretch targets, some Black Belts miss their goals, even if their failure represents an improvement over past performance. What is the response within GE, which places such high expectations on its Black Belts?

General Electric sees missing a target not as failure, but rather as a triumph to be celebrated. Here is what Jack Welch says:

> *Punishing failure assures that no one dares. Because this [GE] management team has been together for a long time, trust has grown, and trust is an indispensable ingredient that allows a business to set big stretch targets. GE business leaders do not walk around all year regretting the albatross of an impossible number they hung around their own necks. At the end of the year, the business is measured not on whether it hit the stretch target, but on how well it did against the prior year, given the circumstances. An exciting by-product of stretch behavior is the enormous surge of self-confidence that has grown across our company as people see themselves achieving things they once suspected were beyond them.*

Self-confidence and stretch thinking were two of the key factors that precipitated General Electric's decision to launch Six Sigma—its greatest stretch goal of all.

When Larry Bossidy talks about Black Belts at AlliedSignal, he reminds audiences that Black Belts are assigned tough stretch targets, and that they can't be punished for not scoring 100 percent every time. He also points out that failure is most often linked to management's lack of support, particularly when the data exist to support change. It is management's responsibility to assign Black Belts to projects with clearly defined goals. Champions and Black Belts working to implement the Six Sigma Breakthrough Strategy will fail if senior management lacks understanding and commitment, and does not allow the Black Belts to make the changes needed.

Long before Six Sigma ever appeared on Polaroid's horizon, the
company's founder, Edwin H. Land, stated, "The first thing you naturally do is teach the person to feel that the undertaking is manifestly
important and nearly impossible. . . . That draws out the kind of drives
that make people strong, that put you in pursuit intellectually."

Black Belts who have proved themselves want to be thanked and
trusted for their judgment. They want to be recognized for the fire
that burned within, when those around them responded only to fires
that were built under them. Freedom breeds creativity; creativity
breeds corporate contributions, and everyone wins. It's up to management to structure environments for success.

CHAPTER FIFTEEN

Preparing an Organization for Six Sigma

People hate change. Change of any kind is a struggle with fear, anger, and uncertainty, a war against old habits, hidebound thinking, and entrenched interests. No company can change any faster than it can change the hearts and minds of its people, and the people who change fastest and best are those who have no choice.

—ROBERT FREY, PRESIDENT, CIN-MADE CORPORATION

Robert W. Galvin, son of Motorola's founder, once said that the intelligence of an organization is inversely proportional to its size. The larger a company, he believed, the more obtuse its actions and decisions, and the greater its propensity for making blunders. Individually, people within companies may act intelligently, but collectively they can act with shortsightedness and ineptness. It is the role of leaders to sidestep this tendency.

Strong emotions can be created inside companies when the old paternalistic ways of doing things clash with a new reality. Many don't believe that change can be for the better. They see anything new and different as creating chaos, rather than being an improvement. Dismantling a corporate culture and asking employees to embrace a new working style is a tough task. Employees who have been doing the same job successfully for many years may feel entitled to cling to the past.

Why Companies Behave the Way They Do

Author Rita Mae Brown defines insanity as doing the same thing over and over again but expecting different results. When Mikel worked at Motorola's Government Electronics Group in Scottsdale, Arizona, one of the wave solder machines—a machine used to coat printed circuit boards by moving the boards through a flowing wave of molten solder—suddenly began producing a large number of solder defects for no apparent reason. After being plagued by the quality problem for several weeks, the area manager pulled a group of engineers together for a powwow. At some point during the meeting, an engineer pointed out that one of the machine's side panels was missing; when the panel was reattached, the machine miraculously began working again without as many defects. Skeptical that this was the solution to the ongoing problem, Mikel suggested that the engineers run several statistically designed experiments on the machine to ferret out the root of the problem.

Several weeks later, Mikel returned to check on the engineers' progress in fixing the faulty wave solder machine. As he approached the wave solder machine, he saw the panel positioned back into place with wide yellow-and-black-striped tape and a large sign posted in the middle of the panel warning that under no circumstances was the panel to be removed. Three months later, the operations manual had been amended to instruct employees to make sure that the side panel to the wave solder was always in place, even if it required taping it on. In this case, the experiment was never run. The engineers relied on their intuition, the problem reoccurred, and another meeting took place to discuss the situation. By this time the previous "solution" had been forgotten, but it still remained in the operations manual and was viewed as essential—while the engineers searched for another "solution."

Situations like this happen in organizations repeatedly. Persistent problems never go away because employees aren't taught how to properly measure, analyze, improve, and control processes. Every disaster is followed by a flurry of tampering and new rules, and regulations are implemented that guarantee that the old problem (and probably several new ones) will occur again because the root causes have not been removed. Companies of all kinds embrace solutions to problems that have no bearing on the problem.

B. F. Skinner and the Superstitious Dance

American psychologist B. F. Skinner would have called the situation described above a "superstitious dance"—behavior that results from and is maintained and reinforced by activities that are not interdependent. Skinner demonstrated this phenomenon by placing pigeons in a box with a feeding mechanism that randomly delivered food pellets regardless of how the pigeons behaved. The pigeons, however, began to correlate certain activities with receiving food. For instance, if a pigeon raised its wing and food appeared, it would correlate raising its wing with being fed. However, if the pigeon began pecking its beak against a wall or scratching its foot when another food pellet appeared, it might modify its behavior to re-create the most recent action that delivered the food. This behavior is known as operant conditioning. In other words, the pigeon falsely believed that repeating its most recent behavior, whether it was raising its wing, pecking its beak, or scratching its food, would result in being fed—hence the term "superstitious dance."

While behavior that is rewarded tends to be strengthened, often the behavior that occurs immediately prior to the reinforcement is coincidental. Imagine, for instance, that a baseball player hits his bat against the ground three times in a row just before hitting a home run. The hitting of the ground is, of course, coincidental to the batter hitting a home run, but the player may see a correlation. Because the player makes this association, he may hit the ground three times every time he is at bat in the future. And because he will be at least partially reinforced for this behavior—batters overall get a hit 25 percent of the time—his ground-hitting behavior will probably be maintained.

Gambling casinos are further proof of Skinner's superstitious dance. Although the slot machines are set to pay off just enough to maintain the high rate of behavior that keeps the casino lucrative to its owners rather than its customers, and although in theory customers know this, not many can resist returning to the slot machine that has just paid a big dividend. Other winners, believing they have depleted their luck on a winning machine, will move on to another machine in hope of repeating their success.

In companies, many employees will associate their last behavior with a result. When a combination of knobs produces a desired result, those same knobs are twisted again and again in the same way. When the yield goes back down, the knobs are twisted back to the position that first worked. Because of bad information and the wrong metrics, most companies cultivate and perpetuate many kinds of superstitious dances within their organization.

Behavior Is a Function of Values

Our actions and behavior are a function of our values and beliefs. Values reflect beliefs, which, in turn, determine how we view the world around us. Not only do values create the bedrock of any corporate culture and provide its philosophy for achieving success, they provide a sense of common direction and guidelines for individual day-to-day behavior. Since value systems create perceived options and behavior, organizations striving to reach Six Sigma must learn new shared values. When those values are reinforced with performance metrics and goal lines, they become ingrained. When the metrics are tied to the reward and recognition system, the value becomes a bedrock and will change only when the system of measurements and rewards changes.

When Six Sigma becomes a value—or the bedrock of a company's belief system—a bond of trust is created between the organization and its customers. It is important that companies understand how the values and philosophy of Six Sigma may differ from the beliefs, values, and priorities that were emphasized within an organization prior to its implementing Six Sigma. Here again, values, beliefs, and priorities are reflected by what companies measure and reward.

Since behavior is a function of values, companies and employees need to agree on values and understand how these values drive behavior. If employees know what their company stands for and how they are to uphold those standards, they are much more likely to make decisions and behave in ways that support the organization's goal. In companies where every employee has at least some rudimentary knowledge of Six Sigma, coupled with the appropriate metrics, people are much more likely to feel that their contribution to the organization is important. They can trace their contribution to the movement of a measurement that is valued by the company. When employees are recognized and rewarded for these kinds of contributions, the needs of the individual are aligned with the needs of the organization. Employees are motivated because life within the company has meaning for them, and strong organizational leadership is created.

Changes in the acceleration of technology, the legal system, acceptable social behavior, economics, and education have created widely varying value systems within organizations.

In his book *The People Puzzle: Understanding Yourself and Others,* business consultant Morris Massey writes:

> *Literally everything is sifted through the gut-level value systems operating in each of us. Values are subjective reactions to the world around us. While some items are purely functional and can be viewed rationally and objectively (chalkboards, picture books, lightbulbs, rulers, etc.), most items involve a subjective reaction, especially when our feelings come into play. Gut-level value systems automatically filter the way we view most things around us. Your filters operate in degrees and shades of good/bad, right/wrong, normal/not normal, or acceptance/rejection.*

RESULTS CHANGE CULTURES;
CULTURES DON'T CHANGE RESULTS

Romanian-born Joseph M. Juran, one of the masterminds behind the Japanese approach to quality, believes that if Japan, as a nation, had not suffered through a significant emotional event when it lost in World War II, the country might not have been as receptive to change. Its focused efforts to recover made it willing to listen to a Westerner (Joseph Juran) who had something to say about quality. Prior to World War II, "Made in Japan" meant shoddy products. Fifty years later, "Made in Japan" means world-class quality. As Juran describes it, when he spoke in Japan at the invitation of the Japanese Federation of Economic Organizations and the Japanese Union of Scientists and Engineers in 1954, he told the Japanese no secrets. In fact, his words, and those of Dr. Edwards Deming, were no different from what he had been telling American audiences for years. The difference was how Japanese audiences heard and interpreted them.

Significant emotional events have two critical elements: personal impact and clarity. Personal impact occurs only when we internalize and think about the consequences—both positive and negative. Clarity occurs when individuals make the connection between what is happening to them and how it was triggered by values-based behavior. This means that we cannot create significant emotional events in others unless we reach them on a direct and personal level. For example, when a business measures quality only at the end of its process, that quality often looks fairly good. However, when the measurements occur at multiple points along the process and then are aggregated, the picture becomes more dismal. When measurements look good, little action is taken to create improvement. Only hard, unmistakable data can force an organization to reassess values and beliefs.

Significant emotional events take place when it becomes apparent that old practices no longer work and the path is cleared for new beliefs and values to be introduced and accepted. There is a direct correlation between behavioral change and the consequences of not changing. Values and beliefs are a response to what we believe is necessary to our survival. Since organizational values determine what people will or will not do within an organization, people need to see how their values drive behavior, and how those values impact their individual jobs and ultimately the organization. *Business measurements drive values; values determine how people work; how people work determines profitability.*

Six Sigma firmly establishes what a company will value—best-in-class quality, customer satisfaction, and profitability—and how it can measure and improve those values. Company values determine performance and profitability. Performance and profitability are the keys to unlimited growth. Employees flourish when they know they are creating goods and services of incomparable quality. In the end, an organization's sigma level is an indicator of how strong its values are. Six Sigma links measurements with values that drive an organization's actions, which, in turn, set improvement in motion.

Getting a company to embrace common values is not a simple task, and often an organization's understanding of what it means to have common values is limited to a corporate handbook and posters tacked to walls. Perhaps the clearest example of what it means to bring disparate individuals together and ask them to embrace common values is the military. When Mike joined the Marines as a new lieutenant, his infantry platoon was composed of a group of young men with different values, levels of education, aptitudes, motivations, and beliefs. Yet in order to achieve their mission, each man had to work with others to create a coherent unit. And each man had to learn to cope with a wide range of possible combat situations that could involve different opponents, threats, missions, and locations. They all knew that survival meant working together with a common focus. Achieving Six Sigma requires many of the same qualities. Mutual trust, shared values, good internal communications, effective judgment under pressure, rapid group response, continuous debriefing, reappraisal, and reinforcement through management's emotional and financial backing are crucial to the success of a company's implementation of the Breakthrough Strategy. The behavior of those responsible for implementing the Breakthrough Strategy should exemplify their beliefs and values in action.

Retrofitting a Culture Is Tough

The European electrical engineering conglomerate Asea Brown Boveri (ABB) underwent a series of mergers and reorganizations while simultaneously implementing Six Sigma. The organization's vitality threatened to crumble as employees were repeatedly thrown into new and turbulent situations. Resistance to change within ABB was strong. CEO Percy Barnevik described the organization's attempt to change human behavior in this way:

> *You have to exploit your success stories to break resistance. We human beings are driven by habit, history, and the rearview mirror. If you want to break direction, you have to shake people up, not by threatening them, not by offering a bonus, but by illustrating in a similar situation what can be accomplished.*

Employees have understandable and rational reasons for resisting change. They ultimately filter a potential change through their value system to see how it will impact them. In this sense, change is a balancing act—to the left are favorable outcomes, to the right are unfavorable outcomes. The role of leadership is to move the balance point without knocking employees off the high wire. This can often be accomplished through product benchmarking data and process baselines. People see where they are and where they must go. When one company sees how others have excelled, it begins to realize that it, too, can achieve breakthrough.

Criticism can be an inevitable consequence of significant change. But an atmosphere that encourages employees to voice concerns is also an atmosphere that encourages employees to break the mold and be innovative. For instance, to motivate administrative personnel to solve problems more quickly at ABB's rotor factory in Barr, Switzerland, the president of ABB's Power Generation unit forced an entire floor of white-collar administrators out of their austere, separate office building and into the noisy, dirty factory. Initially disoriented and antagonistic, the vociferous staff gradually saw how the move was benefiting them. Factory workers no longer had to leave the factory to report problems such as machine breakdowns to administration's headquarters. And administration now understood that silence in the factory eloquently signaled problems needing immediate attention.

What companies have found is that by allowing criticisms of Six Sigma during its implementation, employees are given opportunities to express their fear. When fears are properly addressed through training sessions, internal newsletters, and so on, the doors are opened for employees to be educated regarding new values and beliefs.

General Electric's Jack Welch believes that organizations change only after a new idea is clearly defined. Once that idea is communicated over and over again so that it reaches a critical mass, it will gain enough momentum to ultimately change core values and, thus, behaviors.

Here is what Welch has to say about employee motivation and input:

> *The only way I see to get more productivity is by getting people involved and excited about their jobs. You can't afford to have anyone walk through a gate of a factory, or into an office, who's not giving 120%. I don't mean running and sweating, but working smarter. It's a matter of understanding the customer's needs instead of just making something and putting it into a box. It's a matter of seeing the importance of your role in the total process. . . . When people see that their ideas count, their dignity is raised. Instead of feeling numb, like robots, they feel important. They* are *important.*

Most organizations don't know how to deal with the behavior or the underlying emotions and values that are expressed when employees are forced to change. Work is an emotional experience, and emotionally healthy people can't turn their feelings off when they walk out the office door at the end of each day. But once employees understand the purpose and value of implementing Six Sigma and the Breakthrough Strategy, their resistance begins to dissolve and they become energized at the prospect of having more control over their jobs and being able to contribute productively to the goals of their organization. Simply stated, they feel empowered to institute beneficial change. When this occurs, breakthrough is at hand.

Bombardier Challenges Old Beliefs

Bombardier Inc. was founded in Canada in 1942 as a manufacturer of snowmobiles. It has since become a diversified global manufacturer of recreational products (such as its Sea-Doo personal watercraft), mass-transit systems, business jets, and regional aircraft. It is also a rapidly growing financial services business and a business focused on the maintenance and support of transportation-related products. It operates manufacturing facilities in eleven countries and has 47,000 employees. After the death of his father-in-law and the company's founder, J. Armand Bombardier, chairman Laurent Beaudoin took over the family business in 1966. Three years before stepping down as president and CEO in February 1999, Beaudoin made the decision to roll out Six Sigma across the company's five business groups over a three-year period, beginning in the winter of 1996.

Although Bombardier possesses a very defined culture—it values inventiveness, innovation, entrepreneurship, and decentralized management—the company as a whole consists of many different business entities, each with its own history, outlook, and management philosophy. To an extent, Bombardier has supported this climate by minimizing the integration of corporate-level structures into each business. Beaudoin described the company like this:

We would rather lose some synergy across the groups than hamper decision making and entrepreneurialism within them. However, if and when there is a strong need for sharing, the corporate center will intervene, and often I will get personally involved.

Launching Six Sigma was one such intervention.

Bombardier's radar screens showed a number of urgent issues—issues that Beaudoin and his group presidents believed that Six Sigma could address. One important reason was the need to accelerate improvement across all of the businesses. But other reasons were equally compelling: the conviction that Bombardier needed to accelerate knowledge sharing across its rapidly growing, decentralized organization, and the fact that it needed an effective way to train a new generation of leaders. For Bombardier, Six Sigma was a pragmatic blend of practical projects that could improve the bottom line by eliminating the root causes of defects through the use of hard data and analytical tools, while fundamentally changing the way people perceived and thought about the future of the business.

A challenge not unique to Bombardier is how to create change so that it delivers immediate results with a lasting impact. Bruce Miyashita, a former McKinsey & Company consultant who spent nearly a decade helping organizations improve their process performances, joined Bombardier with the task of functioning as a Champion to help drive the Six Sigma initiative across the company's five business groups. Miyashita talks candidly about the challenges Bombardier continues to face in its Six Sigma implementation:

When I joined Bombardier in early 1997, it was because I viewed the company as one with huge potential. The proof of this was Laurent Beaudoin's commitment to implement Six Sigma. Our challenge was to fight what Executive Vice President Yvan Allaire calls the "success breeds failure" syndrome; to see the need for change even when, by most indicators, things have never been better; and to see how much untapped opportunity exists if we focus our resources in the right places with the right tools, data, and know-how. This is the first hurdle—to help people see the need for, and the benefits of, change. This is especially true when you set a goal of 3.4 defects per million opportunities. Initially, that goal sends an almost eerie silence across an organization as people try to create a mental bridge between the way things are done now, and the process, product, and ser-

vice design that will have to be built to reach six sigma levels of quality. But I firmly believe that as we place information, knowledge, and tools into people's hands, positive things will begin to happen. The company's entrepreneurial instincts will kick in, and people will start to experience new possibilities not only for themselves but for the organization.

We need to balance top-down direction with what takes place in the factories. On one hand, too much top-down direction can squelch innovation. On the other hand, too little direction from the top can cause an effort like Six Sigma to stumble. We feel very strongly that within Bombardier, Six Sigma must be built on its common methodology and language. This is the only way we know how to facilitate knowledge sharing. For example, when someone talks abut how they have used a particular tool or when someone talks about process capability, word starts to spread and others can quickly take and adapt these lessons to their own functions, plants, or even businesses. Additionally, as Bombardier creates or acquires new businesses, we have a methodology to integrate new businesses and cultures with already existing businesses and cultures. Rather than each division reinventing the wheel, we take our employees through the rigors of learning the Breakthrough Strategy, thereby creating a network of knowledge and expertise that continually works because there is a common language and common points of reference.

My own experience is that there are many more similarities than differences between functions, sites, and businesses than people want to admit. It seems to be part of human nature to emphasize our differences, rather than our likenesses, particularly when we are asked to change. Of course, there are specific industry and customer nuances that need to be recognized, but at the process level everything is pretty much the same. This is why we have made a highly visible effort to involve all parts of the organization in Six Sigma, rather than limiting the initiative to manufacturing and engineering. I've seen too many companies *limit the tools and concepts of Six Sigma to their manufacturing sectors, and ignore the immense potential the initiative carries for administrative and service processes as well.*

While you definitely want to experience early wins to reinforce learning and potential gains, organizations need a "stick-to-it" attitude, particularly in the early days of implementation. Senior management needs to continually reinforce, improve, and push the implementation forward. We recognize that Bombardier is still in the early phases of implementation and that much needs to be done to teach our employees that Six Sigma is a prism that can be viewed from many different angles. With the support of our CEO and group presidents ensuring that our Six Sigma initiative is not compromised or diluted, I believe we have the potential to not only create real and lasting improvements but perhaps push Six Sigma into uncharted territories.

Motorola's Art Sundry, whom we met in Chapter 1, was Motorola's sales manager for the fastest-growing, most profitable Motorola business when he stood at the 1979 officers' meeting and announced that his customers didn't like Motorola's quality. We believe that the reason why Sundry's pleas for better quality opened the door to Six Sigma within Motorola had to do with leadership and timing: then-president Bob Galvin believed that the company's expectation levels were too low, and Motorola's management was finally ready to listen. The company realized that customers were no longer just buying the Motorola name. They wanted a package of features that included quality, exceptional service, competitive prices, and a warranty program that would quickly repair or replace defective products.

If It Ain't Broke, Why Fix It?

Traditional quality programs use metrics to focus on the past. For example, first-time yield or final yield tells how well a process performed, while rolled throughput yield tells companies how likely it is that they will be able to produce a defect-free product. Using metrics to highlight history is analogous to steering a boat by looking at its wake. Companies need to be proactive, not reactive, in their work. While these programs allow mistakes to be corrected, they do not prevent mistakes from reoccurring. Imagine driving your car forward while looking only through your rearview mirror. It won't be long before you find yourself in a ditch. Six Sigma is a predictive strategy that allows companies to combine history with current performance. By applying the philosophy and tools of Six Sigma, companies can drive themselves into the future. It's a way of asking, "How will we perform tomorrow?" If the answer is that you will not perform as well as you need to, companies can measure and modify their processes to improve performance. The future is in driving the car by looking forward, and not through the rearview mirror.

Many successful companies using traditional quality methods ask, "Why should we pursue Six Sigma?" This is a fair question, since implementing Six Sigma represents a long-term commitment, particularly for troubled organizations. Yet people and organizations have no incentive to change when things are going smoothly. It's human nature to alter behavior only when a crisis is at our doorstep. But the corporate boat gets rocked when people are suddenly told that their past successes no longer count enough and are told to start fixing what ain't broke. Changing behavior in an organization that has not experienced a significant emotional event is difficult. It's an easy thing to lead an organization when the coffers are nearly empty and people are in fear of losing their jobs, but to create a sense of urgency in an organization when profits are skyrocketing and shareholders have never been happier is another story. Again, benchmarking data and process baselines can help. Regardless of profitability, when people see that they are only "average," they believe they can (and want to) do better. Information and data can effectively "unfreeze" the apathy that keeps an organization static.

To achieve Six Sigma, an organization must endure extensive psychological changes. We have found that it takes between three and five years for Six Sigma to become entrenched in even the most progressive organizations. Employees are forced to undergo fundamental changes in how they view and accomplish their jobs. While the Six Sigma Breakthrough Strategy has proven itself to be an effective methodology to direct and facilitate organizational change, it cannot be accomplished without strong commitment and involvement from everyone within an organization, and especially top leadership. However, the discipline and dedication necessary to implement Six Sigma must be tempered so that it doesn't break a company's spirit. This spirit can be broken when people are commanded to do something without understanding why. It's only when people are properly and judiciously trained in the Breakthrough Strategy that they understand how Six Sigma will benefit themselves as well as the company.

Getting People on Board with the Breakthrough Strategy

GE's success with Six Sigma is due in part to Jack Welch's belief that implementation requires true believers. There is no room for anyone who is not an A player. In GE terminology, "A" players are those with a vision and the ability to articulate that vision to others so vividly and powerfully that it also becomes their vision. GE accepts nothing but A players in every leadership position throughout the company.

Despite the media hype over Six Sigma, taking a company to a six sigma level of quality is not a glamorous process. However exciting the process, it is a never-ending fight against intellectual rigidity and requires new skills and experience. In fact, statistics have shown that the fallout rate among Champions and Black Belts is nearly 25 percent during the first two years of implementation. The chief reason for this is management's failure to put the finest and brightest employees into Six Sigma leadership roles. When companies populate their Six Sigma ranks with marginal performers, they get marginal results. We have seen this lead to a "renewed" Six Sigma implementation, an effort that is harder and riskier to implement because it is the second time around for the concept.

Companies will see faster results when the Six Sigma Breakthrough Strategy is implemented uniformly and simultaneously across an organization, much in the way that General Electric and AlliedSignal launched their programs. When profits and market share are at stake, companywide implementation is the only way to achieve breakthrough quickly and profitably. However, a leading business within a company can be selected to spearhead Six Sigma—an approach many companies have had a great deal of success with.

Jack Welch's general theory of leadership is closely tied to what needs to take place within companies launching the Six Sigma Breakthrough Strategy:

> *Look, I only have three things to do. I have to choose the right people, allocate the right number of dollars, and transmit ideas from one division to another with the speed of light. So I'm really in the business of being the gatekeeper and the transmitter of ideas.*

Leaders trying to change behaviors and culture can draw wisdom from science and nature. Quantum physics teaches that the atom is made up not of the solid billiard balls of the schoolroom model but of electrons, neutrons, protons, neutrinos, quarks, mesons, and other particles. Moreover, we can never know both the velocity and mass of particles in subatomic physics. The ambiguity and randomness of the subatomic world is a lot like the ever-changing world in which leaders operate. The language of chaos theory also applies to business. While the behavior and thought processes in organizations may appear repetitious and uniform, an organization may also appear as chaotic and unpredictable as hurricanes and tidal waves in the natural world. Leaders must learn how to work both environments. While to a large extent they cannot control the random and ambiguous changes that affect their organization, they can spell out a cohesive corporate message and make sure it is imprinted on every worker. Leaders can re-create the machinery of their organizations so that the business continues to move forward, with the different parts pulling and pushing on one another to produce a new outcome.

Summary

The success of any Six Sigma initiative is largely driven by the following factors: Does your company's leadership understand and are they completely behind implementing Six Sigma? Is your company open and ready to change? Is your company hungry to learn? Is your company anxious to move quickly on a proven idea? Is your company willing to commit resources—people and money—to implement this initiative? Is your organization and its people ready and able to re-create its values so that there are no roadblocks to achieving the vision of Six Sigma?

Traditionally, organizations compare current performance with past performance, not with what might have been or what is yet to be. Six Sigma tears down the structures that protect existing systems. The Breakthrough Strategy gives organizations a road map to business situations not yet on the horizon or issues that are so unprecedented that there is no time to learn by trial and error. People can't change unless they are made aware of their current reality. Awareness of this reality comes through the accumulation of unquestionable evidence known as data. New measurements create new data, and new data (when properly analyzed and interpreted) lead to new knowledge. In turn, new knowledge leads to new beliefs, and new beliefs lead to new values. New values, when cultivated through success and properly reinforced, create passion. And passion is the root of profound change.

WHAT ARE THE VALUES OF A SIX SIGMA ORGANIZATION?

ISSUE	CLASSICAL FOCUS	SIX SIGMA FOCUS
Analytical perspective	Point estimate	Variability
Management	Cost and time	Quality and time
Manufacturability	Trial and error	Robust design
Variable search	One-factor-at-a-time	Design of experiments
Process adjustment	Tweaking	Statistical process-control charts
Problems	Fixing	Preventing
Problem solving	Expert based	System based
Analysis	Experience	Data
Focus	Product	Process
Behavior	Reactive	Proactive
Suppliers	Cost	Relative capability
Reasoning	Experience based	Statistically based
Outlook	Short-term	Long-term
Decision making	Intuition	Probability
Approach	Symptomatic	Problematic
Design	Performance	Producibility
Aim	Company	Customer
Organization	Authority	Learning
Training	Luxury	Necessity
Chain-of-command	Hierarchy	Empowered teams
Direction	Seat-of-pants	Benchmarking and metrics
Goal setting	Realistic perception	Reach out and stretch
People	Cost	Asset
Control	Centralized	Localized
Improvement	Automation	Optimization

SIX SIGMA CONVERSION TABLE

Sigma Value	Defects Per Million Opportunities	Sigma Value	Defects Per Million Opportunities	Sigma Value	Defects Per Million Opportunities
0.00	933,193	2.20	241,964	4.40	1,866
0.05	926,471	2.25	226,627	4.45	1,589
0.10	919,243	2.30	211,856	4.50	1,350
0.15	911,492	2.35	197,663	4.55	1,144
0.20	903,199	2.40	184,060	4.60	968
0.25	894,350	2.45	171,056	4.65	816
0.30	884,930	2.50	158,655	4.70	687
0.35	874,928	2.55	146,859	4.75	577
0.40	864,334	2.60	135,666	4.80	483
0.45	853,141	2.65	125,072	4.85	404
0.50	841,345	2.70	115,070	4.90	337
0.55	828,944	2.75	105,650	4.95	280
0.60	815,940	2.80	96,800	5.00	233
0.65	802,338	2.85	88,508	5.05	193
0.70	788,145	2.90	80,757	5.10	159
0.75	773,373	2.95	73,529	5.15	131
0.80	758,036	3.00	66,807	5.20	108
0.85	742,154	3.05	60,571	5.25	89
0.90	274,253	3.10	54,799	5.30	72
0.95	291,160	3.15	49,471	5.35	59
1.00	308,537	3.20	44,565	5.40	48
1.05	326,355	3.25	40,059	5.45	39
1.10	344,578	3.30	35,930	5.50	32
1.15	363,169	3.35	32,157	5.55	26
1.20	382,088	3.40	28,717	5.60	21
1.25	401,294	3.45	25,588	5.65	17
1.30	420,740	3.50	22,750	5.70	13
1.35	440,382	3.55	20,182	5.75	11
1.40	460,172	3.60	17,865	5.80	9
1.45	480,061	3.65	15,778	5.85	7
1.50	500.000	3.70	13,904	5.90	5
1.55	480,061	3.75	12,225	5.95	4
1.60	460,172	3.80	10,724	6.00	3
1.65	440,382	3.85	9,387		
1.70	420,740	3.90	8,198		
1.75	401,294	3.95	7,143		
1.80	382,088	4.00	6,210		
1.85	363,169	4.05	5,386		
1.90	344,578	4.10	4,661		
1.95	326,355	4.15	4,024		
2.00	308,537	4.20	3,467		
2.05	291,160	4.25	2,980		
2.10	274,253	4.30	2,555		
2.15	257,846	4.35	2,186		

Note: This table includes a 1.5σ shift for all listed values of Z.

Notes

Preface

p. xii   *"Six Sigma companies . . . greater customer satisfaction"*: Morgan Stanley, Dean Witter, Discover & Co., company update by Jennifer Murphy, June 6, 1996.

Chapter One: Why Six Sigma?

p. 15   *For some companies . . . sales price*: James Harrington, 1987 Poor Quality Cost, Marcel Dekker, Inc. American Society for Quality Press.

p. 17   *If this same company . . . current operation income*: James Harrington, 1987 Poor Quality Cost, Marcel Dekkler, Inc., American Society for Quality Press.

p. 18   *"Six Sigma gave our company . . . rather than the defects themselves"*: Interview with Joseph J. Kasabula, Quality Strategy Manager for Product Development and Worldwide Manufacturing, Polaroid Corporation, March 16, 1998.

Chapter Three: Being Better Is Cheaper

p. 28   *"To err is human . . . it was even fun"*: Robert W. Galvin, *The Idea of Ideas*, Motorola University Press, 1991, p. 67.

p. 29   *In fact, while 82 percent . . . cost of quality*: Results of a survey of the Cost Management Group of the Institute of Management Accountant located in Montvale, N.J.

p. 37   *Businesses that achieve . . . ten time improvements in profitability*: Facts from the PIMS Data Survey in 1992 and the U.S. Government General Accounting Office Report of 1991.

One Company's Experience: General Electric 2000

p. 40   *During his . . . in 1998*: John A. Byrne, "How Jack Welch Runs GE": *Business Week*, June 8, 1998, pp. 90–106.

p. 47   *"Today people expect . . . dollars"*: Hal Clifford, "Case Study: Six Sigma": *Continental* magazine, November 1997, pp. 64–67.

p. 55   *Wal-Mart, a key GE customer . . . says Watson*: "GE Races Ahead to Quality Improvement": by Kiyoshi, Tokuda and Koichiro, Sakai, *Nikkei Business,* September 8, 1997, pp. 34–41.

p. 56   *"We had a billing system . . . our investment"*: John F. Welch, Jr. Speech presented at the General Electric Company 1997 Annual Meeting, Charlotte, North Carolina, April 23, 1997.

Chapter Four: Benchmarking: Discovering Who Is Really Best

p. 63   *AlliedSignal CEO . . . one thing better than Allied*: Harvard Business Review, "The CEO as Coach: An Interview with AlliedSignal's Lawrence A. Bossidy": by Noel M. Tichy and Ram Charan, March–April 1995, v. 73, n. 2, p. 68.

p. 64   *"In industries where performance . . . and implement them"*: Price Waterhouse Review, "Black Belt Manufacturing: An Interview with Lawrence A. Bossidy, Chairman and Chief Executive Officer, AlliedSignal Inc.,": 1997.

p. 65   *Motorola's development . . . under two hours*: What America

Does Right: Lessons from Today's Most Admired Corporate Role Models, by Robert H. Waterman, Jr., Plume Books (paperback version), 1994, p. 255.

One Company's Experience: Polaroid Flashes Back

p. 100 *"If you go back . . . results every time"*: Interview with Howard Worzel, April 15, 1998.

p. 102 *"The Breakthrough Strategy . . . quick and powerful"*: Interview with Mike Hart, an engineer in Polaroid's Consumer Imaging Manufacturing Division, March 24, 1998.

Chapter Ten: The Six Sigma Players

p. 196 *"General Electric . . . other corporate accounts"*: Doubletree Hotels has merged with Promus Corporation, but the hotel still operates under the name of Doubletree.

One Company's Experience: AlliedSignal's Journey to Six Sigma

p. 216 *"We can't tell. . . tremendous lessons"*: Richard A. Johnson, Director of Six Sigma for AlliedSignal Inc.

p. 219 *"One of the flaws . . . new blood"*: *Price Waterhouse Review,* "Black Belt Manufacturing: An Interview with Lawrence A. Bossidy, Chairman and Chief Executive Officer, AlliedSignal Inc.": 1997.

p. 225 *"You can see the 'before' . . . make improvements"*: Richard A. Johnson, Director of Six Sigma for AlliedSignal Inc.

p. 225 *"If you look . . . benchmark themselves"*: Richard A. Johnson, Director of Six Sigma for AlliedSignal Inc.

p. 228 *"He drives home . . . value is increased"*: "So, Mr. Bossidy, we know you can cut. Now show us how to grow": by Shawn Tully, *Fortune,* August 21, 1995, v. 132, n. 4, p. 70.

Chapter Thirteen: Project Selection Guidelines

p. 241 *"In its early days . . . allowances for this"*: Interview with Ken Pickering, a Program Manager for Polaroid Corporation's Chemical and Coatings Manufacturing unit, May 6, 1999.

p. 247 *For example, a company's finance . . . shorter periods of time*: *What America Does Right: Lessons from Today's Most Admired Corporate Role Models,* by Robert H. Waterman, Jr., Plume Books (paperback version), 1994, p. 255.

Chapter Fourteen: The Psychology of Six Sigma

p. 257 *Larry Bossidy claims . . . what we think of them*: Harvard *Business Review,* "The CEO As Coach: An Interview with AlliedSignal's Lawrence A. Bossidy": by Noel M. Tichy and Ram Charan, March–April, 1995, v. 73, n. 2, p. 68.

p. 258 *To emphasize . . . potential of his employees*: John A. Bryne, "How Jack Welch Runs GE," *Business Week,* June 8, 1998, pp. 90–106.

p. 258 *Watson Wyatt Worldwide . . . publicly traded companies*: The Watson Wyatt Worldwide study referenced is entitled "Competencies and the Competitive Edge": published by Watson Wyatt Worldwide, 1998.

p. 259 *At GE, pioneers . . . moved into the "big jobs"*: General Electric Company, 1998 Annual Report, p. 5.

p. 260 *Jack Welch never . . . demand action*: Business Week, "How Jack Welch Runs GE: A Close-up Look at America's #1 Manager": June 8, 1998, pp. 92–104.

p. 260 *Another Watson Wyatt Worldwide . . . recognizing performance*: Figures were presented in Watson Wyatt's "WorkUSA" study, published in August 1997.

p. 262 *Setting stretch goals . . . past performance*: John F. Welch, Jr., "Shun the Incremental: Go for the Quantum Leap": Hatfield Fellow Lecture at Cornell University, reprinted in *Financier,* July 1984.

p. 263 *"Punishing . . . suspected were beyond them"*: John F. Welch, Jr., General Electric, letter to shareholders, February 10, 1995, p. 10.

p. 263 *When Larry Bossidy . . . support change*: Fortune, "So, Mr. Bossidy, we know you can cut. Now show us how to grow." August 21, 1995, v. 132 , n. 4, p. 70.

Chapter Fifteen: Preparing an Organization for Six Sigma

p. 269 *"Literally . . . acceptance/rejection"*: The People Puzzle: Understanding Yourself and Others, by Morris Massey, Reston, A Prentice-Hall Company, 1979, p. 4.

p. 270 *Romanian-born Joseph M. Juran . . . personal level*: Joseph M. Juran, "Made in the U.S.A.: A Renaissance in Quality": *Harvard Business Review,* July–August, 1993, p. 43.

p. 272 *"You have to exploit . . . accomplished"*: Gail E. Schares, "Percy Barnevik's Global Crusade": *Business Week/Enterprise,* 1993, p. 20.

p. 272 *For instance, . . . immediate attention*: Gail E. Schares, "Percy Barnevik's Global Crusade": *Business Week/Enterprise,* 1993, p. 20.

p. 273 *"The only way . . . are important"*: Control Your Destiny or Someone Else Will, by Noel M. Tichy and Stratford Sherman, Harper Business, 1993, p. 248.

p. 274 *"We would rather . . . personally involved"*: Interview with Laurent Beaudoin, McKinsey Quarterly, 1997, no. 2.

p. 275 *"When I joined . . . uncharted territories"*: Conversation with Bruce Miyashita, director, Strategic Initiatives, Bombardier Inc., June 18, 1998.

p. 280 *"Look, . . . transmitter of ideas"*: "How's Business? Where Leaders Come From": by Marshall Loeb, *Fortune,* September 19, 1994.

Index

Design of Experiments (DOE), 134
Deutsch, Carol, 157
DiCamillo, Gary, 92, 96
Digital Electronics, 21
Doubletree Hotels, 196
Drewes, Robert W., 36
Dupont Chemical, 1, 110

E

Eastman Kodak, 20
Effectiveness *vs.* efficiency, 90–91
Engineering/design process and
    documentation, 38
Entitlement, 120, 244
Executive management:
    Champions (*See* Champions)
    role of, 172
    Senior Champion, 172–73, 178,
        190–93
    support by, 217–18, 226–27,
        241–42
    vision and values of, 189–90
External failure costs, 32, 33, 35

F

Failure:
    cost of, 32–35
    psychology of, 262, 263
Fattori, Ruth, 50
Final outcomes *vs.* process, 17–18
Final yield, 81, 84
    contrasting with rolled through-
        put yield, 85
    traditional use of, 82
Financial gains, monitoring, 175–77
Financial targets, 2
First-pass yield, 81
First-time yield:

contrasted with throughput yield,
    84–87
reasons for continued use of, 90
traditional use of, 81–83
Five Sigma wall, moving past, 149–53
Focus, creating, 167–70
Foxboro, 234–38
Functional benchmarking, 65

G

Galvin, Robert, 14, 19–20, 230,
    265, 277
General Electric 2000, 4–5, 16, 21,
    29–30, 39–59, 110, 139–40,
    190, 279
    Aircraft Engines division, 48
    Capital Fleet Services, 51–54
    Capital Mortgage Insurance
        division, 49, 50–51
    Capital Services division, 5,
        49–51, 232
    Commercial Finance division, 51
    Customer Dashboard tool, 46–47
    decision to pursue, 41–42
    Design for Customer Impact
        (DFCI) initiative, 55, 58
    Global Consumer Finance divi-
        sion, 51
    Green Belts at, 45, 48, 52–54,
        195–96
    impact of, 58–59
    investment in, 42–43
    Leadership Development Insti-
        tute, 42
    Lighting division, 55–57
    Medical Systems division, 44,
        57, 155–64
    Mortgage Insurance division, 51
    Plastic division, 250–54

Process technology, 77
Process variation:
  long-term *vs.* short-term capabil-
    ity, 141–43
  shift and drift factor, 142–45
  sources of, 146
Producibility, 78
Product, focus on, 167–68
Product design capability, 118
Profitability, 1–3, 7, 16
Project Champions, 173, 178–79,
  190, 191
Project cost savings, focus on, 167
Project management system, 127
Project Master Black Belts, 174
Project performance, 126–27
Project selection, 239–56
  focus and, 239
  low-hanging fruit, 246, 248–49
  measuring projects, 243–46
  at operational level, 125–26
  prioritizing projects, 246–49
  process-level case study, 249–54
  project criteria, 242–43
  sample chart, 255–56
  strategic alignment and, 239–42
Project team members, 175
Promotion, promise of, 259
Psychology, 121–22, 257–64
  compensation, 258–59
  motivation theory, 260–62
  promise of promotion and, 259
  stretch goals, 262–64
  written and verbal recognition,
    259–60

Q

Quality:
  cost of (*See* Cost of quality)

new definition of, 5–9, 31
Quantitative benchmarking, 65–67
Questions, role of, 72–74, 117

R

Recognition, written and verbal,
  259–60
Recognize stage, 108, 111, 112
  business level application, 115–17
  operational level application,
    123–25
  process level application, 130
Reiner, Gary, 44, 46–47
Resources required, 246
Rolled throughput yield, 83
  application of, 87–88
  contrasting with final yield, 85
  defined, 84
  relationship to cost, 89–90

S

Schroeder, Richard, 20
Seagate, 190
Senior Champion, 172–73, 178,
  190
Service industry, 47–49, 230–38
Shift and drift factor, 142–45
Short-term *vs.* long-term capability,
  141–43
Sigma capabilities, approximation
  of, 14–15
Sigma scale of measure, 118
  benefits of higher levels, 17, 18
  measuring performance on (*See*
    Performance measurement on
    sigma scale)
  significance of higher levels,
    13–14

MIKEL HARRY, Ph.D., is the founder and chief executive officer of the Six Sigma Academy, Inc. He was one of the original architects of Six Sigma while working at Motorola in the 1980s. He later served as corporate vice president at Asea Brown Boveri Ltd. He received his B.S. and M.A. from Ball State University and a Ph.D. at Arizona State University. He lives in Scottsdale, Arizona.

RICHARD SCHROEDER is president of the Six Sigma Academy, Inc. A former vice president at Motorola and AlliedSignal, he joined Mikel Harry at the Six Sigma Academy in 1996. Today, Mikel Harry and Richard Schroeder implement Six Sigma programs at major corporations throughout the world. He lives in Scottsdale, Arizona.